CHILDREN, CHILD ABUSE
AND CHILD PROTECTION

CHILDREN, CHILD ABUSE AND CHILD PROTECTION

Placing Children Centrally

by

The Violence Against Children Study Group

JOHN WILEY & SONS, LTD

Chichester · New York · Weinheim · Brisbane · Singapore · Toronto

Copyright © 1999 by John Wiley & Sons Ltd,
Baffins Lane, Chichester,
West Sussex PO19 1UD, England

National   01243 779777
International   (+44) 1243 779777
e-mail (for orders and customer service enquiries):
cs-books@wiley.co.uk
Visit our Home Page on http://www.wiley.co.uk
                   or http://www.wiley.com

Other Wiley Editorial Offices

John Wiley & Sons, Inc., 605 Third Avenue,
New York, NY 10158-0012, USA

WILEY-VCH Verlag GmbH, Pappelallee 3,
D-69469 Weinheim, Germany

Jacaranda Wiley Ltd, 33 Park Road, Milton,
Queensland 4064, Australia

John Wiley & Sons (Asia) Pte Ltd, 2 Clementi Loop   #02-01,
Jin Xing Distripark, Singapore 129809

John Wiley & Sons (Canada) Ltd, 22 Worcester Road,
Rexdale, Ontario M9W 1L1, Canada

Library of Congress Cataloging-in-Publication Data

Children, child abuse and child protection: placing children
   centrally / by the Violence Against Children Study Group; [contributors, Cath
   Adams . . . et al.].
        p.   cm.
   Includes bibliographical references (p.   ) and index.
   ISBN 0-471-98641-0 (pbk.)
     1. Abused children—Services for—Great Britain.   2. Child welfare—United
   States.   3. Child abuse—Great Britain.   4. Social work with children—Great
   Britain.   I. Adams, Cath.   II. Violence Against Children Study Group.
   HV751.A6C59   1999
   362.76'8'0941—dc21
                                                          98-37307
                                                          CIP

British Library Cataloguing in Publication Data

A catalogue record for this book is available from the British Library

ISBN 0-471-98641-0

Typeset in 10/12 pt Palatino by Best-set Typesetter Ltd., Hong Kong
Printed and bound in Great Britain by Biddles Ltd, Guildford and King's Lynn
This book is printed on acid-free paper responsibly manufactured from sustainable
forestry, in which at least two trees are planted for each one used for paper
production.

This book is dedicated to the memory of Wendy Marshall,
a valued colleague and friend, who died on
26 March 1997

CONTENTS

ABOUT THE AUTHORS

Cath Adams is a Detective Inspector with West Yorkshire Police and manages Domestic Violence and Child Protection Units in Bradford, Huddersfield and Halifax. She has had over 20 years experience with the police and has taken a lead role in establishing domestic violence and child protection services within the West Yorkshire force and in developing inter-agency training. In 1994, under a United Nations initiative, she set up the Women and Child Abuse Unit in Namibia.

Anne Ashworth is a Family Court Welfare Officer with Greater Manchester Probation Service, currently undertaking postgraduate studies in this area of practice at Bradford University. She has worked for the last 20 years in a variety of probation settings and as a psychiatric social worker. She has written several articles and been involved in training on domestic violence.

Eric Blyth is Reader in Social Work at the University of Huddersfield. He is a founder member of the Violence Against Children Study Group. In addition to co-authorship of *Taking Child Abuse Seriously*, he has been co-author of *Coping with Child Sex Abuse: A Guide for Teachers* (Longman), *Social Work with Children: The Educational Perspective* (Addison Wesley Longman), and co-editor of *Exclusion from School: Inter-professional Issues for Policy and Practice* (Routledge) (all with Judith Milner).

Helen Cooper is employed part-time as an Education Social Worker by Kirklees Metropolitan Council and also as a part-time social work lecturer at the University of Huddersfield. Her work has mostly been with children and families in a variety of different settings. Her special interests are the teacher's role in child protection issues, the role of social work in an education setting and anti-bullying strategies in schools. The latter has involved writing leaflets for parents and guidelines for schools. She has recently started teaching part-time on the Open University Diploma in Social Work programme.

Marcus Erooga is Manager of the NSPCC Lancashire East Child Protection Team and Child Care Centre, having worked in Child

Protection for the last 12 years. He is a co-editor and contributor to *Sexual Offending against Children: Assessment and Treatment of Male Abusers* (Routledge). He has written a number of articles on Child Protection and is an Associate Editor of the *Journal of Sexual Aggression*.

Brid Featherstone is a qualified social worker and worked in the area of juvenile practice for a number of years before becoming a social worker and a manager in child protection. She is currently a lecturer in the Department of Applied Social Studies at the University of Bradford. Her current research is on women's violence to children. She is co-editor of *Violence and Gender Relationships* (Sage).

Lorraine Green is a researcher and part-time lecturer in psychology and sociology at the University of Huddersfield, having previously studied social administration and social work at Cardiff and Birmingham Universities. Her current research is in the area of sexuality, sexual abuse and residential child care.

Jeff Hearn is Professorial Research Fellow in the Faculty of Economic and Social Studies, University of Manchester, and Visiting Research Professor of Sociology at Äbo Akademi University, Turku, Finland. As a founder member of the Violence Against Children Study Group, he is co-author of *Taking Child Abuse Seriously* (Unwin Hyman). Other recent books include *Men in the Public Eye* (Routledge), *'Sex' at 'Work'* (Prentice-Hall)—with Wendy Parkin, *Violence and Gender Relations* (Sage), *Men, Masculinity and Social Theory* (Unwin Hyman), and *The Violence of Men* (Sage).

Christine Horrocks is Lecturer in Psychology at the University of Huddersfield. She has previously been employed by local education authorities in the youth service and working with minority groups and young offenders. Her current research is an investigation of the transitional experience of young people leaving local authority care, about which she has recently published in relation to exclusion from school.

Jocelyn Jones is the Director of the Child Protection Studies Centre at Leicester University. She has extensive experience in social work practice, management and education. Her research interests centre on the empowerment of child victims and she has published and presented papers at national and international conferences on this theme. She also writes on current issues in post-qualifying education and training and is currently working on the development of competence-based workplace learning and assessment for children and families' social workers.

Kate Karban is Senior Lecturer in Social Work at Leeds Metropolitan University. She has been involved in teaching and research concerning residential child care. Prior to this she worked with children and families and in mental health social work in field and group care settings.

Nancy Kelly is Lecturer in Psychology at the University of Huddersfield, where she teaches on undergraduate, postgraduate and vocational programmes. Her current research interests focus on risk assessment and decision-making in social work practice and she currently provides training on risk assessment in child protection and probation practice.

Helen Masson is Principal Lecturer in Social Work at the University of Huddersfield. She has worked in both voluntary and statutory social work agencies in the field of child care/child protection and now teaches on qualifying and post-qualifying courses for social workers and other professionals. She is a founder member of the Violence Against Children Study Group and co-author of *Taking Child Abuse Seriously*.

Judith Milner is a freelance solutions counsellor. She works mainly with individual children and young people who have experienced violence, but also with staff and ex-residents of children's homes in the aftermath of police investigations into institutional abuse. She is a founder member of the Violence Against Children Study Group and co-author of *Taking Abuse Seriously*. With Eric Blyth she has been co-author of *Coping with Child Sexual Abuse: A Guide for Teachers* (Longman), *Social Work with Children: The Educational Perspective* (Addison Wesley Longman), and co-editor of *Exclusion from School: Inter-professional Issues for Policy and Practice* (Routledge). She is co-author of *Assessments in Social Work* (Macmillan) and has contributed to *Surviving Childhood Adversity: Issues for Policy and Practice* (Dublin Social Studies Press) and *Violence and Gender Relations* (Sage).

Jenny Myers is a part-time tutor in the Child Protection Studies department at Leicester University and part-time National Training and Development Officer with the NSPCC. She is a qualified social worker with experience of practice management and inter-agency training. She is currently working on helping providers of residential care for disabled children to develop preventive strategies, policies and standards, to reduce the risk of institutional abuse.

Teresa O'Neill is an experienced guardian *ad litem*, freelance trainer and lecturer. She has had extensive experience in social work practice, management and training and has trained as a psychotherapist. She is currently at the University of Bristol completing doctoral research with young people in secure residential care.

Wendy Parkin is Principal Lecturer in Social Work at the University of Huddersfield. She has a background of both generic and specialist child abuse social work practice in addition to research and publications in the field of sexuality, gender, emotion and organisations. Her current research topic is sexuality and residential care. She is a founder member of the Violence Against Children Study Group and co-author of *'Sex' at 'Work'* (Prentice-Hall).

Gurnam Singh is Senior Lecturer in Social Work at Coventry University. He was previously employed by Bradford Social Services Department as a social work practitioner and staff training and development officer. He has undertaken research and written about various aspects of anti-racist social work theory and practice. He is currently working on doctoral research that is attempting to develop new insights and configurations on anti-racist social work by utilising poststructuralist and postmodern theory.

Suzanne Smith is a qualified nurse and health visitor and is employed as Named Nurse–Child Protection for Leeds Teaching Hospitals NHS Trust after having held the same post for the Leeds Community and Mental Health Trust. She undertook her health visiting training at the University of Huddersfield and has also completed the University's MA programme in Child Protection.

Allison Waddell is the manager at a young carers project in the North West. She has had previous experience working with children and families in local authority residential settings and as a child protection social worker in the voluntary sector. She is involved in teaching and training in child protection and work with children and young people. She has completed the MA programme in Child Protection at the University of Huddersfield.

ACKNOWLEDGEMENTS

Jocelyn Jones would like to thank the University of Leicester for the award of study leave in 1998. She would also like to thank the Faculty of Social Sciences Research Committee for its financial support of an earlier study which contributed towards her chapter.

The group wishes to thank Liz Saville for the preparation of this manuscript and for coping admirably well with virtually every word-processing package known to humankind.

INTRODUCTION

Taking Child Abuse Seriously, written by the Violence Against Children Study Group and published in 1990, resulted from a collective effort to examine the complexity of child abuse—in its perpetration, in professional practice, in policy development, and in its analysis through social theory. Actively attempting to break down conventional academic and practice-focused divisions, the book addressed practice, policy and theory in relation to a range of topic areas including the relationship between state and family in contemporary Britain; women, gender oppression and child abuse; men's violence; racism, cultural relativism and child protection; notions of dangerousness; and the process of inter-agency work.

Taking Child Abuse Seriously sold well and was reprinted in 1993, and received very favourable reviews. However, during the 1990s, further significant developments have occurred that have had important impacts on current and future child protection theory, policy and practice. These include:

- The implementation in 1991 of the Children Act 1989, with its associated Regulations and Guidance which were formulated in part in response to the findings of a number of child abuse inquiry reports during the 1980s, culminating in the Cleveland inquiry into child sexual abuse (HMSO, 1988). The Act has sought:

  to strike a balance between the rights of children to express their views on decisions made about their lives, the rights of parents to exercise their responsibilities towards the child and the duty of the state to intervene where the child's welfare requires. (HMSO, 1991, p. 1)

  The child's welfare as the paramount consideration, notions of significant harm, principles of parental responsibility and the need to work in partnership with parents and avoid court action wherever possible have exercised the minds of policy-makers, practitioners and agency managers, and the judiciary as they have struggled to implement the new legislation.
- New concerns and inquiries about other kinds of abuse, including ritual and organised abuse (SSI, 1990; Secretary of State for

Scotland, 1992); institutional abuse and abuse by professionals (e.g. Levy and Kahan, 1990; Kirkwood, 1993).

- Publication of further central government guidance on inter-disciplinary working such as Working Together (Home Office, DOH, DES, Welsh Office, 1991), all of which has been made more complicated by education and NHS reforms and the introduction of market forces to public sector services which have contrived to fragment the 'welfare network'.

- Since the mid-1990s increasing concerns and debate about the focus of current child protection practice with calls for the empha-sis to be shifted onto child and family support, to children in need, and a redirecting of resources away from the 'front-end' of heavy investigative work (Audit Commission, 1994; HMSO, 1995).

- Major political changes, not least the overwhelming defeat of the Conservative government on 1 May 1997 after 18 years in office and the ushering in of a Labour government. However, the new government has seemingly adopted many of the policies of its predecessor, resulting in increasing pressures on local authori-ties to maintain services in the face of ever-diminishing resources and continued uncertainty about the long-term future of key agen-cies within the child protection network, such as social services departments and local education authorities.

Thus much has changed and is in the process of change since 1990, with the result that, although still relevant in some respects, *Taking Child Abuse Seriously* does not reflect issues and developments at the end of the 1990s. This, therefore, has prompted the Study Group to resurrect itself in a reconstituted form to collaborate in a publication that attempts to address contemporary debates. As with the original text, the group has gone about its work with the firm assumption that prac-tice in, and theorising about, child protection occur and have to be understood, critiqued and developed in relation to broad social and political changes.

So what of the constitution of the current Study Group? Five of the original group remain and fourteen have been welcomed into the col-lective. All but five of the group live or work in close proximity; twelve are, or have been, practising social workers and the group now includes a health visitor and a police inspector. Most of the group are actively involved in teaching social work students and in research into social work. Four of the group are men and differences of ethnicity, family circumstances, sexual identity and other dimensions have contributed to debate.

The process of producing the book has been a collaborative venture, assisted by information technology, land mail and fax. The chapters have been subject to collective comment and discussion within the sections of the book, thus increasing the chances of the cross-fertilisation of our differing practical, intellectual, disciplinary and political positions. Similarly, the process of editing has been shared within the group.

As with the first book, the characteristic theme of this text is the simultaneous engagement with, on the one hand, current debates in social theory and social research (for example, around gender, sexuality, race, class, disability and age) and, on the other hand, the development of improved policy and practices in child protection. This book is therefore written not only for students, researchers and academics, but also for practitioners and policy-makers.

The second major theme of this book is the placing of children centre stage—at the centre of policy and practice, and at the centre of discourses. There is an increasing literature on childhood studies (e.g. Hendrick, 1997; James and Prout, 1997; James, Jenks and Prout, 1998), a literature that demonstrates the only fairly recent emergence of notions of childhood and the changing nature of adult social constructions of childhood over time. Since the early eighteenth century, most models of childhood that have informed policy and professional practice have been constructed within both a deficit and a developmental model. In other words, children have been viewed as being in the process of 'becoming adults' and as such therefore as undeveloped, irrational, inadequate and inferior. Consequently they are perceived as being in need of care and protection, delivered by well-meaning, powerful adults, both professional and familial, who 'know best'.

Shifts in policy and practice mirror a more general change in the understanding of children and childhood. Rather than simply seeing children as young, small, dependent humans who are developing into adults, within a developmental or socialisation framework, there is increasing interest in focusing on children as social actors and on children's experiences in their own right. This involves rethinking children's worlds as more than just dependencies or subsets of adult social worlds. It is also part of the broad attempt to more fully appreciate the historically-specific of 'childhood'. In terms of child abuse and child protection, this perspective necessitates not only 'taking child abuse seriously' but also taking children and children's experiences seriously.

The third theme relates to the need to explore the margins of the child protection system and in particular how child protection interconnects or overlaps with other systems. Other systems include those with a specific institutional base, such as health, police and education, as well as more diffuse systems, such as those around ageing and disability. An enduring contradiction exists between the case for extending child protection models and approaches into other areas of policy and practice, and the case against 'imperialism' in policy and practice. Analysis focuses on whether some systems might become extensions of the child protection system or on the possibility and the nature of separations between different systems.

The book is divided into four sections. Part I places children's issues as central and covers the treatment of black children, children as carers and children who sexually abuse. Gurnam Singh, in 'Black Children and the Child Protection System', argues that any serious attempt to understand the relationship between black children, families and communities and the child protection system must go beyond simplistic, but still very dominant, uni-dimensional reductionism of cross-cultural differences. Through an extensive examination of the research evidence the chapter develops a powerful argument for the development of anti-racist practice models centred on a non-essentialist understanding of ethnicity. In so doing it seeks to show how practitioners can work effectively in 'partnership' with black children, families and communities.

In 'Young Carers—the Contradictions of Being a Child Carer', Eric Blyth and Allison Waddell describe the emergence of a new 'welfare category'. They draw on recent research and practice experience to connect developing thoughts and policies regarding 'young carers' with those in child protection. They conclude that welfare agencies need to utilise resources and legislative powers to provide support and protection to, and promote the rights of, 'young carers' both as children and as carers, and to avoid the perpetration of institutionalised abuse of 'young carers' and their families. Helen Masson's chapter, 'Children and Adolescents who Sexually Abuse', highlights the implications of child-on-child sexual abuse for assumptions about childhood and 'age-appropriate' sexual knowledge and behaviour; the relationship between adolescent sexual offending and other forms of juvenile offending; the dual perspectives needed on young people as sexual offenders and as children in need of protection; and indicates ways forward in developing models of practice and consistent patterns of response.

Part II focuses on issues of gender and generation. It covers the place of women and children in the child protection system; domestic violence, and the relationships between child abuse and protection and elder abuse. Brid Featherstone, in 'Mothering and the Child Protection

System', draws on case material and current research involving women who have been violent towards their children. Her chapter focuses on how women are positioned as managers, front-line workers and service users within professional discourses, arguing that such positionings can be destabilised, as well as supported, by other positionings such as mother, wife, lesbian, childless, and heavily influenced by the presence or absence of men and children. In 'Child Protection and Domestic Violence: Pointers for Practitioners', Anne Ashworth and Marcus Erooga make a case for taking a more nuanced approach to domestic violence and assessing risk to children which acknowledges the complexities of violence in intimate relationships beyond the current orthodoxy of it being simply an abuse of male power. They build on emerging feminist/pro-feminist thinking, arguing for practice and development and practice-inspired research which uses an open definition of domestic violence capable of responding to the diversity of family situations.

Jeff Hearn's chapter, 'Ageism, Violence and Abuse', focuses on both theoretical and practice perspectives that link the abuse of children and of older people. He suggests that these relationships can be approached both through theoretical perspectives on the social construction of age and ageing, and through practice and policy perspectives on interventions against different forms of violence and abuse. The chapter analyses the interrelations of age with other social divisions and the fundamental importance of the gendering of these processes.

Part III of the book considers issues of multidisciplinary and interagency working, focusing on case conferences and the interrelationships between child protection and schools, health services, and the police. Nancy Kelly and Judith Milner, in 'Decision-Making in Case Conferences—Meeting Whose Needs?' explore the impact of groupthink and prospect polarisation in child protection decision-making. Application of the concepts illustrates that 'two (or more) heads are not necessarily better than one' in risk assessment and management. The notion of competing and conflicting needs of children and families in child protection is addressed. The implications of conflating children's and adults' needs in the decision-making process are discussed.

In 'Schools and Child Protection', Eric Blyth and Helen Cooper provide an analysis of the emerging and expanding role of schools, and of the teaching profession in particular, within the child protection system. They highlight features that have not, hitherto, been connected with child protection, including the scope schools provide for the perpetration of abuse, child-on-child, child-on-adult and adult-on-child abuse. The authors argue that a range of pressures effectively limits the contribution that schools and teachers may make to inter-agency child protection strategies and that any re-evaluation of their role has to be considered within the context of contemporaneous developments regarding pupil behaviour and management, and the wider 'moral panic' concerning the behaviour of the young. Sue Smith debates child protection work from a health visiting perspective in 'Primary Prevention in Child Protection: The Role of the Health Visitor'. Within an historical context, principles of health visiting and the nature of primary, secondary and tertiary prevention as applied to child protection are outlined. Although highlighting the contribution to service provision which may be made by a professional who is generally perceived as a universal, non-stigmatising visitor to families, difficulties of evaluating the effectiveness of primary prevention are also discussed. The risk of erosion of the health visitor role in child protection is emphasised, given the demands of changing NHS structures and the pressures imposed by market forces within the health service.

Cath Adams and Christine Horrocks, in 'The Location of Child Protection in Relation to the Current Emphasis on Core Policing', outline the development of police child protection units and provide a critical evaluation of the relationship between child protection and 'mainstream' police culture. The chapter highlights the implications of perceptions of 'women and children work' for management and support within police forces; career development and experiences of stress amongst child protection workers; resourcing child protection work within the police force, including the provision of training, and threats and challenges to working practices posed by 'mainstream' police practices.

The final part of the book provides an overview of the residential care system that is supposedly part of the child protection system in that children are placed there to protect them. Research is presented that demonstrates the particular nature of these settings and how they can contribute to the further exploitation of children through direct abuse, sex/gender power systems or neglect of basic rights. In ' "Being There": Residential Care of Children and Young People', Christine Horrocks and Kate Karban locate residential care within wider child care and child protection systems and explore the notion of 'parenting' in relation to children who are 'looked after'. The shortcomings of care offered by the 'corporate parent' are acknowledged, while at the same time the tensions surrounding the provision of residential care are recognised. A particular feature is the need to take into account the socio-historical legacy of residential services as well as the continuing issues of inequality and discrimination that affect both the context and the internal dynamics of providing residential care for children and young people. Extracts from interviews with young people emphasise that the views of young people are essential if services are to be able to develop and respond to the continuing need for high-quality care, providing an environment that promotes participation and self-determination.

Lorraine Green and Wendy Parkin, in 'Sexuality, Sexual Abuse and Children's Homes—Oppression or Protection?', draw on recent qualitative research to examine the links between how sexuality and sexual abuse issues are perceived and responded to in contemporary children's homes and children's subsequent vulnerability to sexual abuse and exploitation. The children's past family and 'in care' backgrounds; personalised beliefs around gender and sexuality and associated behaviour; the social construction of childhood and child/adolescent sexuality; the myth of the asexual and agendered organisation and the institutionalisation of the settings are identified as interlinking factors that contribute to and exacerbate the potential for exploitation. The chapter analyses the part each of these factors plays, using both illustrative research examples and theorisation of these in terms of majority themes to substantiate and explain the issues. Jenny Myers, Teresa O'Neill and Jocelyn Jones, in 'Preventing Institutional Abuse: An Exploration of Children's Rights, Needs and Participation in Residential Care', draw on literature from institutional abuse inquiries to analyse whether recommendations made can actually protect children in residential care. They argue that a move towards a children's rights model may reduce the risk of institutional abuse. The chapter concludes with recommendations for practice that could help reduce the future likelihood of institutional abuse, by providing examples of how a model based on children's participation might be incorporated into the structure.

As will be evident from these chapter summaries, and from the chapters themselves, no quick and easy solutions are available to what are complex and multi-dimensional phenomena. Our aim is, in part, to overview this complexity and the uncertain political, moral and social context within which practitioners and managers attempt work with children, families and others. However, what we have also tried to do is to make some suggestions for factors that should be attended to when considering possible refinements in policy and practice as well as also making suggestions for such refinements. In any such work the voice of children, their perspectives and opinions should be actively sought as central to future debates and decision-making.

REFERENCES

Audit Commission (1994) *Seen but not Heard: Coordinating Child Health and Social Services for Children in Need*, HMSO, London.

Hendrick J (1997) *Children, Childhood and English Society 1880–1990*, Cambridge University Press, Cambridge.

HMSO (1988) *Report of the Inquiry into Child Abuse in Cleveland 1987*, HMSO, London.

HMSO (1991) *The Children Act 1989. Guidance and Regulations. Volume 1, Court Orders*, HMSO, London.

HMSO (1995) *Child Protection: Messages from Research*, HMSO, London.

Home Office, Department of Health, Department of Education and Science, Welsh Office (1991) *Working Together Under the Children Act 1989: A Guide to Arrangements for Inter-agency Co-operation for the Protection of Children from Abuse*, Home Office, London.

James A and Prout A (eds) (1997) *Constructing and Reconstructing Childhood* (2nd edn), Falmer Press, London.

James A, Jenks C and Prout A (1998) *Theorizing Childhood*, Polity Press, Cambridge.

Kirkwood A (1993) *The Leicestershire Inquiry 1992*, Leicestershire County Council, Leicester.

Levy A and Kahan B (1991) *The Pindown Experience and the Protection of Children: The Report of the Staffordshire Child Care Inquiry 1990*, Staffordshire County Council, Stafford.

Secretary of State for Scotland (1992) *The Report of the Inquiry into the Removal of Children from Orkney in February 1991*, HMSO Edinburgh.

Social Services Inspectorate (1990) *Inspection of Child Protection Services in Rochdale*, SSI/DOH, London.

Violence Against Children Study Group (1990) *Taking Child Abuse Seriously*, Unwin Hyman, London.

I

PLACING CHILDREN'S ISSUES AS CENTRAL

1

BLACK CHILDREN AND THE CHILD PROTECTION SYSTEM

Gurnam Singh

INTRODUCTION

From the mid-1970s through to the 1990s the issue of child abuse has become a major preoccupation of societies throughout the western hemisphere. Within this period, there has been a gradual shift towards a more systematic and proceduralised approach to state involvement in the protection of children (Parton, 1991; Corby, 1993). In Britain, primarily as a consequence of well-publicised instances of the deaths of children on *at risk registers* and the uncovering, by professionals, of sexual abuse by family members on a large scale, particularly centred around the Cleveland affair (Butler-Sloss, 1988), an intricate and wide-ranging child protection system has been established around the Children Act 1989. This shift also saw the broadening of the concept of child abuse to incorporate sexual and emotional abuse in addition to established concerns with physical abuse and neglect.

What is perhaps most significant, notwithstanding the fact that two of the most publicised child deaths involved black children (Jasmine Beckford and Tyra Henry), is the scant attention given to the questions of 'race' and racism, both in terms of the life experiences of black children and more specifically in relation to institutional responses to the needs of black children and families. For example, the work of Barn (1993) and Thorpe (1994) provided clear evidence of the way black families are much more likely to receive social work intervention where control and surveillance, rather than care and support, are the primary motives.

In requiring authorities and professionals to attend to cultural factors

Children, Child Abuse and Child Protection. Placing Children Centrally, by The Violence Against Children Study Group.
© 1999 John Wiley & Sons Ltd.

in working with children and families, the Children Act 1989 was seen as representing a landmark in that it was the first positive piece of welfare legislation in Britain which specifically recognised the existence of a multicultural society (Ahmad, 1990). In recognising that two of the basic principles of the Act, protecting children and families from unwarranted intervention and 'partnership', do indeed reflect anti-racist concerns, Stubbs (1991) warns that the origins of these are not derived from black critiques but:

> from a 'new right' Thatcherite (and post-Thatcherite) orthodoxy on 'the family' which finds it hard to see black families as 'good' families. The Children Act does nothing, therefore, to challenge constructions of black family pathology which underpins racist social work practice. (Stubbs, 1991: 226)

In the context of the media onslaught on progressive anti-oppressive thinking during the late 1980s and early 1990s in the guise of political correctness having 'gone mad' (Singh, 1994; Dominelli, 1997) one can see how the Children Act 1989 was in fact more driven by 'new right' moral panics about the preservation of 'the family'. The concern of the government was to make professional intervention more accountable to the court system, coupled with a wish to recentre the traditional nuclear family against the relativising tendencies of feminists and anti-racists in their challenge to the notion of the 'normal family'. This was to be done by developing very narrow approaches to child protection and focusing most attention on 'dysfunctional', 'abnormal', 'danger-ous' or 'inadequate' families (Dale, Davies, Morrison and Waters, 1986). As Saraga (1993) points out, such a strategy provided an ideal mech-anism for avoiding the more complex and damning explanations of child abuse:

> By focusing on intervention, much more difficult questions about family life, and about the ways that children are abused or neglected through lack of social provision, through poverty, or by racism, are avoided. (Saraga, 1993: 48)

Through an analysis of research, theory and practice this chapter aims to examine the relationship between black children, families and the child protection system. The first section sets out the historical per-spective, providing the backdrop to the central core of the chapter that will constitute a critical analysis of the relationship between child abuse and 'race'. To assist with this critique extensive use will be made of available research. The final section will engage in an analysis of con-temporary debates surrounding the critiques of Eurocentricity in child protection and the demands for the development of models centred on ethnic diversity and anti-racist perspectives. In doing so it will seek to highlight how practitioners can work more effectively in 'partnership' with black children, families and communities.

Before proceeding, I feel the need to clarify the use of the term 'black'. Throughout the chapter, the term 'black' will refer to all visible minorities. By doing so I am aware that the term is not unproblematic and has been subject to much debate in recent times (Anthias and Yuval-Davis, 1992). For example, in highlighting the increasing internal social and economic diversification of the constituent members of the 'black' community, compelling critiques of the inability of the concept 'black' to articulate the specificities of the needs, problems and experiences of different ethnic minorities in Britain have been made (Modood, 1994). On the other hand, as I have argued elsewhere (Singh, 1992), by focusing attention away from 'cultural differences' and towards issues of power and oppression, the concept 'black' formed the backbone of an anti-racist politics and practice which in the late 1980s and 1990s undoubtedly enabled some black families to become beneficiaries of social work intervention and not merely its victims (Singh, 1992). It is because I maintain the belief that it was precisely through a radical anti-racist politics underpinned by a collective black voice that the social spaces from which the celebration of difference was and is made possible that I continue to appreciate the value of the term, whilst recognising that it has limited analytic properties.

HISTORICAL BACKGROUND

Three different but equally problematic perspectives have historically characterised most public policy discussions about the provision of child protection services to members of minority ethnic communities in Britain: First, by abstracting clients from their social contexts and neglecting to attend to the issues of 'race', culture and ethnicity, it has been argued that the needs of minorities are no different to the rest. What has been termed the colour-blind, or Eurocentric, model has acted to ignore the complex relationship between 'race', class, and gender out of which the specificities of black children's oppression can only be truly understood. Although it is perhaps less evident today, up to the late 1970s much of social work practice with black children and families was rooted in what has otherwise been termed as the assimilationist perspective.

The second perspective, in attempting to develop a 'racial' or cultural dimension to the analysis and treatment of child abuse, has tended to focus on the problems *within* black families. The kinds of frameworks emerging out of this perspective have often ended up promoting a series of misleading and often dangerous constructions of black family functioning. What has been termed the 'black family pathology perspective', evident in much of the social work and health literature of the 1970s and 1980s, sets out to map the particular features of African-Caribbean and Asian family forms disrupted by cultural transition and dislocation as an explanatory model for child abuse and family dysfunction.

Popularly termed the 'multicultural perspective' this model posited a series of stereotypical representations of black families. Thus, African-Caribbean families were perceived as being 'decadent', 'culturally deficient', 'disorganised' and 'disintegrating'; with the high incidence of single parenthood, offending behaviour and low educational achievement being seen as evidence for this assertion. The Asian family, on the other hand, has been portrayed as an island of morality in a sea of decadence and immorality. It attempts to take a positive view of the Asian community which, in contrast to broader trends in society of chronic family breakdown—evidenced by high divorce rates and the growth of single parenthood—and the contingent problems of juvenile delinquency, homelessness and so on, has managed to retain a sense of piety, financial independence and social and familial cohesiveness. The problem with such families is seen to reside in their rigid traditional conservative outlook which may result in narrow repressive 'feudal' regimes within the family (Stubbs, 1989).

The third perspective, seen as representing a critique of the pathological model set out above, attempts to develop a positive picture of black families. By using the apparently low take up of existing services by minority ethnic groups as evidence, it has been argued that some minority ethnic communities prefer to 'look after their own' within various extended family and community arrangements; that they are strong precisely because of their ability to survive under the pressures of social deprivation, poverty and racism. Intervention would only act to destabilise and weaken the internal community mechanisms for dealing with family affairs. A kind of 'radical non-intervention model' so evident in the Tyra Henry case (Channer and Parton, 1990) has resulted very often in black family problems being neglected and black children being unprotected. In pointing out the problematic nature of state intervention into black family life, MacLeod and Saraga (1988) argue that whilst doing nothing is not an option, when intervening, professionals must be prepared to confront the question of racism:

> We cannot, however, simply be anti-interventionist, thinking we are being progressive, because this does mean closing our eyes to the abuse

of children in families; but we do have to take cognisance of the implications of state intervention. (MacLeod and Saraga, 1988: 45)

RESEARCH EVIDENCE

Each one of the positions outlined above is characterised by inadequate responses to both the complex nature of racism and the various needs of black children and families; responses that at best represent a set of misleading stereotyped analyses of black families that ignore the many changes, conflicts, and struggles that they are undergoing and in which they are engaged. More seriously, there is the recurring theme of an overly punitive response to the needs of black children and families. For example, a recent study on three Social Services Departments carried out by Barn, Sinclair and Ferdinand (1997), evaluating the implementation of requirements within sec.22 (5) of the Children Act 1989 (the section requiring service providers to give due attention to the clients' 'racial origin and cultural and linguistic background'), highlighted significant and worrying trends:

- The high numbers of South Asian referrals around child protection and 'looked after' cases
- African-Caribbean children entering care much more quickly than other groups
- An increased tendency to label black women as suffering from mental illness

In the absence of useful research bringing together the issues of 'race', culture and child protection, it is difficult to establish a broader picture of the black experiences of the child protection system. Whilst there is some evidence of small-scale, mostly unpublished evaluative studies taking place within local authorities, in relation to substantial centrally funded research by bodies such as the Department of Health, 'race' has received scant attention (Barn, 1993). On the other hand, whilst a great deal of child protection research has tended to ignore 'race' and culture, similarly, a great deal of 'race and ethnic studies' research has avoided focusing on child protection. Indeed the whole subject of 'race' and social work has been contested, overall, on ideological and political grounds, rather than on serious academic research.

One can only speculate about the reasons for this lack of research. However, possible explanations for this gap may include: first, an orthodoxy which states that child abuse is a universal phenomenon; that 'children are children' and that 'abuse is abuse' regardless of culture, race or anything else—a view that ultimately results in a 'colour-blind' approach. Second, as much of child protection research is dominated by white liberal academics who may have a concern about their ability to research black clients and fear that their work could be used to exacerbate racism, a tendency exists on their part to keep well away from the subject of 'race'. For example Herman (1981) provides such a justification for deciding not to interview black women in her empirical study of *Father–Daughter Incest*:

> We made the decision to restrict the interviewing to white women in order to avoid even the possibility that the information gathered might be used to fuel idle speculation about racial difference. (Herman, 1981: 68)

Of the reliable research that has been conducted, the overall picture is that black children are more likely to receive inadequate services in comparison to their white counterparts (Bebbington and Miles, 1989; Rowe, Hundleby and Garnett, 1989; Barn, 1993). For example, in her study of the public care system Barn found that:

> social workers approached cases of black children and families with a greater degree of negativity than those of white children and families. Such negative attitudes operated to the detriment of black children and families. (Barn, 1993: 59)

The hegemony of the empiricist positivist approach is very evident in much of the research on child protection; particularly in relation to US research, but increasingly in Britain as well. This tends to involve large-scale studies of child abuse statistics trying to assess the prevalence of abuse within a given society. Now because of definitional problems (i.e. what constitutes abuse) and the fact that most abuse— particularly sexual abuse—goes undetected, there tend to be massive variations in the estimates. Kelly, Regan and Burton (1991) for example, on a sample of 16–21 year olds from different ethnic backgrounds, found that, using broad definitions of abuse, nearly two thirds of all women and one third of all men reported at least one experience. For more serious incidents of abuse such as forced sex, rape and masturbation the figures dropped to one in 25 women and one in 50 men.

The significance of these figures is that far from being 'abnormal' behaviour, sexual behaviours amongst children and parents seem to occur in the majority of families. Similarly we are also reminded of the work of Campbell (1988) in her analysis of the Cleveland affair, in which she asserts that the vast majority of sexual—and for that matter—physical abuse is not committed by sadistic, pathological, mentally disturbed individuals, but by 'normal' people:

> What the sexual abuse crisis of the 1980s has forced us to confront is that the perpetrators aren't dangerous strangers, lunatics exiled from settled communities. They're the men we all know, not so much the outcasts as the men in our lives, respectable dads, neighbours, stockbrokers and shop stewards, judges and jurors. They are men of all ages, races, religions and classes. (Campbell, 1988: 5)

So, very often, scientific data do nothing more than obscure a phenomenon that is very much about perception and public discourse; which may or may not be connected to the lived realities of children. The important point is that the notion of what constitutes child abuse can (and does) vary across both time and space, and amongst different cultural groups. Given this fact it is difficult to see how an analysis of 'the drama' of child abuse as individual pathology and family dysfunction can be sustained. Nevertheless, much of the serious research funding continues to be directed at projects setting out to identify the characteristics and psychopathology of 'abusers' and 'abusive families'.

To counter the pathology model, there is a small but growing body of research, mostly undertaken by feminists, seeking to explain child abuse as a social phenomenon. Rooted in a feminist-oriented epistemology, this body of research has set out to develop an analysis that explains child abuse as an act of oppression where there is an abuse of power and authority by others (usually adults) in which a child's human rights are violated. Crucially, it sets out to make a link between child abuse and the structures of oppression based upon a politicised analysis of gender, age, 'race' and class power relations within society. Unfortunately, even within this paradigm there has been a tendency by white feminists, under the slogan of 'universal sisterhood', to minimise or ignore the issue of 'race' and difference (Carby, 1982).

The key point of disagreement has been related to questions about the role and status of the family. While white feminists have identified the family as being a crucial site of women's oppression black feminists have felt the need to defend the black family in the face of white racism and in critiquing Eurocentric conceptualisations of it:

> A key source of counter-attack to the feminist critique of the family has come from black feminists who have vocalised their defence of the black

family-household as an arena of solidarity and resistance against racism
both in Britain and the USA. (Tang-Nain, 1991: 9)

Clearly, this position does not suggest that the black family household
is not a source of oppression for women and children. Indeed, the very
foundations of progressive child protection work are rooted in a belief
that, while embodying dynamics of oppression characteristic of the
wider society, the family can also be a source of love, care and security.
In other words, one is trying to avoid simultaneously both a patholo-
gised and a glamorised view of the black family. In helping to find a
path between these equally problematic constructions Channer and
Parton (1990) state:

> Too often, black families are either pathologised or excused on the
> grounds of 'cultural relativism' practice, which leans towards 'blaming
> the victim'. The need is, we emphasise, to individualise and subjectify
> them, within an understanding of structural racism, in a search to under-
> stand more fully in what ways people are different but the same.
> (Channer and Parton, 1990: 116)

Moreover, part of the way in which black families and individuals may
be different will inevitably be the way they will view white state institutions. In other words, deviant behaviour, far from providing evidence
of abnormality and dysfunction might, in fact, represent 'normal' and
predictable responses to particular social situations. For example,
whilst not desirable, it may be quite rational for a black child living in
an all-white community to deny their blackness, particularly where
drawing attention to this aspect of their identity is likely to create
hostile responses from their peer group. Therefore, by attempting to,
as it were, relativise behaviours it does not mean that anything goes.
On the contrary, behaviours, particularly if they are causing harm to
others, must be confronted. However, a relativist position does highlight the dangers in drawing any conclusions about family functioning
based on white middle-class norms. It demands that professionals
penetrate the lives of their clients in such a way that each other's world
view, if not lived, can be acknowledged and understood.

PHYSICAL ABUSE AND NEGLECT

One way to begin to compile some useful data on child abuse and 'race'
is by making statistically based comparisons of black and white children, in care, on at risk registers, in types of placement and so on.
Whilst some studies have attempted to do this, most are very unreli-

able as they are dependent on efficient monitoring of ethnic background. Moreover, there is the problem of defining useful categories for monitoring. Concepts such as 'race' and 'ethnicity' have been operationalised in very problematic ways in much of the research. This process of decontextualising these concepts from their social origins and presenting them as objective facts is particularly characteristic of epidemiological research on black people. The problem with such epistemological approaches, rooted in quantitative scientific/positivist modes of enquiry, is that complex sets of social relations are reduced to crude, and very often meaningless, variables (Sheldon and Parker, 1992; Stubbs, 1993).

Nevertheless, in spite of the methodological problems, several American and a smaller number of British studies examining 'race' do exist. Available statistics are inconclusive as to whether black children are over- or under-represented (Corby, 1993). Some research indicates a disproportionately higher number of children registered from ethnic minorities (Creighton, 1992) although other more localised studies paint a different picture (King and Trowell, 1992; Coventry Child Protection Committee, 1994).

While not surprising, one of the most worrying findings from research is the higher propensity of black families compared to white families to be investigated for reasons of neglect. Studies by Saunders, Nelson and Landsman (1993) in the US found that whilst black African American families were more likely to be reported for child neglect, agencies were less likely to engage positively with those families until the problems became chronic. There are some indications that similar patterns of child protection work with black families and the lack of effective preventive work are being repeated in Britain (Barn, 1993).

In his comparative research of child protection cases in Western Australia and Wales, Thorpe (1994) found that child protection workers in both countries were spending most of their time policing the parenting habits of extremely disadvantaged people whom he felt were more in need of practical and financial support. Moreover, he found that only 25% of children were entering state care due to physical, sexual or emotional abuse. The remaining 75% were deemed as being 'at risk' or 'neglected'. The most striking statistic in Thorpe's research in Australia was the fact that nearly 70% of all families investigated were headed by lone mothers and almost 50% were black Aborigines, who make up 3% of the population. He concludes that the child protection system, as it has developed in recent years, is more geared up to being used to impose standardised norms of parenting on a diverse population than to protecting children from abuse and harm.

SEXUAL ABUSE

The amount of research into the incidence of sexual abuse and black families is minimal. This is perhaps not surprising for, coupled with the sensitive nature of the subject within many non-English speaking communities, the language and concepts associated with sexual abuse simply do not exist. This of course does not mean that sexual abuse does not exist, but the way it might be talked about or explained may be very different. Language and conceptual difficulties are a great source of difficulty for both practitioners and researchers and, coupled with cultures in which the open discussion of sexual matters (abuse or not) can be seen as a taboo, obtaining useful information is extremely difficult.

Nevertheless, in contrast to physical abuse and neglect, previous American studies (Finkelhor and Baron, 1986) and more recent British studies tend to indicate a disproportionately lower incidence of reported cases of sexual abuse amongst black communities. In their examination of the child protection system in England, based on a national postal survey and a detailed examination of a number of localities with substantial minority populations, Gibbons, Conroy and Bell (1995: 40) found that:

> Black and Asian families were over-represented among referrals for physical injury compared to whites (58% v 42%), and under-represented among referrals for sexual abuse (20% v 31%).

While one may speculate that cultural variations in child-rearing practices may account for some of these differences, one wonders whether the statistics also provide further evidence of cultural stereotyping on the side of professionals, based on the misplaced belief, fed by certain cultural theorists and anthropologists, that incest and abuse are 'normal' in some minority families and cultures (Nelson, 1987: 48). Moreover, one may ask whether this under-representation is not also related to certain myths about the sexual and moral decadence of 'western culture' in contrast to 'God fearing' black and Asian families and communities. Thus child sexual abuse is understood as a by-product of western sexual promiscuity. As we have seen with the exposure of Catholic priests in Ireland or the activities of staff in 'elite' English boarding schools, the idea that certain cultures, institutions and families may be of a higher moral order very often provides a perfect smoke-screen for concealing abuse and disarming its victims.

In debates about child protection and 'race' discussions about black patriarchy have been conspicuous by their absence. Indeed one is prompted to suggest that some practitioners and authorities, in their half-hearted efforts to involve 'the community', have allowed male patriarchs, in the guise of 'community leaders', to act as brokers and guarantors in cases of child abuse, thus blurring the thin boundary between 'working in partnership' and 'collusion'. The most obvious example of this combination of white cultural racism and black patriarchy can be seen in the spurious but well rehearsed explanation for the phenomenon of Asian girls running away from home because of 'cultural conflict' and forced marriages (Ahmed, 1986). In a study on homelessness and the phenomenon in question, Patel found that far from the received wisdom, in addition to general family conflict: 'like many other young women in general, the young black women interviewed were running because of physical violence, emotional and sexual abuse' (Patel, 1994: 35).

CHECKLISTS

Another approach within the quantitative paradigm can be linked with attempts to identify the characteristics of abusers and abusing families by isolating sociological and psychological variables associated with abuse such as: family constitution, income, history, sexual relations, domestic violence and so on. Some research attempts to operationalise 'race' and cultural variables. However, whilst a lot of time and money has gone into very prestigious research, more often than not definite conclusions cannot be drawn.

In challenging some of the reductionism of Kemp, Silverman, Steel *et al.* (1962) and their claims to single causal factors, other researchers using this approach from a more eclectic perspective have attempted to show a multiplicity of variables associated with child abuse. Out of this research, it is possible to isolate four essential factors that can be associated with child abuse: social isolation, stress, socio-economic status, and cycle of violence (Gelles, 1982; Parton, 1985). However, as Gelles (1982) warns, it is critically important not to see these factors as *causes*, but as indicators or associations that are based on statistical averages and often on dubious samples. There is other evidence to suggest that nearly half of all abusing families tend to fall outside all of the indicators, again reinforcing the point that abuse, particularly sexual abuse, is extremely difficult to predict.

Specifically in relation to physical abuse and neglect, one factor which seems to be consistently repeated is that of low income and high poverty (Garbarino, 1976). For example, Sedlack (1992), investigating 'maltreatment' based on a national US sample, found that children of low-income families were at greatest risk of maltreatment. If one looks at the low socio-economic position of most black families in both Britain and the US, it is not surprising that they are more likely to be over-represented in cases of physical abuse and neglect.

PREVENTION

In terms of preventive work with black families, evidence suggests that, where positive engagement is made, risk of abuse can be drastically reduced. For example, research conducted by Tracy and Clark (1974) on single parent, black families in Philadelphia who were referred for physically abusing their children, found that an intervention pro-gramme focusing mainly on the mothers and their support needs led to drastic reductions in re-referral rates. Trained outreach workers—who were mostly middle-aged black women from within their clients' own community—were introduced to the families to offer a negotiated and contracted plan of friendship and practical support rather than 'therapy'. Their work in the home involved behavioural techniques such as modelling and positive reinforcements, practical steps to reduce life stresses and advocacy on behalf of the parents. Clearly, such non-punitive social work intervention, coupled with the creative and flexible use of human and material resources, can be very effective in the prevention of abuse in black communities and families.

Sadly, the experience of black families has tended to be characterised by miscommunication, lack of trust and insensitivity, particularly where a plethora of professionals is involved. For example, Bogle (1988), reflecting on her work with black women at the Brixton Black Women's Centre, sets out the problems that can result from the closer proximity of the police in child protection investigations:

> Black women, in trying to protect their own children, face racism from the police which can compound the abuse already suffered by the chil-dren. Black mothers do not want to put their children at risk through this yet they wish justice for their children. (Bogle, 1988: 134)

IMPLICATIONS FOR PRACTITIONERS— DEVELOPING ANTI-RACIST PRACTICE

Up to this point, I have commented on the broader context in which the relationship between black children and families and child protec-tion agency responses to child abuse may be understood. A detailed analysis of the research evidence has formed the basis of the discussion and overall a negative picture of current practice has been painted. At a time when social work itself seems to be at a crossroads and professionals are struggling to stay afloat under mountains of bureaucracy, I am acutely aware of the need to make some suggestions and offer some possibilities for developing practice. The final part of the chapter, whilst endeavouring to offer some pointers for practice, will, at the risk of being accused of pessimism, reinforce the message that any hope of meaningful change requires a broader analysis of the historical role of state institutions into the lives of minority communities and their struggles against oppression.

Whilst no doubt there are many examples of good anti-racist practice, Gordon's (1989) historical study of family violence and the role of 'child protectors' suggests that being pessimistic is perhaps wise if not desirable. In examining the case records of three child protection agencies in Boston, US, covering 80 years up to the 1960s, she found a constant litany of discriminatory attitudes and action against non-white clients spanning the whole period. Whilst one would hope that things have progressed, many of the examples she highlights do indeed reverberate with the experiences of black clients up to the present period.

Lack of adequate translators was a chronic problem. The most common result was the conclusion that clients were stupid or ignorant because of their inadequacy in answering questions or following instructions. Sometimes the caseworkers could not gather basic family information accurately because of their lack of language skills. Often case records were duplicated because, due to mistakes in spelling foreign names, workers did not find a previously existing record.

> Social workers often disdained many aspects of the ethnic and religious cultures of their clients; for most of the period of this study, the child protectors were overwhelmingly native-born white Protestant. Most caseworkers, reflecting the cultures in which they had been raised, assumed subnormal intelligence among their poorer clients. The records abound with derogatory references, even when made with kind intent. (Gordon, 1989: 14)

So clearly, whilst 'race' has been an ever present feature in social work intervention into black families, more often than not it has been addressed in problematic ways. Nevertheless, any assessment of the needs of black children and families must include a 'racial' dimension. This does not mean that professionals should be merely seeking to understand abuse as a manifestation of cultural and/or family norms. It demands that professionals attend to factors that traverse the confines of the immediate and extended family. In developing an anti-racist perspective assessment of needs and risk must be much more expansive. There is a need to recognise that abuse and significant harm for black children can, and very often does, take place through bullying, racial and sexual harassment, within institutional care, and by alternative carers as well as within the family (Jones and Butt, 1995).

In working with black children survivors professionals must attempt to unravel and understand the abuse through a complex analysis of cultural forms, socio-economic and psycho-social contexts, 'race', gender and any other factor (e.g. disability) which might have some bearing on power relations both intrinsic and extrinsic to the family (Droisden, 1989). In building on their understanding of power and powerlessness, professionals must seek innovative ways to empower black children to be able to talk about their experiences; where, for example, Asian girls do not have to make the choice between 'running' away from home and disclosing sexual abuse, or where the fear of family members being threatened with deportation does not force children and mothers into a Hobson's choice of continued family violence versus oppressive intervention by state authorities.

Far too often black children and families have experienced social work intervention in negative ways, and sometimes the damage caused has not been realised until it is too late; when the child has been isolated from her family, community, culture and social support networks. Abuse can have a very disorientating impact on children, particularly if it is coming from loved ones. For black children who have been abused the psychological trauma is very often amplified by the daily bombardment with racist stereotypes about black people. Particularly in cases of sexual abuse, as Droisden (1989) observes, for black children who may already be suffering from a poor self-image there can very often be a doubling of negative messages, resulting in a child feeling that they are 'bad' and 'dirty' not only, as it were, on the outside but also on the inside.

> In the end it can become impossible to unravel whether your feelings of unworthiness are due to the abuse or the racism . . . They merge and intensify each other. For survival, they need to be unravelled. (Droisden, 1989: 161)

The resources for helping black children, particularly in relation to questions of identity, are very often to be found within their own community. In relation to developing partnership within black communities, professionals must be aware of the important developments that are taking place. Organisations that have traditionally been dominated by the patriarchs and have been used primarily for purposes of religious worship and ceremonies are beginning to diversify. What seems to be emerging, particularly with the greater involvement of second and third generation British born black people, is a greater readiness to develop community welfare, education and training provision, including confidential counselling services, day care and child protection services. It is important that child protection agencies and workers support such initiatives, not only through financial backing but also by offering their expertise and skills to assist in, for example: making applications for funding and planning permission; setting up effective management/administrative structures and providing access to training and other resources such as information technology. It is only through such positive engagement with black communities that trust and partnership can emerge, and some of the misconceptions about child protection workers can be removed.

CONCLUSION

The dominant orthodoxy within the child protection system—one that treats child abuse as a consequence of family dysfunctioning—persists (MacLeod and Saraga, 1988). The power and status of professionals, coupled with the ever-growing technical jargon and ingrained—and often unconscious—ideas of 'normal' families and resource limitations, have served to limit black children's and families' opportunities for receiving appropriate intervention and support. Such a view is supported by much of the research evidence examined in this chapter. It has been argued that the major failure of the dominant liberal multi-cultural approach has been its tendency to misunderstand the complex nature of black identity, which is often reduced to a set of ill-thought-out stereotypes. On the other hand, concerns have been raised that a certain self-righteous anti-racist orthodoxy, with its tendency to avoid questions of culture, difference and diversity, has also failed to connect with the real lives of black children and families in Britain.

Child protection work is very demanding and complex and there are no easy answers. Indeed, social workers are in one sense both victims and survivors of what has become a highly proceduralised and punitive system for intervening in the lives of families who are very often suffering from a multitude of social problems on top of family conflict. Because of the daily rigour of work it can become very difficult for professionals to see beyond the presenting problems, nevertheless the social production of child abuse must be understood in its complexity. Whilst attending to the immediacy of human suffering, alongside factors concerning familial and carer abuse, child protection professionals must build into their equation such factors as poverty, racial violence and harassment, institutional racism and community safety.

REFERENCES

Ahmad B (1990) *Black Perspectives in Social Work*, Venture Press, Birmingham.

Ahmed S (1986) Cultural racism in work with Asian women and girls, in Ahmed S, Cheetham J and Small J (eds) *Social Work with Black Children and their Families*, Batsford, London.

Anthias F and Yuval-Davis N (1992) *Racialized Boundaries*, Routledge, London.

Barn R (1993) *Black Children in the Public Care System*, Batsford/BAAF, London.

Barn R, Sinclair R and Ferdinand D (1997) *Acting on Principle: An Examination of Race and Ethnicity in Social Services Provision for Children and Families*, BAAF, London.

Bebbington A and Miles J (1989) The background of children who enter local authority care, *British Journal of Social Work*, **19**: 349–368.

Bogle M T (1988) Brixton Black Women's Centre: Organising on child sexual abuse, *Feminist Review*, **28**, Spring, special issue on sexual abuse: 132–135.

Butler-Sloss E (1988) *Report of the Inquiry into Child Abuse in Cleveland*, HMSO, London.

Campbell B (1988) *Unofficial Secrets*, Virago, London.

Carby H (1982) White women listen! Black feminism and the boundaries of sisterhood, CCCS, *The Empire Strikes Back, Race and Racism in the 70s*, Hutchinson, London.

Channer Y and Parton N (1990) Racism, cultural relativism and child protection, in Violence Against Children Study Group, *Taking Child Abuse Seriously*, Unwin Hyman, London.

Corby B (1993) *Child Abuse: Towards a Knowledge Base*, Open University Press, Milton Keynes.

Coventry Child Protection Committee (1994) *Annual Report 1993/94*, Coventry.

Creighton S J (1992) *Child Abuse Trends in England and Wales 1988–1990 and an Overview from 1973–1990*, NSPCC, London.

Dale P, Davies M, Morrison T and Waters J (1986) *Dangerous Families: Assessment and Treatment of Child Abuse*, Tavistock, London.

Dominelli L (1997) *Sociology for Social Work*, Macmillan, Basingstoke.

Droisden A (1989) Racism and anti-Semitism, in Driver E and Droisden A (eds) *Child Sexual Abuse, Feminist Perspectives*, Macmillan, Basingstoke.

Finkelhor D and Baron L (1986) High risk children, in Finkelhor D (ed.) *Sourcebook on Child Sexual Abuse*, Sage, New York.

Garbarino J (1976) A preliminary study of some ecological correlates of child abuse: The impact of socio-economic stress on mothers, *Child Development*, **47**: 178–185.

Gelles R (1982) Child abuse and family violence: Implications for medical professionals, in Newberger E (ed.) *Child Abuse*, Little, Brown, Boston.

Gibbons J, Conroy S and Bell C (1995) *Operating the Child Protection System*, HMSO, London.

Gordon L (1989) *Heroes of Their Own Lives—The Politics and History of Family Violence*, Virago, London.

Herman J L (1981) *Father–Daughter Incest*, Harvard University Press, Cambridge, MA.

Jones A and Butt J (1995) *Taking the Initiative*, NSPCC, London.

Kelly L, Regan L and Burton S (1991) *An Exploratory Study of the Prevalence of Sexual Abuse in a Sample of 16–21 Year Olds*, Child Abuse and Women's Studies Unit, University of North London.

Kemp C H, Silverman F N, Steel B B, Droegemueller N and Silver H K (1962) The battered child syndrome, *Journal of the American Medical Association*, **181**: 17–24.

King M and Trowell J (1992) *Children's Welfare and the Law: The Limits of Legal Intervention*, Sage, London.

MacLeod M and Saraga E (1988) Challenging the orthodoxy, *Feminist Review*, **28**, Spring, special issue on sexual abuse: 16–55.

Modood T (1994) *Changing Ethnic Identities*, Policy Studies Institute, London.

Nelson S (1987) *Incest: Fact and Myth*, Stramullion, Edinburgh.

Parton N (1985) *The Politics of Child Abuse*, Macmillan, London.

Parton N (1991) *Governing the Family: Child Care, Child Protection and the State*, Macmillan, Basingstoke.

Patel G (1994) *The Porth Project: A Study of Homelessness and Running Away Amongst Black People in Newport, Gwent*, The Children's Society, London.

Rowe L, Hundleby M and Garnett L (1989) *Child Care Now: A Survey of Placement Patterns*, BAAF, London.

Saraga E (1993) The abuse of children, in Dallos R and McLaughlin E (eds) *Social Problems and the Family*, Sage, London.

Saunders E, Nelson K and Landsman M (1993) Racial equality and child neglect: Findings in a metropolitan area, *Child Welfare League of America*, **LXXII**, 4: 341–354.

Sedlack A J (1992) *Risk factors for child abuse and neglect and the likelihood of official investigation*, paper presented at Ninth International Congress on Child Abuse and Neglect, Chicago, September.

Sheldon T and Parker H (1992) 'Use of ethnicity' and 'race' in health research: A cautionary note, in Ahmad W I U (ed.) *The Politics of 'Race' and Health*, Race Relations Research Unit, University of Bradford, Bradford.

Singh G (1992) *Race and Social Work: from 'Black Pathology' to 'Black Perspectives'*, Race Relations Research Unit, University of Bradford, Bradford.

Singh G (1994) Anti-racist social work—Political correctness or political action, *Social Work Education*, 13 April, 1: 26–31.

Stubbs P (1989) Developing anti-racist practice—problems and possibilities, in Blagg H, Hughes J and Wattam C. *Child Sexual Abuse: Listening, Hearing and Validating the Experiences of Children*. Longman, Harlow.

Stubbs P (1991) The Children Act 1989: An anti-racist perspective, *Practice*, **5**, 3: 226–229.

Stubbs P (1993) 'Ethnic sensitive' or 'anti-racist'? Models for health research and service delivery, in Ahmad W I U (ed.) *'Race' and Health in Contemporary Britain*, Open University Press, Buckingham.

Tang-Nain G (1991) Black women, sexism and racism: Black or anti-racist feminism? *Feminist Review*, **37**, Spring, 1–22.

Thorpe D (1994) *Evaluating Child Protection*, Open University Press, Buckingham.

Tracy J J and Clark E H (1974) Treatment of child abusers, *Social Work*, **19**: 338–342.

2

YOUNG CARERS—THE CONTRADICTIONS OF BEING A CHILD CARER

Eric Blyth and Allison Waddell

INTRODUCTION

The unique status of 'young carers' both as carers of sick and disabled and family members and as children means they can benefit from services from a range of agencies provided under a variety of statutes: the Children Act 1989, the NHS and Community Care Act 1990, the Carers (Recognition and Services) Act 1995, and the Disability Discrimination Act 1995. As a group, therefore, it might be presumed that young carers are well catered for. The reality according to Dearden and Becker (1998) and the authors' experiences of young carers projects in the North of England, is considerably different. Members of their own families and professionals may ignore the needs of young carers, exploit their role within the family, and even punish them for being carers. This chapter analyses definitions of young carers, identifies contradictions in the perceived role and status of young carers, and highlights the different responses to them by health and welfare professionals.

LEGISLATING FOR YOUNG CARERS

Recognition as a carer under the Carers (Recognition and Services) Act 1995 entitles the carer to request a separate assessment of their needs when the care recipient is being assessed. It also introduces the right of the carer to stop caring and can provide access to a range of services for the person cared for. However, official definitions of caring are essentially task-focused, the Carers (Recognition and Services) Act 1995

Children, Child Abuse and Child Protection. Placing Children Centrally, by The Violence Against Children Study Group.
© 1999 John Wiley & Sons Ltd.

defining a carer as an individual providing 'a substantial amount of care on a regular basis', while the Department of Health offers a working definition of a 'young carer' as

> a child or young person who is carrying out significant caring tasks and assuming a level of responsibility for another person, which would usually be taken by an adult. The term refers to children and young people under 18 years caring for adults (usually their parents) or occasionally siblings. It does not refer to young people under 18 years caring for their own children. Nor does the term refer to those children who accept an age appropriate role in taking responsibility for household tasks in homes with a disabled, sick or mentally ill parent. (SSI, 1995)

Problems associated with this approach to young carers are that some young carers may be excluded because their caring activities do not meet local authority criteria of 'significant', or that whatever they do is regarded as 'age appropriate'; while exclusive concern with task performance may ignore the *impact* of caring on the carer.

In practice, agencies involved with young carers have tended to consider both the impact of caring on the young person as well as the actual caring tasks performed in determining whether to identify particular young people as carers. As a result the term 'young carer' has been applied to young people who do not necessarily have 'significant' levels of caring responsibilities but who, nevertheless, are affected emotionally, socially, educationally, or physically by living with someone who is disabled, has learning difficulties, has mental ill-health, is physically ill, abuses substances or has HIV/AIDS-related illnesses (Webster, 1992; O'Hagan, 1993; NCH Action for Children, 1995).

Attempts to raise the profile of young carers have not, however, been immune from criticism. Olsen (1996) warns that the emergence of 'young carers' as a new welfare category fails to discriminate between children and young people in a variety of family circumstances, some of whom may be defined as young carers, while others are not. He argues that further research is required to explore how the experiences of children living with a disabled parent differ from those of children who live in other households—particularly children who assume responsibilities for caring or undertake household tasks for reasons other than those associated with a recognised disability or illness. Olsen also claims that the focus on young carers has diverted attention from the needs of, and devalued, disabled people. On the other hand, accounts of adults who were previously young carers indicate that young people have taken hitherto unrecognised responsibilities for the informal care of family members for many years (e.g. Aldridge and Becker, 1993). Currently many young carers remain hidden (Alexander, 1995; Frank, 1995).

Potential reasons for the reluctance of young carers and their families to acknowledge their role in providing care have been well articulated: denial of the disability or illness; denial of its effects on the young person; a failure to recognise the responsibilities carried by the young person; a preference for maintaining the *status quo* and thus avoiding potential disruption to daily routines, individual caring roles and family composition which might be put at risk by outside intervention; or fear of the consequences of official identification and possible intervention. When professionals are involved they may justify inaction by imposing stereotyped norms about the role of children in families in terms of gender, race, class, religion, culture and status, and fail to listen to the child (e.g. Greater Manchester Black Young Carers Working Group, 1996) or may subject them to inappropriate and/or punitive forms of intervention (Aldridge and Becker, 1993; Hinchliffe, 1995).

The government has acknowledged that some young people may not provide the level of care to meet the criteria of 'carer' but that their development may nevertheless be impaired as a result of their circumstances, suggesting these children may be regarded as 'children in need' under provisions of the Children Act 1989 (Part III Section 17) (DOH, 1995a, b; DOH and DFE, 1996). The Children Act does not define 'children in need', the government determining that this was best left to individual local authorities according to local *need* (although it clearly provides much scope, especially in the context of constraints on public services, for such definitions to be framed according to local *resources*). While a review of local authority young carer policy documentation revealed that 55 out of 71 local authorities providing information had addressed the issue of young carers at some level, only 11 indicated they would define a young carer as a child 'in need' (SSI, 1996). Furthermore service provision for 'children in need' varies between local authorities, suggesting that young carers are frequently marginalised and afforded low status and priority unless they are regarded as children who require protection.

Although the possibility of providing for young carers under a multifaceted legislative framework might promote flexibility, it could be argued that such diversity reduces the potential for a consistent approach. SSI, for example, noted 'a considerable amount of delay . . . (in accessing) . . . straightforward services' for families of young carers because of the organisational divide between adult and children's services with different allocation priorities and approaches to provision, and found 'confusion amongst staff about their roles and responsibilities regarding young carers' (SSI, 1996: 25).

Such concerns were reinforced by a judicial review involving the London Borough of Newham (1996) for failing to take into account the needs of a young carer when determining service provision for a disabled parent, and legal action against the London Borough of Tower Hamlets in two similar instances (Field, 1996; *Disability Now*, 1997). It might be expected that these rulings would encourage consideration that is more sensitive by Social Services Departments when assessing the needs of young carers and disabled care recipients. However, the extent of local authorities' responsibilities to provide services under community care legislation was subsequently thrown into confusion following a House of Lords ruling that Gloucestershire County Council had acted lawfully in withdrawing community care services because of insufficient resources (Clements, 1997).

Alternatively, if potential risks are identified, the caring arrangement may be challenged and other strategies may be suggested or imposed, for example home care, alternative placement, or adaptations to the home. The judicial review of Newham Council's actions determined that the local authority was failing a family in need and the Social Services Department was instructed not only to undertake assessments of individual family members under the Carers (Recognition and Services) Act 1995, the Children Act 1989 and the Chronically Sick and Disabled Persons Act 1970, but also to 'ensure that the arrangements to give effect to its service provision decision are put in place timeously'.

Furthermore, support and resources provided as a result of an assessment under the NHS and Community Care Act 1990 are likely to be specific (e.g. aids and adaptations, home care) and/or time-limited to address the particular needs of the adult. The support package may fail to address the range of needs associated with parenting and, therefore, be incongruent with the type of support required for the family as a whole, such as could be available within the provisions of the Children Act 1989, Part III, Section 17.

Given the comparatively recent recognition of young carers as a group and the difficulty of applying a set of characteristics to assist identification of individuals, it is perhaps not surprising that the present response to them by professionals is piecemeal and inconsistent. The reasons are inherently complex but indicate the contradictions in the status of children who care.

CONTRADICTIONS IN THE STATUS OF YOUNG CARERS—CHILDREN AS 'CARERS', 'IN NEED' OR 'AT RISK'?

The point at which a young carer may be regarded as a 'carer', 'in need' or 'at risk' may be determined by the label or definition used to describe a particular set of circumstances. For example, Bentovim

(1991) applies the term 'emotional abuse' to children who are 'inducted into parental caretaking roles'. This feature is associated with children who undertake a range of caring tasks for parents and others who have mental ill-health difficulties or who misuse substances (O'Hagan, 1993), and Mahon and Higgins (1995) suggest that such 'role reversal' constitutes a caring task. Similarly Bentovim (1991) considers that children who do not have opportunities to play or develop relationships and whose personal development is restricted are 'emotionally abused' while young carers researchers (Aldridge and Becker, 1993; Blyth, Saleem and Scott, 1995) cite these features as possible consequences of caring.

Although the young person may appear to cope well with their circumstances, they may not realise their full potential. The difficulty in determining the impact of caring with regard to unrealised potential is evident. Youngsters who do not cope well may not succeed in managing the emotional or physical pressures of the caring relationship, leading to deterioration in their own mental and physical well-being. They may become withdrawn, aggressive, develop disturbed or self-harming behaviours or miss school, thereby attracting attention to the overt presenting 'problems'.

Further, it is likely that, unless the child is disabled or considered to be 'at risk', children in general would not be the focus of professional interventions. By virtue of their age, children lack legal rights to autonomy and are considered the dependants of their adult carers until they attain the age of 18. Despite the emphasis of the Children Act 1989 and the United Nations Convention on the Rights of the Child to give status to the voices of children, adults can override the *wishes* of children if it is considered to be in their *best interests* to do so. Consequently, the needs and rights of the young carer both as a child and as a carer may be undermined either by the person with parental responsibility or by professionals not only used to assuming they know what is in children's best interests but also having a mandate to give this effect. Professional assessment and intervention will need to promote the child's right to choice—to continue with, or withdraw from, caring responsibilities—as well as considering the need for action to protect the child if it is considered the child's safety and well-being are at risk.

Some behaviours and health conditions of the care recipient may attract a more deliberate, structured response by professionals, and there is evidence that a more punitive and reactionary approach is taken in families where it is considered that children may be 'at risk' because of the life-styles and/or unpredictability and potential instability of the parent (Weir, 1994; Alexander, 1995; Wallace, 1995). Sone (1997) suggests that social workers may be 'trigger-happy' with child protection procedures when parents have one of a range of problems widely differing in nature, such as learning difficulties or the misuse of drugs or alcohol.

The source and reason for referral to agencies, and the philosophy of the organisation receiving the referral, are also likely to be significant in the initial stages, for example children living in families where there are some mental health conditions, or alcohol or drug use, may be viewed as children 'at risk'. Child protection procedures will demand a particular course of statutory intervention that disregards the caring role and relationship and which focuses on the ability of the parent to provide a 'good enough' standard of care for the child. The initial assessment of the family circumstances is on the level of risk and need to protect.

Lewis (1997) notes that where parents have mental health difficulties different approaches are taken by mental health and children and families' teams. Mental health professionals are likely to focus on the medical conditions of the adult rather than on their needs as a parent and so make a referral to Children's Services to address matters relating to the child. Social workers need to balance the rights of the parent and the risks to the child. However, where there is a difference in opinion between the teams, the need to protect the child will take priority. Coombes (1997) suggests that difficulties of co-operation between professionals are compounded by the need to work within different legal frameworks and the absence of multidisciplinary training.

Risk assessment frameworks such as those advocated by the Department of Health (1990) support the notion that mental illness and substance misuse are associated with predictions of neglect and physical abuse of children, while studies of child abuse tragedies (e.g. Department of Health, 1991) indicate a correlation between mental ill-health, substance misuse and child abuse that should not be ignored when working with children and families. Nevertheless child abuse is rarely attributable to these factors alone (Falkov, 1997). A number of characteristics and situations have been identified that may indicate increased risks when presenting simultaneously (see, e.g., O'Hagan, 1993; Reder and Lucey, 1995). The timing of professional intervention is, therefore, likely to be significant in these circumstances if the child's welfare and development are to be promoted and preserved without the need for statutory action. Waddell (1996) notes that a statutory referral may be more likely if the parent is perceived as unwilling to engage with professionals. Additionally, the younger the child, the more likely it is that child protection action will be pursued.

In contrast, parents with a chronic illness or physical disabilities who may be emotionally 'absent' or whose irritability might be heightened at times of acute pain, distress or hospitalisation do not appear to be viewed with the same scrutiny or concern. Thoburn (1997) distinguishes the support offered to parents who are regarded as having more 'acceptable' conditions, for example, multiple sclerosis or visual impairment, and a punitive approach to those who are regarded as 'less deserving', for example, those who misuse substances. However, Segal and Simpkins describe how disability and illness may adversely affect the self-worth of the person cared for, which may contribute to a stressful situation and increase risks of inadequate or unacceptable care of the child:

> People who feel like this may at times actually want to attack their children; to make the children suffer as they suffer themselves. At one extreme they may feel they do not care any more, do not want to bother, and they may withdraw from parental responsibilities, this in itself can result in apparently unintentional cruelty, such as neglect. At the other extreme, there may be a more obvious attack. (Segal and Simpkins, 1996: 98)

The Department of Health asserts that:

> the fact that particular parents suffer from limitations such as low intelligence or physical disablement is not relevant to whether the care they are providing is reasonable. What is expected is the care that the average or reasonable parent would provide for that child. It follows that if a parent cannot cope with a child because of personal difficulties, he or she will be acting unreasonably if help is not sought, such as local authority services, including accommodation for the child. (DOH, 1989; para. 1.35)

However, such help is not always forthcoming. Parents with learning difficulties are more likely to receive different (more punitive) treatment, based on assumptions that they are: 'incapable of providing good enough parenting and many service providers see only evidence that supports this preconception' (Booth and Booth, 1994: 15), a conclusion endorsed by *Community Care* (1992) and Valios (1995).

Parker and Olsen (1995), on the other hand, remark that children of *single* disabled mothers are most likely to be subject to child protection intervention as they tend to be regarded as unable to offer appropriate care for their children. They comment on the tendency of professionals to focus on these mothers' inability to undertake parental activity and thus unfairly disregard their desire to parent. The result is that the disabled parent is blamed for their circumstances and discriminated against. Disabled activists (see also Keith and Morris, 1995; Olsen and Parker, 1997) argue that resources should be targeted at the disabled person and that the mother should be assisted and supported to perform her parenting role and to live independently, thus removing the dependency on her child to care for her. Such intervention would promote the principles of the Children Act 1989 Part III Section 17.

However, while it is not prudent to suggest that the following comments are representative of all families living with disability, illness or other health problems, it must be noted that studies including parents of young carers (Aldridge and Becker, 1994; Walker, 1996; Waddell, 1997) have highlighted a range of parental views and attitudes about the young person's role in caring for them or another member of the family. These include: acknowledgement of the child's limited freedom; the negative impact of caring on their child's education; damage to the child/parent relationship; 'loss of childhood'; parents' rejection of external formal sources of support; and parents' description of themselves as a 'burden' on the young carer. In short, the impact on a young person of caring for a member of the family is complex and cannot be addressed effectively without consideration of the individual needs and aspirations of *all* the family members.

Other situations that could result in different professional responses are highlighted by Waddell (1996). She notes that children who perform physical caring tasks, such as lifting and turning a family member, may be at risk of causing themselves physical injury and of impairing their physical development. Professionals may focus on and support the caring task, for example, by providing instruction on lifting and handling techniques or providing aids and adaptations to assist the process and thus condone the behaviour and the role of the young carer. Such an approach may result in criticism of agencies for supporting a young person in this way if the young person subsequently injures himself or herself.

Messages from research (DOH, 1995c) indicate that few families are offered informal support prior to child protection intervention and that professionals tend to withdraw quickly if care proceedings are not instituted. This suggests that children who are affected by the disability or ill-health of a family member are unlikely to be the focus of Social Services or other formal support or intervention unless they present some identifiable 'difficult' behaviours or are considered to be exposed to an unacceptable level of risk within the home.

Thus if children who have caring responsibilities are not the focus of Social Services Departments' attentions, at best they may be referred to a dedicated young carers project if one exists within the local area, at worst they may be ignored and denied services and support. Analysis of the circumstances of approximately 80 young carers who were in contact with a young carers project in the North West in 1996/1997 indicated that over 27% of the families were not in contact with any other welfare agencies. Furthermore, only five children (from three families) were allocated their own social worker during their involvement with the project. In four instances, this resulted from their being accommodated by the local authority when their home circumstances changed, and one young person was allocated a social worker following a number of child protection referrals. Another two youngsters received non-teaching support in school in an attempt to manage their behaviour in class. Some family members of the remaining young carers had social work support, for example, where the siblings of young carers had physical disabilities or learning difficulties, while a few parents had a social worker allocated from the adult Social Services team, specialist social worker or community health worker to address their own needs arising from their disability or long-term mental health problems. Others had brief contact with Social Services at points of crisis or when being assessed under community care legislation but otherwise were not involved with any statutory welfare agency.

The absence of professional intervention and/or support noted in this project reinforces other evidence that, regardless of the family member's illness or disability and the caring roles and responsibilities of the young carers in this particular local authority, the children and young people were considered neither to be 'in need' nor 'at risk' by other professionals, echoing conclusions reached by Blyth, Saleem and Scott (1995).

Despite the drive to refocus children's services to provide more family-oriented support (Audit Commission, 1994; DOH, 1995c) the tendency to prioritise work with those who appear most 'at risk' and who require an immediate response is understandable given public and political expectations that Social Services Departments should assume the lead role in protecting children, although the effectiveness of the child protection system in preventing them from suffering significant harm in the long term is increasingly questioned.

Paradoxically, children and families who would benefit from access to services now (but who do not receive them because they are afforded insufficient priority) may be the recipients of compulsory action and involuntary intervention in the future.

The experience of the authors is that referrals to young carers projects do not generally arise as a result of an assessment of need via either children's legislation or the Carers (Recognition and Services) Act 1995. Without statutory responsibilities and powers, and in the absence of clear policies and protocols, young carers workers rely on the goodwill of statutory agencies to work together to offer appropriate support to young carers and their families.

CONCLUSION

Inconsistencies in identifying and responding to 'young carers' are exacerbated by a number of factors. First, the term 'carer' is generally considered to relate to predominantly physical, tangible tasks, thus hindering understanding and acceptance of the more abstract elements of caring, or the effects of someone else's disability, illness or health problem on a young person. Second, the language used to describe 'young carers' in families conflicts with the language used in the field of child protection. Depending on professional or agency orientation a young person in a given situation may be perceived as either a 'young carer' (implying role and responsibility) or 'at risk' (implying dependency, lack of responsibility and vulnerability). Thus the relationship between child and parent, 'young carer' and (dependent) person cared for, is substantially, albeit subtly, changed; although it is accepted that children may be adversely affected by another's disability or illness, there is a danger that this may be perceived as inherently posing a threat to the young person's well-being. While some young people may require protective intervention, for others, with appropriate support, the experience may have positive effects, for example enhanced skill development, increased self-worth and confidence. Third, despite models and suggested frameworks for balancing preventive and protection services, professional perceptions of 'carers', 'children in need', and 'children at risk' tend to be diverse, if not polarised. Although a young person may be both a 'young carer' and 'at risk' it is unlikely that the principles and methods of working with 'young carers' would be applied in this case.

Young carers and their families are not, of course, the only ones whom the welfare net fails adequately to support. The Department of Health has formally acknowledged the imbalance in service provision between, on the one hand, child protection and, on the other, preventive services to children 'in need' (DOH, 1998). It is to be hoped that the government's intentions that 'assessment of the needs of children and their families will be a key element' in the delivery of appropriate services (DOH, 1998: 1.3) will encompass all children and their families and successfully challenge countervailing pressures imposed by legislative tensions, resource constraints and competing agency priorities.

REFERENCES

Alexander H (1995) *Young Carers and HIV*, Children in Scotland, Edinburgh.
Aldridge J and Becker S (1993) *Children Who Care: Inside the World of Young Carers*, Loughborough University, Loughborough.

Aldridge J and Becker S (1994) *'My Child, My Carer': the Parents' Perspective*, Loughborough University, Loughborough.

Audit Commission (1994) *Seen but Not Heard: Co-ordinating Community Child Health and Social Services for Children in Need*, HMSO, London.

Bentovim A (1991) Significant harm in context, in Adcock M, White R and Hollows A (eds) *Significant Harm*, Significant Publications, Croydon.

Blyth E, Saleem T and Scott M (1995) *Kirklees Young Carers Project, October 1994–June 1995: Report to Kirklees MC*, University of Huddersfield, Huddersfield.

Booth T and Booth W (1994) *Parenting under Pressure: Mothers and Fathers with Learning Difficulties*, Open University Press, Buckingham.

Clements L (1997) Rule of law, *Community Care*, 10–16 April, 19–20.

Community Care (1992) Mother was unjustly treated, *Community Care*, 2–9 January, 2.

Coombes H (1997) cited in Sone K, Mother love, *Community Care*, 22–28 May, 26–27.

Dearden C and Becker S (1998) *Young Carers in the UK: A Profile*, Carers National Association, London.

Department of Health (1989) *An Introduction to the Children Act 1989*, HMSO, London.

Department of Health (1990) *Protecting Children: a Guide for Social Workers Undertaking a Comprehensive Assessment*, HMSO, London.

Department of Health (1991) *Child Abuse: a Study of Inquiry Reports 1980–1989*, HMSO, London.

Department of Health (1995a) *The Carers (Recognition and Services) Act 1995: Policy Guidance*, Department of Health, London.

Department of Health (1995b) *The Carers (Recognition and Services) Act 1995: Practice Guide*, Department of Health, London.

Department of Health (1995c) *Child Protection: Messages from Research*, HMSO, London.

Department of Health (1998) *Working Together to Safeguard Children: New Government Proposals for Inter-Agency Co-operation*, draft consultation paper, Department of Health, London.

Department of Health and Department for Education (1996) *Children's Services Planning: Guidance*, Department of Health and Department for Education, London.

Disability Now (1997) High court shows it cares, *Disability Now*, March, 1.

Falkov A (1997) *Parental Psychiatric Disorder and Child Maltreatment. Part II: Extent and Nature of the Association*, Highlights No. 149, National Children's Bureau, London.

Field P (1996) Schoolboy 'trapped by burden of care', *The Independent*, 4 March, 5.

Frank J (1995) *Couldn't Care More: a Study of Young Carers and their Needs*, Children's Society, London.

Greater Manchester Black Young Carers Working Group (1996) *Working with Black Young Carers: a Framework for Change*, Carers National Association, London.

Hinchliffe D (1995) *Parliamentary Debates*, 21 April, **258**: 463.

Keith L and Morris J (1995) Easy targets: A disability rights perspective on the 'children as carers' debate, *Critical Social Policy*, **44/45**: 36–57.

Lewis H (1997) cited in Sone K, Mother love, *Community Care*, 22–28 May, 26–27.

London Borough of Newham (1996) *R v. London Borough of Newham ex parte Whittingham*.

Mahon A and Higgins J (1995) *'A Life of our Own'. Young Carers: an Evaluation of Three RHA Funded Projects*, University of Manchester Health Services Management Unit, Manchester.

NCH: Action for Children (1995) *All in the Family: Siblings and Disability*, NCH: Action for Children, London.

O'Hagan K (1993) *Emotional and Psychological Abuse of Children*, Open University Press, Milton Keynes, Buckingham.

Olsen R (1996) Young carers: challenging the facts and politics of researching into children and caring, *Disability and Society*, **11**: 41–54.

Olsen R and Parker G (1997) A response to Aldridge and Becker—'Disability rights and the denial of young carers: the dangers of zero-sum arguments', *Critical Social Policy*, Spring, 125–133.

Parker G and Olsen R (1995) A sideways glance at young carers, in Social Services Inspectorate, *Young Carers: Something to Think About: Report of Four SSI Workshops, May–July 1995*, Department of Health, London.

Reder P and Lucey C (eds) (1995) *Assessment of Parenting: Psychiatric and Psychological Contributions*, Routledge, London.

Segal J and Simpkins J (1996) *Helping Children with Ill or Disabled Parents: a Guide for Parents and Professionals*, Jessica Kingsley Publishers, London.

Social Services Inspectorate (1995) *Young Carers*, CI (95) 12, 28 April, Department of Health, London.

Social Services Inspectorate (1996) *Young Carers: Making a Start: Report of the SSI Fieldwork Project on Families with Disability or Illness, October 1995–January 1996*, Department of Health, London.

Sone K (1997) The right stuff, *Community Care*, 13–19 March, 16–17.

Thoburn J (1997) cited in Sone K, The right stuff, *Community Care*, 13–19 March, 16–17.

Valios N (1995) Labelled by the system, *Community Care*, 13–19 July, 7.

Waddell A (1996) *Oldham young carers project: Meeting the needs of young carers in Oldham*? Unpublished MA dissertation, University of Huddersfield, Huddersfield.

Waddell A (1997) *Evaluation of the Oldham Young Carers Project February 1995–December 1996*, Oldham Young Carers Project, Oldham.

Walker A (1996) *Young Carers and their Families: a Survey Carried Out by the Social Survey Division of the Office for National Statistics on Behalf of the Department of Health*, The Stationery Office, London.

Wallace W (1995) 'He ain't heavy, he's my father', *Times Educational Supplement*, 3 March, 3–4.

Webster J (1992) Split in two: Experiences of the children of schizophrenic mothers, *British Journal of Social Work*, **22**: 309–29.

Weir A (1994) Split decisions, *Community Care*, 1–7 December, 18.

3

CHILDREN AND ADOLESCENTS WHO SEXUALLY ABUSE

Helen Masson

INTRODUCTION AND BACKGROUND INFORMATION

Taking Child Abuse Seriously (Violence Against Children Study Group, 1990) made no reference to children and adolescents who sexually abuse others. Indeed it is only during the 1990s in this country that the extent of such abuse has begun to be acknowledged. Drawing on the author's own research, this chapter focuses on children and adolescents involved in sexually abusive activities. After a brief overview of relevant literature on the characteristics of such children, an outline of current policy and practice in this area is given. The challenge young sexual abusers present to traditional notions of childhood is highlighted, as are the tensions existing between child protection and other systems for the management of these youngsters.

The growing research evidence that young abusers account for a significant proportion of reported sexual victimisation has fuelled awareness of sexual abuse by children and adolescents. Much of the early research has come from North America (Ryan and Lane, 1991, 1997; Barbaree, Marshall and Hudson, 1993) but UK findings also indicate that a quarter to one third of reported sexual offences are committed by children and young people under 18 years of age (NCH, 1992; Home Office, 1995). It seems, likely, however, that any official statistics considerably underestimate the size and nature of the problem because typically many incidents of abuse go unreported and many incidents that are recognised as sexually abusive are not dealt with formally and officially recorded.

There are a number of articles and texts which provide detailed

Children, Child Abuse and Child Protection. Placing Children Centrally, by The Violence Against Children Study Group.
© 1999 John Wiley & Sons Ltd.

overviews of research-based profiles of young sexual abusers and their victims (see, e.g., Ryan and Lane, 1997; Openshaw, Graves, Erickson *et al.*, 1993). In this chapter only a brief outline can be attempted. Evidence shows that these sexual abusers may be as young as four years although the majority in treatment are in their middle teenage years. They are also predominantly male and white, the latter characteristic possibly reflecting the likelihood that young black abusers may be dealt with more punitively through the criminal justice system than their white counterparts, ending up in custody rather than in treatment. There is also research evidence that young females can be sexually abusive although the extent is unknown and some commentators have expressed concerns that a search for equivalence may detract from the need to acknowledge fundamental issues of male power and abuse of power in society (Forbes, 1992).

Sexual abuse by children and adolescents has multifaceted causes. It cannot be explained by a single factor such as an abuser's own previous victimisation though such trauma figures in the lives of a significant proportion. Abusive behaviour usually results from a combination of family, environmental and social factors, set in the context of socially constructed definitions of sexually abusive behaviour (NCH, 1992). As regards treatment, theoretical models of work have been developed in the USA and the UK (O'Callaghan and Print, 1994; Hoghugi, Bhate and Graham, 1997; Ryan and Lane, 1997), models that usually combine a clear focus on sex offence-specific work, with complementary packages of individual, group and family therapy. However, it appears, in this country at least, that such treatment facilities are rare, with only a few studies of the outcomes of such services (see, e.g., Buist and Fuller, 1996).

THE CHALLENGE POSED BY CHILDREN AND YOUNG PEOPLE WHO SEXUALLY ABUSE

It is interesting in itself that abuse by children and adolescents has only entered professional agendas relatively recently compared to the 'discovery' of adult forms of abusive behaviour. This is despite research evidence that much abuse is peer abuse (Ambert, 1995). Given current pervasive assumptions about the innocence of childhood, it may be that professionals and public alike find it difficult to accept that children and adolescents are capable of such behaviour. In a very interesting discussion about James Bulger's murder in 1993, James and Jenks (1994) analyse the sensational public and media reaction in this country to the tragic circumstances of this case and argue that for many in society the events that occurred seemed inconceivable, reopening debates about a child's nature and the limits of a child's capacity for action.

The developing literature on the sociology of childhood is outlined in a later publication by Jenks (1996). Jenks argues that throughout the historical and cross-cultural writing on childhood there appear two dominant ways of conceptualising or imagining the child—the Dionysian concept (the child as initially evil, corrupt and in need of curbing) and the Apollonian concept (the child as innocent, needing nurturance and protection). He comments:

> these images are immensely powerful, they live on and give force to the different discourses that we have about children; they constitute summaries of the way we have, over time, come to treat and process children 'normally'. (Jenks, 1996: 74)

Society can be seen as oscillating over time between images of children 'at risk' or children 'as a risk', but largely failing to own both conceptions simultaneously. Such dichotomised thinking, often a feature of wider debates about the state of the family and the social order, can then all too easily result in policy and practice developments which fail to reflect children and adolescents as people with many dimensions to their being.

Jenks argues that the Apollonian child has been the dominant conception in modern society. Little wonder then if evidence of abuse by children and adolescents is difficult to absorb and accept. In such circumstances denial and minimisation of what has happened or punitive, rejecting responses can easily be extreme adult coping strategies. Clearly the public and legal responses to the young killers of Jamie Bulger were of the latter variety, even though there was clear, publicised evidence that these were two unhappy and disturbed children, in need of nurturance, caring and protection. Boswell's (1995) study of similar young people being detained under Section 53 orders (see later) provides ample evidence of the prevalence of abuse and/or loss within this group and she suggests that their subsequent violent behaviour can be seen as manifestations of post-traumatic stress disorder.

It may be even harder to imagine the capacity of youngsters for sexual violence against other children compared to other forms of abuse such as bullying. As an aspect of Jenks's Apollonian image, it may be especially difficult to conceptualise the child as a sexual being, capable of sexual abuse. Freud's ideas about the sexual urges of children were certainly initially controversial and have remained so (Jones, 1955). The prevailing resistance to accepting children as sexual beings may explain the relative lack of knowledge and consensus about stages

of normal sexual development and about how sexually abusive behaviour can be successfully distinguished from either sexual experi-
mentation or sexually inappropriate behaviour. What research exists
indicates that stages and norms are difficult to clarify. Smith and
Grocke in their study *Normal Family Sexuality and Sexual Knowledge in
Children* (1995), found considerable variation in sexual knowledge and
behaviours across children's age groups, with consistent and pervasive
differences according to social class and, to a lesser extent, gender.
Moreover behaviours thought to be indicative of sexually abusive
situations such as excessive masturbation, over-sexualised behaviour,
an extensive curiosity or sexual knowledge and genital touching,
were found to be as common in the 'normal' community group of
families they had studied as in families where sexual abuse had
occurred.

How can professionals make decisions in these contexts which are
simultaneously emotionally charged and unclear? The National Children's Home Committee of Enquiry (1992) discusses key factors, such
as consent, power imbalance and exploitation, that need to be borne in
mind when deciding whether what has happened between two minors
is sexually abusive or not and many professionals find the definition
offered by Ryan and Lane (1991) useful:

> The juvenile sex offender is defined as a minor who commits any sexual
> act with a person of any age (1) against the victim's will, (2) without
> consent, or (3) in an aggressive, exploitative, or threatening manner.
> (Ryan and Lane, 1991: 1)

This definition, however, still allows for a wide variety of interpretations about particular incidents of alleged abuse and their relative
seriousness. In a survey of practitioners conducted by the author
(Masson, 1998) 100 respondents, from a range of professional
backgrounds and all identified as involved in work with young sexual
abusers, were asked to rank two lists of 10 vignettes, each involving
children or adolescents in potential sexually abusive situations.
(The first list is included as a sample in Appendix 1.) Respondents were
asked to rank the vignettes in each list in what they perceived to
be their relative order of seriousness (10 ranking as the most serious).
A summary of their replies to the first list is provided in Table 3.1
that comprises a box plot overview of the data where the units are the
rankings of seriousness and the columns the list of vignettes. At the
extreme end of the vignettes there was considerable agreement
between respondents about levels of seriousness. So, for example,
in relation to the first list of vignettes, all but two respondents rated
the vignette 'a 15-year-old boy who has raped an 8-year-old girl at
knifepoint' as the most serious of the incidents in the list of 10. In con-

Table 3.1:   Box plot

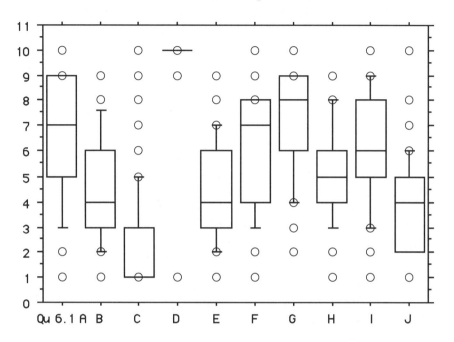

trast, respondents demonstrated a much wider range of opinion regarding their ranking of seriousness for the vignette 'a 17-year-old boy accused of making obscene telephone calls to girls at school'. Specifically the range of rankings varied from one (the least serious of the 10 vignettes) to 10 (the most serious) with 50% of respondents placing their rankings of the vignettes between four and eight, the median value being seven.

In reality, professionals have to weigh up any one incident in the context of its total circumstances including giving due weight to victim statements. Checklists such as those contained in Chapter 21 of Ryan and Lane's text (1997) and the list of questions generated by the NCH Enquiry report (para. 2.8, 1992) may also assist in the process of decision-making. Professional judgements will always be involved in deciding what is or is not abusive behaviour and clearly further under-pinning research into what is normal and abnormal sexual develop-ment and knowledge is needed. Talking to children as subjects about their sexual experiences and understanding of sexuality would seem a particularly fruitful area of study. The potential overlaps between sexually abusive behaviour and other oppressive behaviour such as bullying which Eric Blyth and Helen Cooper discuss in Chapter 8 in this book also merit further study and analysis.

LEGAL PROVISIONS IN ENGLAND AND WALES FOR CHILDREN AND YOUNG PEOPLE WHO SEXUALLY ABUSE

In relation to civil procedures the overarching piece of legislation, the Children Act 1989, does not specifically address the problem of children and young people who sexually abuse. Nevertheless various provisions within the Act may be relevant. The Act obliges Local Authorities to respond to 'children in need' and to take reasonable steps to encourage juveniles not to commit offences. Section 47 places on Local Authorities the duty to make enquiries to enable them to decide whether they should take any action to safeguard or promote a child's welfare. If a child's circumstances and best interests warrant it, then civil proceedings through the courts can be pursued with a view to obtaining a supervision or care order.

However, the emphasis in the Children Act 1989 on working voluntarily in partnership with parents and children to promote children's welfare (all very much in keeping with notions of innocent children needing care and protection) may not be easily applicable in work with young sexual abusers who are ostensibly transgressing society's expectations of acceptable behaviour and who may need directing into treatment. Commenting on the implementation of the Act in 1991, Tony Morrison (Morrison, Erooga and Beckett, 1994) has stated:

> With regard to juvenile sex offenders, the main effect of the Act has been to end criminal care orders at a point where, some would argue, a real purpose had been found for them. This means that a juvenile offender can now only be made subject of a care order if it can be shown that he or she is suffering 'significant harm', as shown by their offending behaviour, rather than because of the harm they cause others . . . this measure may undermine the young person's sense of responsibility for his or her own behaviour. (Morrison, Erooga and Beckett, 1994: 37–38)

Turning to criminal procedures, young people become subject to the criminal law at 10 years of age. If a young person aged between 10 and 17 is believed to have committed a criminal offence, the police have to decide whether to take 'no further action', issue an informal warning, formally caution or institute the process which could result in prosecution through a youth or adult court. Final decisions about prosecution are taken by the Crown Prosecution Service following recommendations from the police who, in the cases of young offenders, should also have consulted with other agencies such as Social Services departments, Probation and Education services, often through juvenile liaison panels.

If a young person is convicted of a criminal offence the courts have sentencing options deriving from various pieces of criminal justice legislation, including, in order of increasing severity: absolute and conditional discharges; fines; attendance centre orders; supervision or probation orders with or without conditions; community service orders of various kinds and a range of custodial sentences, up to Children and Young Persons Act 1933 Section 53 orders (as amended by subsequent criminal justice legislation) for children convicted of offences for which an adult may be sentenced to 14 years' imprisonment or more.

Boswell's study (1995) cited earlier indicates that the backgrounds of many young people sentenced under criminal justice legislation may not be very different from those made the subject of supervision or care orders under civil legislation. Nevertheless there are two distinctive systems of response. This fact presents particular difficulties for those involved in the management of children and adolescents who sexually abuse who, it is suggested, would seem to need both care and protection and curbing and controlling.

CHILD PROTECTION VERSUS YOUTH JUSTICE APPROACHES

A major current debate about how to respond to children and young people who sexually abuse others concerns differing philosophical approaches to the management of young sexual abusers, particularly those over the age of criminal responsibility (Masson, 1995). On the one hand, a Child Protection perspective can be identified which influenced the NCH Enquiry findings (1992) and the wording in Paragraph 5.24 of *Working Together* (1991). This view suggests that youngsters who sexually abuse others are different from other children who offend because they are unlikely to grow out of their problematic behaviour. If untreated they may become adult sexual offenders. Therefore, given the paramount concern to prevent further victimisation of innocent members of the community, young sexual abusers are seen as in need of care and protection and also control and treatment. The best means of securing this is through the Child Protection system of conferencing, registration and reviews, backed up by a legal mandate. Bengis, in Ryan and Lane (1997) comments that one of the assumptions guiding practitioners has been that:

> Legal accountability for sexually abusive behaviour is part of an overall treatment approach. Legal accountability and treatment are not mutually exclusive principles. (Ryan and Lane, 1997: 211)

On the other hand, in contrast, there exists a much longer established Youth Justice narrative that asserts that most young offenders will grow out of their offending behaviour and that much youth crime is situational. Since the publication of the classic text *Out of Care: The Community Support of Juvenile Offenders* (Thorpe, Smith, Green and Paley, 1980) there has been a steady flow of literature about the diversion and decriminalisation of young offenders, with a particular emphasis on the use of the caution and keeping young offenders 'down tariff'. This narrative which indicates a similar lower key, diversionary approach to young sexual abusers, can be seen as part of the traditional welfare ethic that criminal justice professionals have had for all offenders where the prime concern has been humanitarian rehabilitation, rather than community safety (Kemshall and Pritchard, 1996).

The author's own research (Masson, 1998) suggests that practitioners disagree about the validity of these two approaches to work with young sexual abusers and there remains great variation in the ability of local authorities to make workable connections between child protection and youth justice systems of response. The NCH Committee of Enquiry report (1992) had anticipated that child protection responses would and should take precedence over and supersede youth justice systems when managing young sexual abusers but this has not happened. Indeed it can be argued that to provide effective packages of care as well as control for young sexual abusers procedures for intervention have to reflect both child protection and youth justice processes. This requires facilitation of communication and collaboration between various groups of professionals from senior management levels downwards. Such groupings include social workers, youth justice staff, probation officers, psychologists, police and the Crown Prosecution service, and professionals working in field, residential and other settings.

There is some evidence (Masson, 1998) that a synthesis of child protection and youth justice approaches may be emerging, emphasising a differential response dependent on a risk assessment of the young person concerned. Specifically the nature of any intervention should depend on a thorough assessment of the young person in the context of his or her family circumstances (see, e.g., O'Callaghan and Print, 1994), carried out under the auspices of a child protection conference. The assessment should focus on whether further professional intervention is needed, the level of denial exhibited, the estimated risk of reoffending, the young person's social and intellectual skills and assessment of what, if any, legal mandate is required to ensure the public is protected and the young person gets any treatment required. Such assessments may lead to recommendations that some youngsters be prosecuted through the criminal justice system and a legal mandate obtained, some would be better served via civil action under the Children Act 1989, some should be offered treatment without any legal action and some given just a caution. Such risk assessments are increasing in child abuse work generally (Parton, Thorpe and Wattam, 1997) and in other aspects of welfare practice (see, for example Kemshall and Pritchard, 1996). They promise a means of focusing interventions on those who most need care and control, in contexts of increasing numbers of referrals and chronic scarcity of resources, but evidence of their effectiveness in identifying those at most risk has yet to be firmly established.

Attempts to dovetail child protection and youth justice systems will now also need to heed the current major review of child protection policy and practice in this country, following the publication of 14 major pieces of Department of Health funded research (DOH, 1995), and ongoing debates about criminal justice policy. For example, at the Conservative party conference in the autumn of 1995, the then Home Secretary, Michael Howard, proposed a new tough line on serious offenders, including sexual offenders. Subsequently the Audit Commission's report (1996) on more cost-effective and less bureaucratic responses to youth crime was dismissed by the government of the day as too soft although the Commission's views on the potential of 'cautioning plus' schemes would seem to indicate a speedy, humane and potentially effective way of directing some young people who sexually abuse into appropriate treatment schemes. The danger is that the care and control needs of young sexual abusers may well get lost in current political preferences under the new Labour Government for a more punitive 'lock 'em up' approach, redolent of the Dionysian image of the child as evil, corrupt and in need of curbing in Jenks's analysis (1996).

THE CURRENT STATE OF POLICY AND PRACTICE— EMERGING MODELS OF PRACTICE, AND ISSUES OF CONCERN

Notwithstanding the many issues and dilemmas outlined in this chapter what systems of response have developed during the 1990s? In England, in keeping with *Working Together* guidance (Home Office, DOH, DES, Welsh Office, 1991) Area Child Protection Committees (ACPCs) were encouraged by the Department of Health through, for example, conference workshops (DOH, 1993) to take a lead in developing local policies and practices in relation to young people who sexually abuse others. This prompted some ACPCs to include Youth Justice representatives in their membership and discussion of the NCH Enquiry report (1992) was placed on a number of Committee agendas. The author's analysis of ACPC annual reports suggests that between 1990 and 1994 there were increasing levels of activity in ACPC areas in relation to the development of policies and procedures, but with the 1993–1994 ACPC reports indicating some levelling off. Table 3.2 provides summary data.

Table 3.2, notwithstanding the increased activity noted, shows that a significant proportion of ACPC annual reports makes no mention of policies or procedures being developed. Evidence from the author's 1995–1996 survey of 100 practitioners (Masson, 1998) and anecdotal evidence from discussions with organisational representatives and individual practitioners suggests that some of the momentum of the early 1990s has, in fact, been lost. For example, only 54% of the survey respondents said that policy and guidance had been developed locally beyond paragraph 5.24 of *Working Together* (Home Office *et al.*, 1991). The impression also gained is that any progress is very much the result of the energy and commitment of a limited number of individual practitioners and of one or two key organisations, such as NOTA (The National Organisation for the Treatment of Abusers).

Regarding models that have been developed at the local level, the author's research indicates variations very much based on differing approaches to synchronising or dealing with the current child protection and youth justice systems. In the majority of ACPC areas that have produced a model, process is based on child protection systems taking precedence over youth justice systems. In only one or two areas does the reverse apply. A complicating factor for

Table 3.2: Study of ACPC Annual Reports 1990–1994 for references to the development of policies and procedures in relation to children and young people who sexually abuse

	No. of ACPC reports indicating policies and procedures in place (%)	No. of ACPC reports indicating policies and procedures being developed (%)
1990–1992	9	16
1992–1993	15	43
1993–1994	20	44

those responsible for developing models is that the current edition of *Working Together* (Home Office *et al.*, 1991) recommends that a child protection conference should be held in respect of a young sexual abuser, but it is silent on if and on what basis such youngsters should be registered. While researching, the author had various discussions with staff in the Department of Health. It appears in 1994 that the Department of Health was considering changing the four official categories of abuse to include a separate category for young sexual abusers. However, subsequent discussions during 1995 indicate that the Department was backtracking and the Department's current view is that children and young people who sexually abuse should only be registered if they are themselves victims of sexual abuse. This has caused dismay in some local ACPC areas, if only because child protection registration can be seen as a way of accessing necessary resources. Lack of clarity by the Department of Health has added to the problems faced by local multi-agency initiatives in deciding policies. The current work to revise *Working Together* (Home Office *et al.*, 1991) provides a much-needed opportunity to rectify this gap in the guidance.

In a small number of ACPC areas a very clear distinction is being made between children under 10 years of age and those over 10 years of age, with child protection procedures for referral, investigation and management reserved for the younger age group. Only if a young sexual abuser over 10 years of age is also a victim of abuse might he or she be the subject of a child protection conference. This may be an instance of policy-makers and practitioners trying to use the legal age of criminal responsibility to make a distinction between children 'at risk' and children 'as a risk', as discussed earlier in this chapter. A child aged over 10 years is seen as having a clear understanding of the difference between right and wrong and hence having responsibility for their actions. Considerations of the child's background and developmental needs at that point can easily take a poor second place to consideration of the nature of the criminal behaviour, the need to protect the community and to divert and/or punish the offender. In even fewer areas the decision has been taken to respond to referrals of young sexual abusers under Section 17 of the Children Act 1989 as children in need.

Some of the most well established initiatives locally are based on special projects often jointly funded through local authority and voluntary monies. Such projects support the employment of specialist and dedicated staff, rather than any progress being dependent on good will and unpaid time. The problem of such projects is, of course, their often time-limited funding and worries that momentum will be lost if they close.

Notwithstanding the modest progress that has been made in the development of policy and guidance for practitioners, there are many issues of concern amongst professionals working with children and young sexual abusers and high levels of dissatisfaction with existing local arrangements (Masson, 1998). The following comments from practitioners provide a flavour of the reasons for such dissatisfaction:

- There is no proposed or operational model for consistently dealing with either assessment or (particularly) treatment of this group of children/young people. Overall a lack of policy and guidance.
- There is no effective system for linking criminal process with the child protection system.
- Philosophy not thought through. Absence of treatment resources. Training non-existent.
- We have had two working parties on this in five years. Recommendations . . . have been ignored. If several key people leave the authority the provision will reduce dramatically.
- High levels of minimisation/collusion . . . low levels of awareness.

As part of the author's survey of practitioner views respondents were given the opportunity to provide summary information on issues about which they were concerned in relation to children and young people who sexually abuse others. In the list below are those issues, some of which have already been alluded to, which at least 50% of respondents identified as being of concern:

- lack of treatment facilities (77%)
- lack of suitable accommodation/lack of qualified residential social work staff (76%)
- victims and abusers being accommodated in the same residential homes (75%)
- dearth of evaluation studies (67%)
- lack of supervision, consultation and support (66%)
- lack of comprehensive assessment facilities (65%)
- insufficient training (63%)
- concerns about problems of co-ordinating child protection and youth justice systems (58%)
- overuse of instant cautions and cautioning generally (58%)
- lack of clarity about what is normal and abnormal sexual behaviour at different stages of development and associated concerns

about conferring Schedule 1 status in an uncertain research field (57%)
• lack of initial assessment facilities (55%)

CONCLUSION

While there may be increased awareness about the extent of sexual abuse committed by children and young people, and the beginnings of collaborative responses from agencies and professionals, much work remains to be undertaken before consistent policies and practices are firmly established.

As a beginning it is essential those involved in taking matters forward appreciate the complexities of the issues in relation to children and young people who sexually abuse and the need to conceptualise the problem in ways which address children as people who may be both victims and persecutors of others. Research which includes talking to children and young people themselves about their sexual knowledge and their understanding of sexual abuse, together with the study of the accounts of victims of sexual abuse, would provide invaluable background information from which to develop policies and good practice. Similarly, researching the views of young sexual abusers themselves, and their carers, about their experiences and the impact of professional interventions would also assist in the process of monitoring and promoting sound policy and practice.

A review of the current relevance of the recommendations of the NCH Committee of Enquiry report (1992), coupled with monitoring and evaluation activities in relation to existing models of practice, would provide a useful basis from which to set an agenda for action which addresses the management, assessment and treatment of young sexual abusers, including child protection and criminal justice processes. In particular in relation to children over the age of criminal responsibility, the officially recommended child protection route for such cases has to be reviewed to take into account the fact that such youngsters are also subject to the criminal justice system. Resource issues such as those relating to suitable residential accommodation facilities and the training and supervision needs of staff involved in this area of work would also seem to be priority areas. Finally, research into working with young sexual abusers with learning difficulties and young female sexual abusers, two emerging groups of concern, would also usefully complement existing research findings into work with young male sexual abusers.

REFERENCES

Ambert A-M (1995) Toward a theory of peer abuse, in Mandell N and Ambert A-M (eds) *Sociological Studies of Children*, Vol. 7, JAI Press, Greenwich, Connecticut.

Audit Commission (1996) *Misspent Youth: Young People and Crime*, Audit Commission Publications, Abingdon, Oxfordshire.

Barbaree H E, Marshall W L and Hudson SM (eds) (1993) *The Juvenile Sexual Offender*, Guilford Press, New York/London.

Boswell G (1995) *Violent Victims*, The Prince's Trust, London.

Buist M and Fuller R (1996) *A Chance to Change: An Intervention with Young People who have Sexually Abused Others*, The Scottish Office, Edinburgh.

Department of Health (1993) *Report of Area Child Protection Committee Conferences 1992–1993*, DOH, London.

Department of Health (1995) *Child Protection: Messages From Research*, HMSO, London.

Forbes J (1992) Female sexual abusers: The contemporary search for equivalence, *Practice*, **6**, 2: 102–111.

Hoghugi M, Bhate S and Graham F (eds) (1997) *Working with Sexually Abusive Adolescents. A Practice Manual*, Sage, London.

Home Office, Department of Health, Department of Education and Science, Welsh Office (1991) *Working Together Under the Children Act 1989: A Guide to Arrangements for Inter-agency Co-operation for the Protection of Children from Abuse*, Home Office, London.

Home Office (1995) *Criminal Statistics for England and Wales*, Home Office, London.

James A and Jenks C (1994) *Public Perceptions of Childhood Criminality*, paper presented to ESRC seminar at Keele University, 15 April.

Jenks C (1996) *Childhood*, Key Ideas Series, Routledge, London.

Jones E (1955) *Sigmund Freud: Life and Work*, Vol. 2, Hogarth Press, London.

Kemshall H and Pritchard J (eds) (1996) *Good Practice in Risk Assessment and Risk Management*, Jessica Kingsley, London.

Masson H (1995) Juvenile sexual abusers. A challenge to conventional wisdom about juvenile offending, *Youth and Policy*, **50**: 13–21.

Masson H (1998) Current issues in relation to young sexual abusers; A survey of practitioners' views, *Journal of Sexual Aggression*, **3**, 2: 101–106.

Morrison T, Erooga M and Beckett R (eds) (1994) *Sexual Offending against Children: Assessment and Treatment of Male Abusers*, Routledge, London.

National Children's Home (1992) *The Report of the Committee of Enquiry into Children and Young People who Sexually Abuse other Children*, NCH, London.

O'Callaghan D and Print B (1994) Adolescent sexual abusers: Research, assessment and treatment, in Morrison T, Erooga M and Beckett R (eds) *Sexual Offending against Children: Assessment and Treatment of Male Abusers*, Routledge, London.

Openshaw D, Graves R, Erickson S, Lowry M, Durso D, Agee L, Todd S, Jones K and Scherzinger J (1993) Youthful sexual offenders: A comprehensive bibliography of scholarly references, 1970–1992, *Family Relations*, **42**: 222–226.

Parton N, Thorpe D and Wattam C (1997) *Child Protection: Risk and the Moral Order*, Macmillan, Basingstoke.

Ryan G D and Lane S L (eds) (1991) *Juvenile Sexual Offending. Causes, Consequences and Correction*, Lexington Books, Lexington, Massachusetts/Toronto.

Ryan G D and Lane S L (eds) (1997) *Juvenile Sexual Offending. Causes, Consequences and Corrections* (2nd edn), Jossey-Bass, San Francisco.

Smith M and Grocke M (1995) *Normal Family Sexuality and Sexual Knowledge in Children*, Royal College of Psychiatrists/Gorkill Press, London.

Thorpe D H, Smith D, Green C J and Paley J H (1980) *Out of Care: The Community Support of Juvenile Offenders*, George Allen and Unwin, London.

Violence Against Children Study Group (1990) *Taking Child Abuse Seriously: Contemporary Issues in Child Protection Theory and Practice*, Routledge, London and New York.

APPENDIX 1: SAMPLE OF VIGNETTES USED WITHIN THE QUESTIONNAIRE—LIST 1

Rank Order

A 16-year-old boy in local authority accommodation is found in bed with an 11-year-old boy

A 6-year-old boy who has repeatedly touched the genitals of a 6-year-old girl at school

A gang of four 11-year-old boys who mutually masturbate

A 15-year-old boy who has raped an 8-year-old girl at knifepoint

A 10-year-old girl is caught touching the genitals of her 7-year-old sister

A 17-year-old boy is accused of making obscene telephone calls to girls at his school

A 16-year-old girl who has allowed two 13-year-old boys to simulate sexual intercourse with her in return for money

A 13-year-old boy has been accused of indecently exposing himself to his younger brothers aged 10 and 8

An 8-year-old girl who is 'acting out' her own abuse in sexual play with her 4-year-old brother

An 11-year-old boy who encouraged his 8-year-old friend to compare and touch each other's penises.

II

ISSUES OF GENDER AND GENERATION

4

MOTHERING AND THE CHILD PROTECTION SYSTEM

Brid Featherstone

INTRODUCTION

Currently, western cultural commentators appear preoccupied with what is happening to the 'family'. In particular, concern is being expressed about the welfare of children as a result of the growth in divorce and mothers' entry into the paid workforce (see, e.g., Etzioni, 1993, and replies by Campbell, 1995, and Murray, 1995). Men's welfare is also under scrutiny (see, e.g., Phillips, 1997). Women, particularly mothers, are often posed as the source of a multitude of contemporary ills in many scenarios and the implications of changing work and family patterns for them appear neglected in the focus on men and children.

Within contemporary discussions about social work and the protection of children a number of commentators have pointed out that mothers continue to be held disproportionately responsible by social workers for the well-being of their children. Why this is so has been explored mainly in terms of analysing what social workers do or do not do, but how and what mothers themselves feel about their responsibilities, rights and needs requires further exploration (see Hooper, 1992, for an excellent account of mothers' experiences).

This chapter is concerned to explore some of the stories emerging from a range of mothers in contemporary Britain. In particular, it identifies themes of continuity and discontinuity as mothers think about and construct their lives. It explores how such stories can help illuminate some of the issues involved in social work encounters. In particular, it identifies what may be going on when women service users and women workers try to discuss what children need.

Children, Child Abuse and Child Protection. Placing Children Centrally, by The Violence Against Children Study Group.
© 1999 John Wiley & Sons Ltd.

CHANGING TIMES

Women's lives have undergone considerable transformation in terms of employment patterns and demography in recent years (Coward, 1992). Most women of all classes, including mothers, work, although there are important ethnic differences here. As Holdsworth and Dale (1997) point out, African-Caribbean mothers are significantly more likely to be involved in full-time work than other ethnic groups. Family patterns have also changed, with divorce mostly initiated by women on the increase. The number of lone parents has risen significantly (the majority of whom are women). There has been an increase in the number of unmarried partners, and of children born outside wedlock, alongside a growth in the numbers of women refusing or delaying child-rearing.

Crucially, childbirth and childcare are no longer automatic and given aspects of a woman's life cycle. Woman is no longer synonymous with mother although it is still clear that mother constitutes an aspect of identity for the majority of women. A range of social theorists have reflected on the implications of these developments for the well-being of men, children and indeed the cohesion of the wider social order. What do women/mothers themselves say?

There is evidence of considerable diversity in the stories women/mothers feel able to tell. There is also considerable diversity in the explanations advanced for why women/mothers feel as they do. Recent work has explored women who refuse the identity altogether (Bartlett, 1994), stop being full-time mothers (Jackson, 1994) or see it as an expansion of self or as involving a crucial loss of self (McMahon, 1995).

The relationship between motherhood and paid work has, in particular, received some attention. In the next section I will explore two pieces of research—both originate from the author's own attempts to understand their and other mothers' lives but they reach quite different conclusions. Coward (1992) interviewed 150 women in the late 1980s and early 1990s. These included women from a range of class backgrounds although she did not specify the variations in ethnicity within the population studied. It is clear from the case examples that not all were white. She painted a bleak picture, arguing that worry and guilt were central features of the lives of those interviewed. In her view, this was partly due to the fact that women's lives, in the main, had become more difficult than when feminism first became publicly visible in the sixties. Economic developments required an increasing number of women workers but the quality of life for those who worked and for their children was not being addressed. The low paid and those in jobs with no proper conditions of employment were particularly ill served. Poverty was widespread among lone mothers.

She found, however, contrary to the arguments of commentators such as Etzioni, that women were not prioritising paid work over motherhood. Indeed, she noted a phenomenon that to her was disturbing, in which many of the women interviewed identified motherhood and family with all that was 'good' and 'real' and were actively turning away from the priorities of the workplaces. This manifests itself in women working part-time or stopping work altogether. Many women expressed deep dissatisfaction with the competitive ethos of the workplace and felt deeply uncomfortable about their own feelings of competition. This is an important point in that they felt the workplace mobilised their own feelings of competition and therefore they felt uncomfortable. She argues however, that such feelings were re-emerging in family life and pointed to the amount of competition between mothers she observed. As a consequence many found relationships with other mothers quite problematic.

She also found women burying their own needs in their children as has happened traditionally, and therefore running the risk of mis-recognising what their children needed. She found prescriptions around good motherhood still powerful although the changes in women's lives were reflected in the content of such prescriptions— most did not identify the good mother as the 'stay at home mother' but rather as one who enjoyed motherhood. Mothers felt extremely guilty for not enjoying motherhood although she implies that this may be particularly pertinent for middle-class mothers. In terms of men she found women were not challenging men to do more within the home. Rather, they were doing the work themselves or, if they could afford it, passing it on to other women. Her explanation for why this might be so is derived from the work of the feminist psychoanalytic writer Jessica Benjamin. Benjamin (1990) agues that despite the conscious commitments of women to equality the female psyche still tends towards taking on emotional responsibility for men and children while handing on power and responsibility for other areas of life to men. Taking on such emotional responsibility leaves women with considerable emotional burdens, which was manifest in the amount of worrying and anxiety she observed in the women researched.

Despite the apparent conservatism of Coward's message, her book contains numerous examples of how mothers and mothering have actually been transformed. Crucially, mothering is being 'thought' about in a landscape where mothers are aware of other life alternatives rather than being 'done' as if inevitable. Before moving on to look at a further piece of research carried out more recently which looks at mothers' stories it is worth noting Murray's (1995) observations that paid work can act as a protector for women, particularly in terms of maternal depression. This does not necessarily contradict Coward's arguments in that Coward is arguing the retreat to the home is bad for women and children. But it does question whether her findings on how stressful the workplace is are generalisable. It may be that this applies to a smaller number of women, possibly middle-class women, than she recognises. Despite the difficulties of factors such as poor pay there is evidence that many women very much welcome paid work for the social opportunities it provides amongst other benefits (Benn, 1998).

Benn, writing in 1998, argues that Coward's book is a reflection of a particular time. Benn argues that the 1980s and early 1990s were characterised to some extent by 'bourgeois feminist triumphalism'. This meant that women who felt unable to have and do it all felt personally inadequate and sought answers in psychological explanations. She particularly notes the role played by Margaret Thatcher, a working mother who erased her own mother from her biography, and established her competence in a man's world, without ever bringing in or exploring the implications of being a mother herself. In general, no collective solutions were sought in the 1980s as many women tried to fit in and devise their own solutions to motherhood and work. Benn argues, from her research, that it is not women's fear of competition that is the problem but that they have to live in two worlds—the world of work and the world of motherhood. These have different priorities and until recently it appeared difficult to raise questions about the priorities of the world of work.

Benn argues that the last few decades of change, in particular of mothers' entry into the workforce, have meant that women's competence in the world of work is no longer an issue. However, the full implications of what that means for motherhood require a lot of consideration. She argues that the majority of women continue to want to be mothers but no longer in the old way. For example, motherhood is, she argues, for her an act not an act of faith—it is not definitional of her as a person in quite the same way as it was for previous generations of women. Many women, therefore, by implication, want to be paid workers as well as mothers. Indeed, the women on state benefits interviewed were quite clear about the advantages paid work would bring. The research on ethnicity also paints a different picture. Holdsworth and Dale (1997) found that African-Caribbean mothers were more involved in full-time paid work than any other ethnic category and Duncan (1998, personal communication), argues that

African-Caribbean lone mothers identify having a paid job with being a good mother.

Benn appears to be arguing that it is possible to articulate a 'new' vision of and for motherhood today. This vision appears based on her own experience and research she has carried out with women from a range of backgrounds all over the UK. She sees it as possible and important both to challenge and involve men and calls for the development of domestic democracy and a moral ecology. This would comprise a fundamental challenge to the priorities of the workplace and men.

Benn's book appears at the end of a long period of Conservative administration and exhibits an optimism that is missing from Coward's. However, it is more glib in that it appears to promote a voluntaristic approach to mothers and fathers. In particular, she appears, in my view, to underestimate both the political and psychic barriers there may be to constructing a 'new world'.

Before moving to explore what other researchers are saying about other aspects of mothering, it is important to draw out the common features from Coward and Benn despite their differences. For both writers, mothering continues to be very important in many women's lives. Most women continue to feel responsible for their children in a way that does not seem attributable solely to societal prescriptions. It is not just imposed upon women but desired and valued by them also. But there is an important sense also in which motherhood seems to be different—it is thought about in a context of alternatives. As a consequence, more mothers than ever before can therefore think about mothering as being part of their lives rather than constituting their lives.

SUPPRESSED STORIES

The next two writers focused on raise more difficult themes. Jackson (1994), drawing from developments in her own life, interviewed women who felt compelled to leave their children—the mothering process obliged them to recognise that staying jeopardised something fundamental in themselves. Often it appeared they felt compelled to leave to pursue a creative or spiritual quest. Jackson is at pains to point out that this is not a new phenomenon, citing examples from the past as well as the present, although there appears to be a slight increase in recent years. Equally, she feels feminism is not a cause. Although it would appear to me that the articulation by feminists of alternative life-styles, as well as economic developments, make it more part of women's landscapes today.

This phenomenon was also addressed in a television programme 'Mummy doesn't live here anymore' (BBC2, 14 March 1998). A number of women from differing backgrounds spoke of their decision to leave children with partners. Again, one got a sense of both change and continuity from the stories. All talked of making the decision in the context of considering both their own needs and their children's and one woman clearly felt distraught at the loss of her children. The question of what is choice is foregrounded here—there was a sense in which for one woman it appeared she wanted to leave her partner rather than her children but realised the children would be less disrupted if they stayed with him—the others wanted more clearly to leave their children.

Roszika Parker (1995) has opened up another seldom articulated theme in her research. On the basis of her clinical practice and research, she argues that despite the changes in women's lives, ideals around how a woman should be in relation to motherhood remain static. Indeed, the faster women's lives change the more ossified and stereotyped the dominant representations of motherhood have become. These stress self-abnegation, unalloyed pleasure in children and intuitive knowledge of how to nurture (Parker, 1995: 22). However, she argues that ambivalence is central to mothers' experience. Ambivalence refers to the co-existence of loving and hating feelings. She argues that the co-existence of such feelings is not a problem. Indeed, she claims a specifically creative role for mothers and children for what she calls manageable ambivalence. The conflict between love and hate spurs a woman on to think about the relationship, to struggle to understand and know her baby. If a mother only regarded her child either with hostile feelings or with untroubled love, she would not think about the relationship. Ambivalence allows the mother to experience both herself and her child as subjects rather than objects for each other.

However, ambivalence can become unmanageable, which is where some of the difficulties arise. A central factor in this is western society's inability to tolerate ambivalence. Other factors also contribute, although she is undeterministic about these. They include the mother's own experience of being mothered, father's support, physical health, economic pressures, the availability of emotional support and the contribution of the individual child. However, hers is not an approach that lends itself to checklists that can unproblematically identify risk factors. For example, in terms of emotional support, she discovered that some mothers found others a lifeline in affirming their anxieties and supporting their confusion. Yet for others it was in the company of other mothers that they experienced their deepest anxieties and insecurities. Similarly, a partially absent father can be more problematic than one who is not available at all, in the sense that some fathers provided no space for mothers to explore their ambivalence and, indeed, actively censored its expression.

For Parker, the mothering process itself involves mothers in challenging societal ideals but this is rarely articulated publicly and the pain involved remains individualised.

The two pieces of research dealt with here open up discussion on issues which are often hidden or experienced as deeply shameful. Parker's is potentially the most important as it appears to strike chords with so many mothers. (This has become apparent in recent ongoing discussions with social workers and service users—see Featherstone, forthcoming.)

In all, the pieces of research looked at from different perspectives remind us of the following: change and continuity co-exist; ideals of motherhood appear influential but according to at least three pieces of research they are reworked by mothers and Parker opens up the possibility that the process itself forces rethinking even if this is 'hidden'. Recent work such as Benn's is more positive about the role of men but the more psychoanalytically informed work explores the barriers that may exist at a psychic level. Questions of self appear to be important for women but this is not clear cut—for some women selfhood still appears bound up with developing successful children. For a minority, it is only achieved by leaving. Others seem more pragmatic in juggling different identities. Of central importance appears the recognition of diversity amongst mothers today.

WHAT DOES THIS MEAN FOR CHILD PROTECTION?

A number of commentators have argued that mothers are disproportionately focused on within the child protection system and men are neglected or avoided. Mothers are expected to take responsibility for childcare and child protection even when it is the man who is responsible for the abuse. It is as yet unclear to me whether this is affected at all by the status of the man or whether it is a blanket strategy. Is there a difference if the man involved is the father? Is less expected of stepfathers or the man if he is the mother's boyfriend rather than the father of the child? This is of course important, as it could be that in many situations social workers might actually be basing their decisions on the child's attachment history rather than on gender considerations. Although I am aware that gender considerations are implicated in attachment histories.

In terms of *why* it happens, the following issues have been identified as relevant: fear of men's violence, a general lack of clarity
about what should be expected of fathers and constructions of
motherhood (see O'Hagan and Dillenburger 1995; Milner, 1996;
Parton, Wattam and Thorpe, 1997). Much of this work focuses on
analysing what workers do or do not do, thus analysing one side of
the encounter. This is either based on reflections on the writer's own
practice, case examples provided by workers, or the case records of
social workers.

What do mothers themselves think of their treatment by social
workers? There is, as yet, little research. Hooper (1992) asked a specific
group and a proportion indicated satisfaction with the service
they received. Central to mothers' judgements were considerations
about process. Were their views taken seriously and were they allowed
adequate time to process what had happened? None of them seemed
to say they should not have been seen as important. However,
many resented having been seen as solely responsible and having to
shoulder the sole burden of protection.

Important issues are raised here in the context of what some
researchers such as Coward and Benn appear to be saying. Some
(many?) women invest strongly in being 'good mothers'. It is
not simply a 'role' that is experienced as foisted upon them. According to Coward and Benn the content of what it means to be 'a
good mother' is shifting and is being reworked actively by mothers.
Parker appears to say the process necessitates this rework-
ing but mothers are often fearful of articulating the possibility that
being a 'good mother' in practice can encompass holding on to highly
negative feelings about children. Engaging with mothers who
are service users, around what they feel, is highly complex particularly in a context where a child has been hurt. However, they
may not be helped by explanations that suggest that they are
feeling bad because they have been socialised into a particular
maternal role.

Further research is required into what mothers think and feel in a
landscape of change. It also seems important to locate this work con-
textually and to explore the differing perspectives of workers and
service users as they construct their encounters. Wise (1995) has written
of how her definition of a key issue differed widely from the mother's
in a particular case which made developing a shared understanding
of the mother's and children's needs and welfare profoundly problematic. Further work needs to be done here with specific groups
of mothers and workers in exploring how encounters become
constructed.

In the next section I want to look at some of the issues which may arise for workers and service users in forthcoming periods and which have as yet to be fully explored in the social work literature.

MOTHER OR WORKER OR?

Feminists have pointed out that women comprise the majority of front-line social work staff although they are usually managed by men. Hanmer and Statham (1988) have pointed out the potential for woman-centred practice if workers could explore their commonalities with service users while recognising their differences. White (1995) has pointed out that social workers frequently find it very difficult to share with service users. Lawrence (1992) has demonstrated why commonality may not necessarily lead women workers to understand and empathise with women service users. She argues that women workers and service users share a common developmental trajectory that can lead to workers being more punitive towards service users. Raised by their mothers to expect second class citizenship, all women are expected to look after others' emotional needs while ignoring their own. Raised as copers themselves they may struggle with those they see as not coping. Central to this work is the notion of 'need'. Women have needs which are not met in contemporary society and indeed, they are encouraged to deny those needs and look after others. While there are criticisms of this approach to need (Bar, 1987) Lawrence's analysis can illuminate some of the reasons why women social workers might expect a great deal from women and very little indeed from men. Lawrence appears to be indicating that a shared experience as daughters can lead to distancing between women.

To date, the literature has generally focused on the identities of woman being important, although White and Wise appear to say that the worker identity overrides the potential for commonality in the sense that a worker has a range of alternate allegiances towards the agency, policy, procedures and so on.

I want to explore the worker identity slightly differently, by extending it to both parties and exploring what that opens up and closes in terms of understanding the process. It is clear that the current government see entry into paid work as central to their welfare strategies. This will centrally affect many service users in the forthcoming period. Many already work outside the home although it is difficult to get an accurate sense of this. Women social workers are already in paid work and it is probably fair to say many struggle with some of the difficulties outlined by Benn and Coward. It seems that it will become increasingly difficult for social work practice not to take on board the implications of the entry of many mothers into the paid workforce. How will this affect the way service users see themselves? Will it expand their worlds or add to their sense of beleagurement? How will workers respond? Questions about training and childcare strategies are already central in the concerns of the policy analysts (see Lister, 1998). It is questioned whether Welfare to Work strategies will not compound women and children's deprivation and adversely affect quality of life if such strategies are not combined with proper training and well-resourced childcare. The question of what kinds of childcare strategies are developed is likely to prove very pertinent for social workers working with children and families.

The expansion of the paid worker identity will not necessarily lead to greater empathy between service user and social worker. But it may have two indirect effects that are important. One will be that it will support a recognition that woman does not equal mother. Furthermore, as we have seen, there is important evidence that paid work can act as a protector for some women against maternal depression, which may be very relevant for workers who are assessing the needs and welfare of children. Although it is also possible it will lead for some to an unacceptable level of pressure, particularly if not accompanied by supportive strategies.

In the next section I want to explore why a shared motherhood identity currently can lead to distancing rather than engagement and the possibilities for the future in this area.

MOTHERS TOGETHER

Coward (1992) and Parker (1995) both argue that mothers can find it hard to discuss problems with each other when they are struggling with the difficulties of mothering. This also became apparent in some recent research I carried out. When difficulties are alluded to it is often done via humour. Such humorous exchanges are frequently carried out in 'safety', that is between women who have equal status and where a process of 'sussing out' has been undergone.

This is very different from a situation where one woman is in effect, paid, to evaluate the mothering practices of another. There are numerous considerations here that relate to similarities, differences and context. In terms of similarities let us take the notion of ambivalence. Having now talked to over 100 women and some men myself about this notion of Parker's it does appear to strike a chord. Words like 'love' and 'hate' have been argued by some to be too blunt to describe the complexities of the mother/child relationship but there appears to be recognition by all those talked to that enormously complex feelings of both a positive and a negative nature are evoked. Consequently, we have to take seriously the possibility that workers who are struggling with ambivalence themselves may censor its expression by service users. The context is vital here. Deeply defensive, procedural-type approaches have dominated social work with families for some time and it remains to be seen whether a 'new climate' will be ushered in by *Child Protection: Messages from Research* (DOH, 1996). The shift towards 'family support' may offer more possibilities, although it may also reinforce normative assumptions about mothering, if it does not deconstruct the range of feelings mothers can have.

In terms of differences, questions around class and ethnicity are potentially of great relevance here although they are not straightforward. For example, Ribbens (1994) has argued that there are difficulties in using class to understand women's positions. Certainly, sociologically, there have been problems here. Coward, using the term in an untheorised way, argues that all women shared in prescriptions of ideal motherhood but that what she considered middle-class women seemed particularly vulnerable and were prey to considerable guilt. As she does not deal with this in detail one can only make tentative suggestions about the possible tensions that may arise between middle-class workers and working-class service users. Parton, Wattam and Thorpe (1997) have argued that the kinds of constructions of mothering promoted by social work practice are themselves middle class. However, this does not in itself mean they are not shared by a wider population. In terms of ethnicity, issues around involvement in paid work have already been cited as an area of difference. However, in terms of the mothering process itself further research is required.

In the current context where the language of social work permits only a limited number of constructions of motherhood—the available mother—the protective mother—then the introduction of the ambivalent mother potentially involves a considerable change to practice. Resources at the moment reflect current constructions. There is a restricted menu (Parton, Whattam and Thorpe, 1997). Parenting classes or support for mother and child together are staples of most social work interventions—what about time off from each other? offering a babysitter and so on? Welfare to Work will inevitably bring in new considerations albeit in a manner which is imposed from outside. The contemporary discussions about motherhood underway outside the profession and to a lesser extent inside may also have an impact on what happens in the future.

Finally, I would wish to open up for further discussion a fundamental underlying issue. It is unclear from many of the writings whether social workers are being asked to adopt a gender neutral strategy, that is to expect the 'same' from both parents, expect more from men, less from women. Some issues seem straightforward. Milner (1996) argues that women are expected to manage men's emotional difficulties and their dangerousness in the absence of support from workers. That can seem straightforwardly unacceptable. But, in other situations it is less clear what is desired and advocated. O'Hagan and Dillenburger (1995), who are trenchant critics of current social work practice, are less forthcoming on what should be done in relation to men and fathers. Any critique which implies that too much is expected of mothers does need to consider what that implies for the role of men as well as what needs to change societally.

Furthermore, the failure in much of the social work literature to ask mothers themselves has serious implications. The general literature, a fraction of which has been explored here, indicates a complex picture. Recognition of the diversity amongst mothers seems fundamental in order to develop sensitive, anti-oppressive strategies. However, it is imperative that much more research is conducted with mothers who experience the child protection system.

CONCLUSION

There is a range of possible responses to a period of considerable social transition. Nostalgia for an imagined past where roles appeared clearer as well as panic about the present and future are, however, often dominant. Mothers and mothering, unsurprisingly, act as cultural touchstones in such processes. Social workers have always needed to be able to work in the face of ambiguity, uncertainty and unpredictability. This is likely to intensify in the forthcoming period as, for most of us, there appears to be no escape from unpredictability and change, features that are firmly ensconced in complex ways in contemporary family relations.

REFERENCES

Bar V (1987) Change in women, in Ernst S and Maguire M (eds) *Living with the Sphinx*, Virago, London.
Bartlett J (1994) *Will You Be Mother?* Virago, London.
Benjamin J (1990) *The Bonds of Love*, Virago, London.

Benn M (1998) *Madonna and Child: Towards a New Politics of Motherhood*, Jonathan Cape, London.

Campbell B (1995) Old fogeys and angry young men: A critique of communitarianism, *Soundings* **1**: 47–65.

Coward R (1992) *Our Treacherous Hearts: Why Women Let Men Get their Way*, Faber and Faber, London.

Department of Health (1996) *Child Protection: Messages from Research*, HMSO, London.

Etzioni A (1993) *The Parenting Deficit*, Demos, London.

Featherstone B (forthcoming) Mothers' stories, in Fawcett B, Featherstone B, Fook J and Rossiter A (eds) *Feminist Postmodern Perspectives*, Routledge, London.

Hanmer J and Statham D (1988) *Women and Social Work: Towards a Woman-Centred Practice*, Macmillan, London.

Holdsworth C and Dale A (1997) Ethnic differences in women's employment, *Work, Employment and Society*, **11**: 435–457.

Hooper C-A (1992) *Mothers Surviving Child Sexual Abuse*, Routledge, London.

Jackson R (1994) *Mothers Who Leave*, Pandora, London.

Lawrence M (1992) Women's psychology and feminist social work practice, in Langan M and Day L (eds) *Women, Oppression and Social Work: Issues in Anti-discriminatory Practice*, Routledge, London.

Lister R (1998) *Citizenship: Feminist Perspectives*, Macmillan, London.

McMahon K (1995) *Engendering Motherhood*, Guilford Press, New York.

Milner J (1996) Men's resistance to social workers, in Fawcett B, Featherstone B, Hearn J and Toft C (eds) *Violence and Gender Relations: Theories and Interventions*, Sage, London.

Murray L (1995) The politics of attachment: Personal and social influences on family life, *Soundings*, **1**: 65–77.

O'Hagan K and Dillenburger K (1995) *The Abuse of Women in Childcare Work*, Open University Press, Milton Keynes, Buckingham.

Parker R (1995) *Torn in Two: The Experience of Maternal Ambivalence*, Virago, London.

Parton N, Wattam C and Thorpe D (1997) *Child Protection, Risk and the Moral Order*, Macmillan, London.

Phillips M (1997) Death of the Dad, *Observer*, 2 Nov.

Ribbens J (1994) *Mothers and their Children: A Feminist Sociology of Child Rearing*, Sage, London.

White V (1995) Commonality and diversity in feminist social work, *British Journal of Social Work*, **2**: 143–156.

Wise S (1995) Feminist ethics in practice, in Hugman R and Smith D (eds) *Ethical Issues in Social Work*, Routledge, London.

5

CHILD PROTECTION AND DOMESTIC VIOLENCE: POINTERS FOR PRACTITIONERS

Anne Ashworth with Marcus Erooga

INTRODUCTION

Our aim through this chapter is to promote a greater understanding of domestic violence and highlight the importance of this phenomenon as a child protection issue, in order to enhance the confidence and competence of practitioners.

- We will suggest that practitioners are best served by explanations of domestic violence which recognise the complexity and diversity of this vexed social problem, thus promoting a repertoire of responses, rather than those which offer a single explanation and a singular solution.
- We will also argue in favour of interventions which are built on understandings of the significance of wider social divisions around race, sexuality and class in the manifestation and experience of domestic violence.
- Finally, we will assert the importance of linking theory with practice, practice evaluation and research drawing on the totality of families' experiences of domestic violence, not, for instance, solely on that of women survivors.

Questions of terminology and definition excite considerable controversy in this area, particularly where these are linked to a specific political project such as the emancipation of women from patriarchal oppression (Hester, Kelly and Radford, 1996). However, even amongst those who are not explicitly aligned with such gender politics,

Children, Child Abuse and Child Protection. Placing Children Centrally, by The Violence Against Children Study Group.
© 1999 John Wiley & Sons Ltd.

it is generally accepted that the majority of domestic violence is perpetrated by men upon women and that the precise form of abuse can range across a variety of behaviours (Home Affairs Committee, 1991, 1993).

Clearly practitioners must recognise this reality, but it is neither an argument against holding men accountable for their violence, nor an argument against promoting women and children's safety, to say that practice must be capable of differentiating between different types of domestic violence and of responding to domestic violence in other contexts, for example in same-sex relationships, women's violence and elder abuse.

The term *domestic violence* is in common usage, but is also problematic in that it fails to convey the particularities of the behaviour and experiences involved. However, since alternatives are not readily suggested, it is intended to retain the term domestic violence here.

EMERGENCE/REDISCOVERY

The visibility and naming of domestic violence as a social and political issue has been subject to considerable change over time—appearing and then disappearing from public view. Linda Gordon's (1989) historical study of family violence, taking in incest, woman abuse, child abuse and neglect, offers an analysis of these changes which shatters any notion of a fixed understanding of how violence is experienced in families and how society responds.

Gordon's work demonstrates a complex interplay of factors such as poverty, race and gender in shaping the experience of violent conflict in families. She found, for instance, that in late nineteenth-century Boston society violence in families often erupted from struggles over scarce material resources and that women were as capable of reacting violently against their partners as in the reverse—although women often suffered the greater injury. Changes in society through the early to mid-twentieth century saw very different constructions of masculinity and femininity emerging, such as the emphasis on women's peacekeeping/nurturing qualities and the growth of psychodynamic understandings of interpersonal marital relations. These drastically altered the visibility of domestic violence which, after considerable feminist activity a hundred years before, effectively disappeared from view until second wave feminism hit the shores of the late twentieth-century western world. Thus in the UK in the 1970s Erin Pizzey's *Scream Quietly or the Neighbours will Hear* (1974) and the activity of the women's movement generally sparked renewed awareness of the private misery in some women's lives and opened up the whole question of male–female relations.

Lynne Segal (1987, 1990) offers important insights into these processes. They have by no means been a straightforward march of progress towards greater equality and emancipation for women through which domestic violence again became identified as a social issue. These developments actually signalled deep and complex political struggles over women's position in society, the nature of relationships with men, with other women and with children. It was in this context of fierce contestation within the women's movement itself, against the backdrop of economic fragmentation and decline, and significant social change, that radical feminism, a particular feminist position, emerged. This sought to liberate women from their common oppression by emphasising their unity in a struggle against an all-embracing male domination, casting all men as potential aggressors and all men as benefiting from the violence of some.

In this country, Women's Aid, Rape Crisis centres and associated academics have played the major part in raising awareness of the extent and seriousness of men's violence toward women and have presented this as the means by which women continue to be subordinated and oppressed. The analysis of domestic violence which has underpinned this movement has been radical feminist in orientation, with a central assertion that such violence is a defining male characteristic, fundamental to men's power over women in patriarchal society, transcending divisions such as race, class and culture (Hester, Kelly and Radford, 1996; Mullender, 1996).

More recently, violence to women has been linked to the issue of children's welfare and within the radical feminist paradigm has added a further dimension of dangerousness to heterosexual relationships (Mullender and Morley, 1994).

This construction of domestic violence has come to form the dominant discourse in the UK, influencing agencies to develop domestic violence policies which adopt working definitions of domestic violence as being men's violence toward women and explicitly 'an abuse of male power over women' (ACOP, 1992, 1996). In these definitions it is assumed that children's interests are essentially the same as those of their mothers.

Contrastingly, in North America alongside such an analysis there exists a broader perspective which views family violence as a phenomenon which 'encompasses a multitude of diverse negative interactions that occur between different family members and other intimates' (Bamett, Miller-Perrin and Perrin 1997: 276)—elder abuse, sibling abuse, men's violence to women and the reverse—a perspective which arguably more accurately reflects the experience of many survivors.

Whilst the radical feminist discourse presents a fixed male heterosexual explanation (Hester, Kelly and Radford, 1996) the family violence perspective points up the diversity of violence within family settings across age, gender, sexuality (Straus and Gelles, 1990).

Although both have undoubtedly helped expose the pervasive and damaging effects of previously hidden violence within the family setting, arguably neither provides a sufficiently subtle, responsive and flexible framework to promote the pursuit of social justice for all those women, men, girls and boys who are affected in all the diversity of their individual circumstances. New thinking on the subject, which addresses the process by which social problems are constructed and attempts to develop understandings of the complexities, the peculiarities and the ambivalences of domestic violence, is to be found in the work of Featherstone and Trinder (1997). By drawing on feminist and pro-feminist psychoanalysis and poststructuralism they offer a focus on relational analyses of domestic violence, that is the different yet connected perspectives of individual family members, their emotional attachments and desires and the complicated relationship between power and difference by gender, race and class in specific historical contexts.

Such theorising provides a more nuanced approach to domestic violence which moves beyond the fixed essentialism of the radical feminist orthodoxy and the broad generalism of the family violence perspective. Featherstone and Trinder helpfully point up the multidimensional underpinnings of human behaviour, for example psychological, intrapsychic, political and discursive. Practitioners therefore need to engage with the work across a range of dimensions, within a framework which is capable of recognising the discriminatory effects of wider social divisions on perpetrators as well as their victims.

SOCIAL WORK PRACTICE AND DOMESTIC VIOLENCE

Contemporary British research suggests that domestic violence is indeed an issue for social work practitioners to take seriously. Farmer and Owen (1995) report that 60% of cases with physical abuse, neglect or emotional abuse also featured violence to mothers, with domestic violence a feature of the cases with the worst outcomes. In addition, the significance of the abuse of an adult as a risk factor for children is frequently overlooked. Reviewing 'Section 8 Reviews'—Area Child Protection Committee commissioned reports into child deaths, O'Hara (1995) notes that of those involving death through physical assault and/or neglect by carers 'a large proportion of the parents responsible . . . have a history of violence toward their female partners as well as the child concerned' (p. 15). Whilst professionals involved had been aware of the violence toward the woman, this does not seem to have been a factor in risk assessments or protection plans for the child.

How practitioners conceptualise domestic violence and associated child protection issues is both influenced by, and influential over, its construction as a social problem and developing professional responses. The complementary, competing and sometimes conflicting perspectives of enterprises aimed at ensuring domestic violence is taken seriously can be misleading for practitioners and policy-makers when such projects fail to explicate these underlying differences of focus.

A recent study which attempts to inform development of responsive policies and practices in a Social Services Department by examining social worker attitudes to domestic violence (Judge, 1997) exemplifies this confusion. In the introduction, the question of definition and prevalence of domestic violence is dealt with by reference to two studies—one (North American) focuses on violence in families, across gender (Gelles, 1980); the other (British), focuses on men's violence to their women partners, gender-specific (NCH, 1994)—without problematising, explaining or even acknowledging the fundamental differences of focus or methodology between them.

Men's violence, using a restricted definition, is then implicitly adopted into the conceptual framework of the study, its design, execution and evaluation, based on which recommendations for future policy and practice are made.

Social workers' understandings of, and approaches to, domestic violence are then framed solely in terms of 'practice intervention with abused women and their children', echoing Milner's thesis (1993) that men frequently disappear from view in child protection work. Indeed, the social workers in this study were found to have 'substantial knowledge about the impact on children of witnessing domestic violence' (p. 49) but struggled to maintain a focus on the children's needs when dealing with 'such needy mothers'. They expressed considerable frustration over work with abused women and their children, particularly the failure to effect change.

The question of men's position in families experiencing violence and the ongoing work to protect children in these situations does not appear to arise, except as an implied factor in the researcher's identified requirements for future good social work practice, specifically:

> to have knowledge of the sociological studies on domestic violence; an awareness of the power imbalance in abusive families and why women stay; the effects on children, and on the legislation regarding domestic violence. (Judge, 1997: 50)

Such confusion typically reflects the needs of practitioners attempting to respond to social problems, but risks carrying over the confusion and contradictions of the existing body of knowledge into the policy and practice developments of social welfare agencies. This is especially relevant in the UK where much of the literature and research is rooted in the dominant perspective which forecloses the issue of whether men's violence is in fact a unitary phenomenon and whether protection of women and children can be achieved without reference to interpersonal and intrapsychic dimensions of family relations.

Thus, whilst Dobash and Dobash have been leading figures in this field, they have used a closed definition of domestic violence (1992), and studies of work with male perpetrators of violence have done similarly (Dobash, Dobash, Cavanagh and Lewis 1996; Morran and Wilson, 1997). These studies undoubtedly contain important information of which we need to be aware, but the specific focus used also needs to be borne in mind. Presenting domestic violence as exclusively conscious, rational male behaviour is problematic for practitioners working in the real world, where domestic violence may well include apparently calculated abuse, but may also point to more complex dynamics (Goldner, Penn, Scheinberg and Walker, 1990).

Furthermore, such a simplistic explanation of domestic violence fails to match everyday practice experience where there is also a need to understand, for example, violence in lesbian and gay relationships, women's violence and the significance of wider social divisions of race and class.

CHILDREN IN NEED

Professional and public attention is now rightly turning to consider the position of children exposed to domestic violence. In seeking to place them centrally, it is necessary to attempt to understand the meaning and impact such experiences have for them. Just as the construction of domestic violence as a social problem is not a straightforward matter, neither is understanding the effect of children's exposure to such violence, which has not, until very recently, been investigated as an issue separate from their mother's well-being (Mullender and Morley, 1994).

This is evident in much of the research methodology which uses small, highly selective samples of women (Hester and Radford, 1996; NCH, 1994) and takes their accounts as the basis for building generalised knowledge about the impact on children. Caution must be exercised however, in drawing wider conclusions from material where very few children, or others, are directly involved in the research. Studies have also pointed up differential reporting by mothers depending upon the type and level of violence and who it was directed at (O'Brien, John, Margolin and Erel, 1994; Brandon and Lewis, 1996).

However, despite the contradictory and inconsistent nature of the present knowledge base, there is, nevertheless, sufficient reason to believe children are suffering and are deserving of protection from the effects of domestic violence.

Evidence suggests that children are frequently exposed to violence in the home, although precise information about their exposure and the chronicity of the violence is not available except in anecdotal form. The British Crime Survey (1992) reported children witnessing or being in an adjacent room during 90% of domestic assaults. In the NCH Action For Children study (1994) with a sample 108 women, 73% of their 246 children were reported to have witnessed violence and 62% to have overheard it; 10% of those women also said they had been sexually abused in front of their children. Dobash and Dobash (1984) found 30% of assaults had occurred in front of children.

Domestic violence must be viewed as a dynamic experience which includes several people, not just the aggressor and their victim. Even where a child does not directly experience the event, they are likely to witness its outcome—either in the physical injuries or emotional distress of their carer(s) or through material upheaval in the home such as damage to furniture, household equipment and fittings. Children are also likely to be sensitive to more generalised aspects of violent sequences such as controlling and intimidating behaviour, withholding money and resources, destruction of clothing—all of which have been reported by women (e.g. NCH, 1994). They are also likely to be affected by the more subtle aspects of violent episodes, for example Kelly (1994) reports some women knowing when the process leading to an assault was in chain and acting in a way which would provoke the man in order to 'get the inevitable over with'. Discovering what this all might mean for children, their relationships, their understanding of events and overall development is not easy to determine. Even research which has sought to directly include the views of children and others, for example violent men and professionals, has encountered difficulties, because of children's own reluctance to disclose information, concerns about protecting their confidentiality, and differing accounts of the violent situations (O'Brien *et al.*, 1994; Brandon and Lewis, 1996). Placing the violence in its particular context is crucial to understanding the prevalence, chronicity and meaning it has for the *different* members of the family and their *relationships* with each other. Only by doing this can risk be properly assessed.

Not surprisingly, given the uncertainty in trying to determine their exposure, evaluating the effects of domestic violence on children is also far from straightforward. Taking in both British and North American research, there is a wide range of material, and an array of varying interpretations (see e.g., Fantuzzo and Lindquist, 1989).

Broadly speaking, the research findings identify children being affected directly and indirectly, short and long term, emotionally, cognitively and behaviourally. Children can also internalise sadness, fear and anxiety, as well as display externalised aggression, anger and disobedience.

Strikingly, when a list of possible effects on children (see Table 5.1) is considered it can be seen that such effects are far from homogeneous, and whilst profoundly serious psychosocial and physical consequences are reported, these appear to be mediated by a number of possible variables including age of the child, gender, their position/role in the

Table 5.1:   Range of effects observed/reported by children

Internalising/emotional effects	*School/social functioning*
Anxiety/temperament	School problems
Low self-esteem	Social functioning
Shyness	Low empathy
Depression	Poor problem-solving/conflict
Suicide attempts	Acceptance/legitimisation
Withdrawal	Poor cognition
Trauma/stress reactions	
Anger/loss/sadness	*Externalising behavioural problems*
Confusion	
Self-blame	Aggression
Physical problems	Alcohol/drug use

(Adapted from Bamett, Miller-Perrin and Perrin, 1997.)

family, personality, the type of violence experienced, maternal stress and paternal involvement (Jaffe, Wolfe and Wilson, 1990; Johnston and Campbell, 1993; Brandon and Lewis, 1996).

As well as the effects of domestic violence outlined in Table 5.1 on children we cannot proceed without addressing the issue of direct risk of abuse presented to children living in such situations. Research studies have found a correlation of violence toward women partners and physical abuse of children ranging from 70% of women physically assaulted also reporting assaults on children (Bowker, Arbitel and McFerron, 1988) to 45% of children reported for physical assaults having mothers who were also physically assaulted (Stark and Flitcraft,1988). In a review of studies Hughes (1992) found correlations of 40–60% between child abuse and domestic violence.

Vulnerable children in an environment where their female carer is disempowered by their partner's abusive behaviour and associated dynamics may logically be at increased risk from those with a predisposition to sexual assaults on children (see Finkelhor, 1984) and it is therefore possible that further research may reveal a higher incidence of sexual abuse than in families where domestic violence is not a feature. Here again however, research has tended to rely on fixed stereotypes of perpetrator and victim and consequently excludes potentially highly significant variables.

RESEARCH AND PRACTICE DEVELOPMENT

Practitioners and policy-makers now need to turn to research which seeks to examine the overall context of domestic violence, including the range of individual experiences, dynamic interactions and situational factors. Two notable examples will be considered here: Brandon and Lewis (1996) studied community based samples of children identified as suffering or being at risk of suffering significant harm, almost half of whom were living in situations of domestic violence; Johnston and Campbell's (1993) samples comprised families with a background of domestic violence and who were involved in separation/divorce custody disputes.

Both studies used broad non-gender-specific definitions of violence. Brandon and Lewis focused solely on physical assaults whilst Johnston and Campbell also included psychological intimidation. Neither study collected information about emotional abuse between the adults as part of the violence but both acknowledge this dimension and highlight the psychological and interpersonal dynamics as an important feature of the adult and parent–child relationships.

The studies drew on interviews with children, mothers and fathers/partners (as well as professionals in Brandon and Lewis's samples). The emergent picture shows a complex web of relationships and interactions in those families between men and women and between them and the(ir) children. They raise critical issues for professionals involved in work with families experiencing domestic violence, particularly around enquiry, engagement and assessment.

In the Brandon and Lewis study, most families were suffering multiple disadvantage through unemployment, low income and poor or insecure housing. Echoing the stark picture from nineteenth-century Boston painted by Linda Gordon, poverty and struggles around scarce family resources appear as equally significant factors in the 1990s context, highlighting the importance of wider social divisions in mediating families' experiences. The individual case studies also point up the significance of gender as a fundamental component of relationships, whereby constructions of masculinity and femininity place powerful injunctions and contradictions around the individual behaviour of women, men, girls and boys and through their relationships as mothers, fathers, daughters and sons (see also Benjamin, 1993; Parker, 1995; Frosh, 1997).

For professionals making assessments of children's needs in violent family situations and engaging in ongoing work, a gendered understanding is vital to how they approach and talk with family members. The individual case studies cited are testimony to the complexities of parental, sibling and family attachments, and the threat to children's immediate and future well-being posed by *both* mothers' and fathers' behaviour. Violence was both varied and serious, and all adults, including professionals, were found to minimise its significance except when the risk of direct physical injury to a child was identified. They were also found to pejoratively label children's consequent behaviour and children themselves tended toward caution about disclosing or discussing the violence.

In the face of this evidence, discounting the father's perspective and treating, for example, mothers' or indeed children's accounts as more authentic and therefore the route to a better understanding of a violent situation is not only extremely partial but also potentially dangerous. It is imperative that where possible, the perspectives of all family members be taken into account in attempting to assess the situation.

Brandon and Lewis conclude that the absence of support for children in dealing with violence and failure to recognise the cumulative harm from experiencing this, makes acknowledging the possibility of significant harm a central strategy in promoting children's recovery by securing appropriate help.

Within the Children Act definition of 'significant harm', harm is identified as both ill-treatment and the impairment of physical or mental health or physical, intellectual, emotional, social or behavioural development (DOH, 1989). Significant harm is used in the law to refer to avoidable damage to a child which parents could reasonably be expected to take steps to prevent. Such behaviour may be taken as evidence of serious disturbance in the child's living circumstances (Bentovim, 1992) and such children may reasonably be regarded as children in need, not least of protection.

A clearly documented case example of a correlation between domestic violence and other risk is that of Sukina Hammond, killed by her father in 1988 when she was five years old. Three months after a sustained attack against their mother which included her being tied to a chair, viciously beaten and having some of her hair cut off by her partner, the children's father, the names of Sukina (then aged four) and her sister (aged two) were removed from the 'At Risk' register (sic). The professionals involved knew that there had been an 'incident', but the violence to the children's mother by their father does not appear to have been seen as a significant risk factor to the children and detail of the nature and extent of the violence was therefore not sought (Bridge Child Care Consultancy, 1991). This is not described here in order to criticise those workers but as an example of the dislocation in understanding of the interrelatedness of violence and risk issues which continues to be a feature of much childcare practice. It is also a case which highlights the importance of gender, race and class as significant factors in mediating behaviour and family experiences as well as professional responses.

Johnston and Campbell's work takes us further in differentiating various manifestations of violence and the different interactions/relationships which might accompany these. It is their view that:

> Domestic violence appears to be a behaviour or set of behaviours arising from multiple sources, which follow different patterns in different families, rather than being a syndrome with a single underlying cause. Parent–child relationships are likely to vary with the different patterns of violence, and children of different ages and gender are affected differently. There are also several trajectories for recovery and the reconstitution of family relationships and the potential for future violence. (p. 198)

A five fold typology of interparental violence is established around the following criteria:

- typical precursors to violent episodes
- person initiating the attack
- victim reactions
- severity and frequency of abuse
- degree of restraint exercised by the parties
- perpetrator's perceptions of the violence

Ongoing and episodic male battering—is characterised by terrifying and severe violence to women, perpetrated by possessive, domineering men who minimise or deny their violence, blaming the woman, and who become even more dangerous at separation. These men experienced enormous internal tension and exercised little or no restraint.

Female-initiated violence—these women also experienced intolerable internal tension, fed by a perception that the man was holding back. Violence tended to be relatively minor with the possibility of escalation. The men were generally passive, attempting to contain the assaults but also capable of retaliating. Women admitted their actions although they projected blame.

Male-controlling interactive violence—was often consequent upon an argument, with the man characteristically responding by seeking to control and dominate his partner. Men and women were abusive of each other, with the severity of the violence being consequent in part, upon the level of resistance offered. Mutual blaming and 'just deserts' rationalising were common.

Separation-engendered trauma—involved uncharacteristic violent acts during difficult separations/divorces and were either male- or female-initiated. Victims were shocked and frightened by the out-of-character, generally limited violence in their partner, who was remorseful and ashamed.

Psychotic and paranoid reactions—involved both women and men as perpetrators, acting in an unpredictable, sometimes seriously and unrestrained abusive manner. They were driven by disordered mental processes perceiving outside threats or plots against them which justified their defensive attack. Victims were traumatised and intimidated.

In terms of incidence, the most common category was 'separation-engendered trauma', followed closely by 'male-controlling interactive violence', each nearly a fifth of the sample. Next most common and occurring in similar proportions were 'ongoing and episodic male battering' and 'female-initiated violence'. Least common was 'psychotic and paranoid reactions'. A further interesting point from this study is that Johnston and Campbell found a large number of families characterised by high conflict but no reported violence.

For each type of violence identified, Johnston and Campbell profile the parent–child relationships by child's age and gender, and propose differential prognoses for recovery and reconstitution of post-separation family relationships. Besides providing a helpful and illuminating framework for extending understandings of domestic violence, Johnston and Campbell also describe factors vital to assessment of risk and protection planning for children. Fathers who had perpetrated ongoing or episodic violence were considered to be completely unsuited to having sole or shared care of their children, the same applied to fathers and mothers who were psychotic. Furthermore, they felt consideration should be given to either supervising or suspending contact entirely with that parent where the risk of violence is still current, and special care be taken in making contact arrangements so as not to jeopardise the victim parent's safety.

Serious questions were raised about a mother's capacity to act as primary carer where there was female-initiated violence, requiring a thorough assessment before placing children. In the remaining categories, a variety of shared arrangements were held to be appropriate, with the best prognosis being for parents sharing responsibility for their children where there had been no history of violence. However, the traumatic effects of sudden violence around separation were such that therapeutic help was felt to be desirable, before parents could overcome their fears.

Evidence about children's adjustment to their experience of parental violence was found to fit a fairly consistent pattern. The degree of emotional and behavioural disturbance was greatest where there was male violence, boys showing more disturbance in ongoing violent situations, less in male-controlling or female-initiated, and girls being equally likely to be disturbed in both ongoing or male-controlling violence.

The detail of interparental and parent-child dynamics revealed through Johnston and Campbell's work reinforces the view that an understanding of these relationships is not to be found in simplistic, one-dimensional explanations (see Featherstone and Trinder, 1997). Links between maternal/paternal stress and the resultant parent–child relationship are not straightforward and the assumption of an essential harmony of interest between mothers and their children, implicit for instance in the radical feminist analysis, is deeply problematic to the process of assessing children's needs.

Whilst both studies examined here in varying degrees from sampling to analysis touch on issues of gender, race, culture and class, overall analysis is lacking in terms of the interrelationship of these factors with the individual behaviour and interpersonal dynamics including psychodynamic processes found in families, not to mention the variation in family forms which exist. Attention to these dimensions is crucial to the process of safeguarding children's welfare in families experiencing domestic violence. It is crucial also to work undertaken with individual adult carers, for instance on programmes for perpetrators of domestic violence.

CONCLUSION

Returning again to the case of Sukina Hammond, the inquiry report comments on professional difficulty in differentiating between families under stress where there may be an isolated violent outburst and those experiencing more frequent violence. It goes on 'the literature on child abuse, on the whole, ignores this phenomenon' and concludes 'unless we begin to understand these issues our ability to protect children will be seriously impaired' (BCCC, 1991: 87). Published at the beginning of the decade, the comment regrettably remains as relevant at its close.

The research highlighted in this chapter utilised open definitions of domestic violence and so exposed a range of factors significant to the manifestation, experience and consequences of domestic violence. This kind of research points the way towards models of practice capable of assessing risk across a range of circumstances and responsive to the unexpected. Practice which uses closed definitions is more likely to find only what it is looking for.

There is an important distinction to be made however, between avoidable and unavoidable mistakes (Munro, 1996). Munro examines the dangers of closed thinking in child protection work which can screen out important information from the process of risk assessment—thus leading to avoidable mistakes. Within the current developing body of knowledge lies the promise of enhanced confidence and competence for practitioners. It is important therefore, to prioritise practice evaluation and press for further research as our understanding and experience of working with domestic violence develops.

> To change your mind in the light of new information is a sign of good practice, a sign of strength not weakness. (Munro, 1996: 793)

REFERENCES

Association of Chief Officers of Probation (1992) *Position statement on domestic violence*, ACOP, Wakefield.

Association of Chief Officers of Probation (1996) *Position statement on domestic violence* (update), ACOP, Wakefield.

Bamett O W, Miller-Perrin C L and Perrin R D (1997) *Family Violence Across the Lifespan: An Introduction*, Sage, London.

Benjamin J (1993) *The Bonds of Love: Psychoanalysis, Feminism and the Problem of Domination*, Virago Press, London.

Bentovim A (1992) Significant harm in context, in Adcock M, White R and Hollows A (eds) *Significant Harm: Its Management and Outcome*, Significant Publications, London.

Bowker L, Arbitel M and McFerron J (1988) cited in McKay M, The link between child abuse and domestic violence, *Child Welfare*, **73** (1994): 13–23.

Brandon M and Lewis A (1996) Significant harm and children's experiences of domestic violence, *Child and Family Social Work*, **1**: 333–342.

Bridge Child Care Consultancy (1991) *Sukina: An Evaluation Report of the Circumstances Leading to her Death*, BCCC, London.

Department of Health (1989) *An Introduction to the Children Act 1989*, HMSO, London.

Dobash R and Dobash R (1984) The nature of antecedents of violent events, *British Journal of Criminology*, **24**: 269–288.

Dobash R and Dobash R (1992) *Women, Violence and Social Change*, Routledge, London.

Doabash R, Dobash R, Cavanagh K and Lewis R (1996) *Research Evaluation of Programmes for Violent Men*, Scottish Office Central Research Unit, Edinburgh.

Fantuzzo J W and Lindquist C U (1989) The effects of observing conjugal violence on children: A review and analysis of research methodology, *Journal of Family Violence*, **4**: 77–94.

Farmer A and Owen M (1995) *Child Protection Practice: Private Risks and Public Remedies*, HMSO, London.

Featherstone B and Trinder L (1997) Familiar subjects? Domestic violence and child welfare, *Child and Family Social Work*, **2** (3): 147–160.

Finkelhor D (1984) *Child Sexual Abuse and New Theory and Research*, Free Press, New York.

Frosh S (1997) *Fathers' Ambivalence (too)*, in Hollway W and Featherstone B (eds) *Mothering and Ambivalence*, Routledge, London.

Gelles R (1980) *Family Violence*, Sage, Beverley Hills, CA.

Goldner V, Penn P, Scheinberg M and Walker G (1990) Love and violence: Gender paradoxes in volatile attachments, *Family Process*, **29**: 343–370.

Gordon L (1989) *Heroes of Their Own Lives: The Politics and History of Family Violence*, Virago, London.

Hester M, Kelly L and Radford J (eds) (1996) *Women, Violence and Male Power*, Open University Press, Milton Keynes, Buckingham.

Hester M and Radford L (1996) *Domestic Violence and Child Contact Arrangements in Britain and Denmark*, Policy Press, Bristol.

Home Affairs Committee (1991) *Third Report: Domestic Violence*, Vol. I, HMSO, London.

Home Affairs Committee (1993) *Third Report: Domestic Violence*, Vol. II, HMSO, London.

Home Office (1992) *British Crime Survey*, HMSO, London.

Hughes H (1992) Impact of spouse abuse on children of battered women, *Violence Update*, August, **1**, 9–11.

Jaffe P, Wolfe D and Wilson S (1990) *Children of Battered Women*, Sage, Newbury, CA.

Johnston J and Campbell L (1993) A clinical typology of interpersonal violence in disputed custody divorces, *American Journal of Orthopsychiatry*, **63**: 190–199.

Judge C (1997) The attitudes and views of social workers to domestic violence and their response to children who witness it, *The Kent Journal of Practice Research*, **1** (2): 43–51.

Kelly L (1994) The interconnectedness of domestic violence and child abuse: Challenges for research, policy and practice, in Mullender A and Morley R (eds) *Children Living with Domestic Violence: Putting Men's Abuse of Women on the Child Care Agenda*, Whiting and Birch, 1994, London.

McKay M (1994) The link between child abuse and domestic violence, *Child Welfare*, **73**: 13–23.

Milner J (1993) A disappearing act: The differing career paths of fathers and mothers in child protection investigations, *Critical Social Policy*, **38**: 48–68.

Morran D and Wilson M (1997) *Men who are Violent to Women: A Groupwork Practice Manual*, Russell House Publishing, Dorset.

Mullender A (1996) *Re-thinking Domestic Violence: The Social Work and Probation Response*, Routledge, London.

Mullender A and Morley R (eds) (1994) *Children Living With Domestic Violence: Putting Men's Abuse of Women on the Child Care Agenda*, Whiting and Birch, London.

Munro E (1996) Avoidable and unavoidable mistakes in child protection work, *British Journal of Social Work*, **26**: 793–808.

National Children's Homes: Action For Children (1994) *The Hidden Victims: Children and Domestic Violence*, NCH, London.

O'Brien M, John R S, Margolin G and Erel O (1994) Reliability and diagnostic efficacy of parents' reports regarding children's exposure to marital aggression, *Violence and Victims*, **9**: 45–62.

O'Hara M (1992) Domestic violence and child abuse, *Childright*, **88**: 4–5.

O'Hara M (1995) Child deaths in contexts of domestic violence, *Childright*, **115**: 15–18.

Parker R (1995) *Torn in Two: The Experience of Maternal Ambivalence*, Virago, London.

Pizzey E (1974) *Scream Quietly or the Neighbours will Hear*, Penguin, Harmondsworth.

Segal L (1987) *Is the Future Female? Troubled Thoughts on Contemporary Feminism*, Virago, London.

Segal L (1990) *Slow Motion: Changing Masculinities—Changing Men*, Virago, London.

Stark E and Flitcraft A H (1988) Women and children at risk: A feminist perspective on child abuse, *International Journal of Health Services*, **18**: 97–118.

Straus M A and Gelles R J (1990) *Physical Violence in American Families: Risk Factors and Adaptations to Violence in 8145 Families*, Transaction Books, Brunswick, NJ.

6

AGEISM, VIOLENCE AND ABUSE—THEORETICAL AND PRACTICAL PERSPECTIVES ON THE LINKS BETWEEN 'CHILD ABUSE' AND 'ELDER ABUSE'

Jeff Hearn

Child abuse and child protection are gendered, both as personal and interpersonal practices and as an institutional system in and around the state (Hearn, 1988, 1990; Parkin and Hearn, 1989). Indeed the theme of gendering was a major concern of the Violence Against Children Study Group in *Taking Child Abuse Seriously* (see especially Parton, 1990). Conceptual frameworks for understanding the gendering of both the problems and the responses (the 'child abuse–child protection complex') range from individualistic approaches to those that are more societal, structural or poststructural in orientation.

One framework for addressing this gendered complexity is that of public patriarchy, or more precisely public patriarchies (Hearn, 1992). This shorthand refers to the set of structures, processes and practices whereby the historically defined powers of adult men within patriarchy have shifted from the individual, private patriarch to men in the public realms, institutions and organisations. In this context, this means in particular the powers of men in the welfare (Hearn, 1998c), social work and child protection systems (Hearn, 1998a, 1999), including police, lawyers and legal staff, doctors and medical staff, teachers and

Children, Child Abuse and Child Protection. Placing Children Centrally, by The Violence Against Children Study Group.

headteachers, social workers, and child protection workers and managers. Though such analyses might assist rethinking the interplay of the child abuse–child protection complex, they also need to fully address the social construction of age and 'age-d' social actors. It is not enough just to 'add on' a consideration of age and ageism.

Thus this chapter focuses on not just child abuse, age and ageism, but more broadly on the child abuse–child protection complex, 'elder abuse', age and ageism. It draws on the growing recognition of 'elder abuse', along with questions of definition, explanation, intervention, and indeed its own dominant gendered patterns of men mainly abusing women. The first section explores the social construction of age and ageism; the second addresses alternative theoretical perspectives for linking 'young-ageism'/child abuse and 'old-ageism'/elder abuse; and the third section looks in more detail at the similarities, differences, links and divergences between policy and practice around child abuse and elder abuse. Throughout, the interrelations of age with other social divisions are noted, along with the gendering of these processes of ageing and ageism.

AGE AND AGEISM

Age is one of the basic social divisions of this and most other, perhaps all other, societies. This society is ruled by adults (senocracy) (Hearn, 1988), especially adult men (viriarchy) (Waters, 1989) of middle years. Furthermore, age, physical size, disability, and indeed mobility, are all socially constructed, closely interrelated, and also fundamental elements around which this society is organised. Younger, smaller, 'less able' people are distinguished from those who are 'adults', and they in turn are distinguished from older, increasingly smaller and 'less able' people.

The social dynamics and processes of senocracy and viriarchy are themselves very complex, not least because of the fact that however much we are constructed through age, we are ourselves all in a constantly changing relation to that social differentiation. Thus ageism is a shorthand for a shifting set of social relations, in which individuals *change* their social location usually gradually yet also dramatically over their lifetime. Age and ageism are unusual as a systematic form of oppression in that most people are likely to experience both the privileges and damages that flow from it, albeit generally, though strangely enough not necessarily, at different times of their lives; in other words, it is possible to both benefit and suffer from ageism *at the same time.*

When we talk of ageism, it is often not exactly clear what is meant. Bill Bytheway's (1995) *Ageism* is an excellent analysis of different approaches to the concept, and its relation to other concepts, such as 'the aged as minority group' and 'the ageing subculture', over the last twenty years or more. A key initiative was the use of the term, ageism, in the late 1960s United States by Robert Butler, a psychiatrist involved in social campaigns for older people. With colleagues, he identified ageism as:

> a process of systematic stereotyping of and discrimination against people because they are old, just as racism and sexism accomplish this for skin colour and gender. Old people are categorized as senile, rigid in thought, old-fashioned in morality and skills. (Butler and Lewis, 1973: 115)

This approach has in turn been debated and contested on a number of grounds, perhaps most significantly, for unwittingly reinforcing, through a 'new ageism' (Kalish, 1979), the very constructions that are being critiqued. Bytheway himself reviews these and other critiques. On the one hand, he acknowledges the importance of Butler's linking of the individual and the institutional through the recognition of systematic and categorising processes (1995: 33). On the other, he sees such relatively simple approaches to age and ageism as flawed, and instead propounds a more complex set of recognitions that include: opposition to ageist language, and to age as an institutional regulator; realism about physical change in the body over time; and acceptance of the temporal context of lives rather than the maintenance of an us-them mentality (1995: ch. 9; also see Bytheway and Johnson, 1990). The intersections of ageism and sexism, and ageism, racism and sexism, have also been increasingly recognised (Aitken and Griffin, 1996: ch. 3).

Age and ageism affect both children and older people. However, while children are generally increasing their autonomy, older people often experience decreasing autonomy. While, for this and other reasons, there are grave dangers in equating children and older people too closely, there are parallels to be drawn between the social situation of both groups, most obviously in relation to ageism and frequent dependency on others, especially (relatively) younger adults.

Seen now in this context, there has been something of a reluctance, more or less conscious, to directly address the 'obvious' issues of age and ageism in analyses of violence and abuse in general, and child abuse and elder abuse in particular. Indeed the links between violence, abuse and ageism are probably made less often than those between violence, abuse and racism, or violence, abuse and sexism. Age and ageism are themselves constructed in close relations with other social divisions. As discussed in feminist literature on women's ageing and on older women (e.g., Macdonald and Rich, 1983; Thone, 1992), the experience and the social structuring of age and ageism are gendered. Similar conclusions can be derived from examining men's ageing and older men within a critical gendered perspective. Interestingly, while men are a socially dominant group, which in many societies becomes reinforced with age, there are also ways in which many men, with ageing, lose power relative to younger men (Hearn, 1995).

Placing children centrally with a critical analysis of age and ageism involves promoting and creating a social world free of violence and abuse, and that includes reducing and abolishing elder abuse, or more accurately, violence and abuse to older people. How older people are valued in society contributes to creating an environment for children that is with or without violence and abuse. This applies not only within families, in terms of grandparents and other older relatives, but more generally in the way in which older people with whom children have contact are dealt with. Such social relations say much to children about how those people who are relatively or totally dependent on others are valued, and this in turn speaks of, if only indirectly or implicitly, the value that may be given to children and young people. Furthermore, children gradually learn and come to know that they will become old(er). Abuse of older people is another way in which children and young people may themselves be saddened, distressed, violated and abused.

THEORETICAL PERSPECTIVES

Child abuse and elder abuse are not new; they have historically been and indeed remain embedded in the dominant traditions and ways of life of many societies and cultures (Hornick, McDonald and Robertson, 1992), even when, perhaps especially when, 'the young' and 'the elderly' are given special treatment. The reminiscences of Suffolk village life in the early twentieth century given to Ronald Blythe (1975: 23, cited in Adams, 1996: 163) in *Akenfield* include that about an older relative locked in a cupboard all day to prevent her wandering when the family were working on the land. Therefore estimates of prevalence should always be treated with some caution, and within a broad historical-cultural context.

Partly for this reason the very words, 'child abuse' and 'elder abuse' cannot simply be taken at face value; they may carry ideological connotations, and as such need some critical attention. The first of these terms may obscure the use of violence and sexual violence, and gender

differences in the use of that violence; and may even implicitly reinforce a notion that children can legitimately *be used*. It also fails to
engage with the large question of the social construction of smaller,
younger people *as children* (Hearn, 1988). The term, elder abuse, brings
parallel difficulties. While generally taken to include physical/sexual,
psychological/emotional/verbal, and financial/material violations, its
definition is still contested, for example in relations to the 'obligation
of care' (Hugman, 1995). In a similar way to 'child abuse', it is necessary to consider how the term may fail to engage with both gender and
the social construction (and destruction) of older people as 'elderly'.
Indeed critiques of the notions of 'elderly people' or 'the elderly', rather
than, say, older people or older adults (Manthorpe, 1997: 168), have
made themselves felt very unevenly in deconstructing the term elder
abuse. An interesting example in this regard is the shift in naming used
by the Social Services Inspectorate from 'elder abuse' (SSI, 1992) to 'the
safety of elderly people' (SSI, 1993) to 'abuse of older people' (SSI,
1994a). It is now appropriate to recognise that the term, 'the abuse of
older people', or a combination of more specific, more elaborate terms,
for example, 'men's violence to older known people', may be prefer-
able. (While the term 'elder abuse' is flawed I am continuing to use it
along with 'violence and abuse to older people', as the former remains
in such general usage.) Additionally, while both children and older
people may predominantly be the victims of abuse, it is necessary to
remember that they can also be the violators.

In a recent review of elder abuse, Glendenning (1997: 38) notes that
'elder abuse has often been compared or related to child abuse
(Rathbone-McCuan, 1980; Eastman, 1984)'. He continues that: 'This
is because the relationship between the carer or caretaker and the elder
(according to Finkelhor and Pillemer, 1988: 248) is often thought to have
"a parent–child character in the extreme dependency of the elder".'
Indeed some definitions of elder abuse have assumed abuse by a carer.
For example, elder abuse has been defined as 'systematic and contin-
uous abuse of an elderly person by the carer, often though not always
a relative on whom the elderly person is dependent for care' (Cloke,
1983: 2, cited in Froggatt, 1990: 49). While this definition reminds us
that much, though not all, such violence and abuse occurs within the
context of 'care', it is important not to press this point too far. Much
elder abuse is not committed by a carer (Glendenning 1997); in many
cases it is the abuser who is 'dependent' (Wolf and Pillemer, 1989); elder
abuse may be violence in marriage that has been long established
(Finkelhor and Pillemer, 1988; Homer and Gilleard, 1990); and furthermore, the assumption of any simple dichotomy of violence versus
care should be interrogated (Aitken and Griffin, 1996: 4–6).

There are many ways in which the relationship between child abuse and elder abuse can be conceptualised. People may be involved with child abuse and elder abuse, as violators, violated, or both; through the whole range of types of violence and abuse; at particular points in time, or over time; through direct individual experience, or through structural relations; in terms of differences by gender, age, generation and other social divisions and differences (see McCreadie, 1991). A full examination of the relationship of child abuse and elder abuse would take account of variations in all these connections.

However, in developing conceptual frameworks, three dimensions appear to be especially important: first, the experience of connections-in-time, that is, the nature of the experience of both child abuse and elder abuse in its temporal context; second, the social unit through which the connections take place or are experienced, that is, whether the connections are primarily through the experience of particular individuals or through more (post)structural social relations, and third, the extent to which analysis is gendered. From combining the first two dimensions, we may recognise four forms of relationships between child abuse and elder abuse, which I label *individual present experience; individual developmental experience; present structural relations;* and *developing structural relations.* These can in turn be *less* or *more gendered.*

First, child abuse and elder abuse may be connected through the *individual present experience of* particular individuals, as either violators and/or violated, at particular points in time. The most obvious example of this is when the same person is engaging in both child abuse and elder abuse. More arguably, individuals may experience both child abuse and elder abuse at the same time, if only through the witnessing of both.

Second, the focus may be the *individual developmental experiences* of particular individuals, as violators and/or violated, developmentally over time, perhaps over many years, perhaps separated by many years. For example, a person who is a survivor of child abuse may later experience elder abuse. Alternatively, a young person who has experienced violation through child abuse may go on later in their life to abuse older people. Abusers may become more vulnerable over time and may thus become liable to being abused as elders. There are arguments both for and against developmental theory that examines how abused children may become either abusers of children or elders, or indeed abused elders. While some may see this as simply an empirical question, to understand child abuse as a direct cause of elder abuse is likely to be inappropriate and misleading, not least because that might bring us close to blaming the victim. Much of such an approach has been within the framework of 'intra-family cycles of abuse', a perspective that may well neglect gendering and isolate families from societal structures and processes. However, rather than seeing child abuse and elder abuse as directly linked, developmentally and causally, in such ways, it is possible to consider how the experiences of both violated and violators at one part of their earlier life connect with their experiences at a later part of their life.

Third, the connections may be at a certain point in time but not through the common experience of specific individuals—rather through a third element, *present structural relations*. This may occur in the more collective experience of particular families, for example, when child abuse and elder abuse involve different people in different generations of the same family. Thus even though no one individual may actually experience both child abuse and elder abuse, it may be part of the present collective experience of the particular family.

A fourth possibility is that child abuse and elder abuse are not necessarily connected through the experience of particular individuals at specific points in time, but through more complex, *developing structural relations*. Violence and abuse may occur in families in different generations at different times but in such a way that there is not a direct or complete continuity between abuses for individuals or over time. One way of understanding such connections is in terms of there being a constant replenishment of the 'middle years' dominant group, and particularly those who are male, who may become abusers of children or elders.

These four theoretical frameworks are not exhaustive; in each case they need to be used and developed very carefully and critically; in particular they may be *less* or *more gendered*. Early work on both child abuse and elder abuse tended to neglect gender or, in the latter case, focus on the 'abusing daughter'; more recently, there has been extensive study of the clearly gendered patterns of abuse. There are now excellent feminist analyses of elder abuse, in both introductory (Whittaker, 1996) and extended (Aitken and Griffin, 1996) forms. These point out that the majority of elder abuse is by men to women, and especially so for physical and sexual abuse (Miller and Dodder, 1989; Penhale, 1993; Aitken and Griffin, 1996; Whittaker, 1996). Similarly, dominant, patriarchal, heterosexist ways of defining girls and women, especially in relation to the sexual and the domestic, may mean both that girls experience more sexual abuse than boys, and that women do more caring of older people. Men do most violence and abuse to both children and older women, but women may also be abusive doing care. In addition, a gendered approach means taking into account differences between abuse from known others, from strangers, and in institutional contexts.

There are also other more complex issues still. Of particular interest, both theoretically and practically, is the situation of those people at the margin of childhood and adulthood (older children and young adults) and those at the margin of middle years and older age (late middle years adults and younger elders). Such 'transitional' people (rather like transitional economic classes in class analysis) pose interesting challenges to oversimple interventions or theoretical understandings of violence and abuse. A good example of this complexity is the relations between older (elderly) parents and their adult children who themselves may be (becoming) older/elderly (Froggatt, 1985).

Above all it is necessary to challenge the notion of simple, direct, causal links between child abuse and elder abuse, in any narrow sense. Rather there are multifaceted series of connections, whereby the apparently disparate worlds of child abuse and elder abuse, and indeed of children and older people, are drawn together or are affected by the same or similar social forces. In this sense, both may be understood as part of what is usually called 'domestic violence', usually more accurately named 'men's violence (to known women)'. There is increasing recognition of the connections between men's violence to women and men's violence to children (Bowker, Arbitell and McFerron, 1988; Mullender and Morley, 1994), either directly or indirectly, for example, in the children's witnessing of violence. Similarly, men's violence to women as wives, 'girlfriends', partners, ex-partners, or other relations such as children, may also involve, indeed may be, violence to older women; men's violence to older women is part of the bigger picture of men's violence. More generally, both forms of violence, abuse and neglect need to be understood in the context of general patterns of social division, including those of age, class, gender and generation. Further insights might come from the study of ritual or satanic abuse, and of torture (Scott, 1997), in considering how patterns of violence are reproduced that both transcend and differentiate gender and generation.

POLICY AND PRACTICE

Both child abuse and elder abuse may take place both in the home and within institutions. For children, this will generally mean families, nurseries, day-care, schools, sports and social clubs, and children's homes; for older people, their own homes, families with others, day-care, group care, hospitals and other kinds of institutional care. The director of the charity Action on Elderly Abuse, founded in 1993, has suggested on the basis of their helpline experience that at least 100 000 are abused every month in their own homes (Hyder, 1996). For both children and older people there is the possible problem of institutional abuse, that may include abuse through the carrying out of the polices and practices of the institution, and abuse that occurs within the context of institutions, whether by managers, staff, residents or visitors (see Aitken and Griffin, 1996: ch. 4, 153–154; Grant, 1997).

Although the recognition of elder abuse can certainly be dated from the 1970s (Baker, 1975; Ambache, 1997), and figured to an extent in medical, gerontological and social work debate in the 1980s (see Eastman, 1984), it was not until the 1990s that the problem was given clear governmental attention in the UK through the Social Services Inspectorate (SSI, 1992, 1993, 1994a, b). As such, elder abuse has only been substantially recognised subsequent to the reforms of the child protection system in the late 1980s and early 1990s. There is clearly both a wealth of knowledge and experience in child protection, as well as some dangers in any inappropriate transfer of 'lessons' from one field to the other (see Glendenning and Delcalmer, 1997: 223).

On the other hand, there may well be lessons that can be learnt from the practice and research on child protection (e.g., Department of Health, 1995, on informed, sensitive professional relationships; power balance between parties; wide perspectives; supervision and training; enhancing quality of life) that can be relevant for elder abuse, if they are sufficiently interpreted and contextualised, rather than applied uncritically. Jeremy Ambache (1997) and Jill Manthorpe (1997) provide very useful discussions of some more specific questions: public recognition of both problems; policy development from research on 'outcomes of intervention'; training; and liaison between agencies, including the police (also see Stevenson, 1996). There is also, however, the issue of what can be learnt the other way—from experience around elder abuse for child protection, for example, in terms of the 'obligation of care' (Hugman, 1995).

At the level of practice, both child protection and working on elder abuse are extremely difficult and demanding. In both arenas practitioners have to contend with multiple demands, not least in terms of who is to be defined as the primary client/user. Interventions in both may generate contradictory feelings, and restimulations of feelings from earlier parts of their lives, for example, in confronting their own feelings around violence, victimisers and victims (Pritchard, 1992, 1996). Difficulties also stem from the likely complexity of the power relations around care and dependency in both cases. Caring can itself involve both power over and power from the cared for, and power is a fundamental issue for older people, carers and indeed workers.

A central policy and practice issue is whether the child protection system should be extended to elder abuse, whether protection should be seen as the most appropriate model for elder abuse intervention, or whether they should be developed separately. This is partly a question of which agency or agencies should be responsible for intervention with regard to child abuse and elder abuse, and partly a matter of the detailed principles and practices. In some US states the same agencies handle both child abuse and elder abuse (Glendinning, 1997: 38). Furthermore, both problems have often been, and indeed continue to be, constructed within a health, welfare or social work rather than a legal or judicial frame. This can mean that what elsewhere constitute criminal acts can be redefined as acts of 'abuse' or problems of 'welfare' (Hugman, 1995). There have recently been suggestions for welfare agencies to provide protective services for adults requiring care (Holt, 1994; Pringle, 1995), or abuse protection committees for disabled and vulnerable adults (drawing on the US experience of Adult Protection Services) (Ambache, 1997; also see Aitken and Griffin, 1996: 32–33), and there may indeed be a significant demand for this. However, there are also dangers in creating welfare procedures that may undermine the legal status of older adults in both civil and criminal law (Whittaker, 1996: 156, 158). While there is an urgent need 'to build up a body of knowledge based on older women's experiences of abuse and . . . learn . . . from this', there are also problems with creating services for special categories and programmes for older women (Whittaker, 1996: 155–156).

Despite the fact that there are many possible and complex variations in the socio-legal situation of older people facing abuse, not least in terms of money, housing, frailty, dependency, autonomy, and capability of self-care and self-representation, retaining the adult personhood of the older person, wherever possible, is a fundamental principle. For example, as Adams, in his discussion of the 1983 Mental Health Act, notes:

> relatives and friends [may] put pressure on the local authority to have an older person taken into residential accommodation, but [if] the person is unwilling . . . professionals have to take due account of the wishes of the older person and any carers in making an assessment of needs. (Adams, 1996: 163).

Social complexities in the situations of older people cannot be an excuse for reducing the seriousness with which violence, abuse and neglect are treated.

A further area of comparison is around sexual abuse. While this has become a central preoccupation of the child protection system, it has only relatively recently been taken up in relation to older people. On this, Keith Pringle (1995: 113) has commented: 'some provisional British research is . . . demonstrating that sexual abuse in old age, both inside and outside care institutions, may be a major problem . . .'; he continues, more specifically, to note that 'it seems than men may perpetrate most of this abuse too (Holt, 1993, 1994)'. While sexual abuse of older people may occur in both domestic and group care settings, it may be that it is the very old and the very frail who are the most vulnerable to such assaults (Holt, 1994; Pringle, 1995). The question of sexual abuse also highlights the importance of attending to the earlier experiences of older people, both specifically around sexual trauma (Bergström-Walan, 1997), and more generally within reminiscence work.

This brings us again and directly to the recognition of the centrality of gender in both analyses and interventions (Whittaker, 1996; Aitken and Griffin, 1996). I have already noted both men's specialisation in violence and their abuse to older people, especially older women. Among such surveys, that conducted by Lynda Aitken (Aitken and Griffin, 1996: 106–121) is of special interest. This analyses 91 cases of elder abuse (65 of women, 25 of men, 1 unknown) reported by social workers in Northamptonshire. Of the men, 14 suffered from dementia, 12 were abused by their wives, and psychological abuse was the most common form of abuse. Of the women, most were in their 80s, sons were the most frequent abusers, and physical abuse was the most common form. Such studies have to be placed firmly in the context of the imbalance of care for older people; while women do far more such care, it is not unusual for men also to be carers, and men appear to outnumber women in the over-75 age range (OPCS, 1985).

One implication of men's specialisation in violence and abuse, as carers, husbands, sons and other relatives and 'friends', is the need to place under the spotlight the social construction of men and masculinities in relation to violence, care, gender and age. As with child abuse, this applies both to those men who have been violent and abusive and to the more general construction of 'normal' boys and men. This may take for granted that the care of older people is not something to be done by them, and moreover that abusing power is not incompatible with a sense of masculinity. Dominant forms of masculinity and ageism can intersect, through the men's use of age as a form of hierarchy, status, power and violence. Intervention against this needs to be as wide and as thorough as possible. This includes attending to the transformation of men who are workers and managers in agencies (Hearn, 1990, 1998b, 1999).

Similarly, the interrelations of 'race', ethnicity, gender and age need to be foregrounded in addressing both forms of violence and abuse. While the question of the protection of black children from abuse in the context of social work profession that is predominantly white has been put more fully on the policy and practice agenda (Ahmad, 1989), raising parallel issues around elder abuse has been slower (Aitken and Griffin, 1996: 25–27, 48–51, 58–74). This is partly a reflection of the overall lesser development of policy on elder abuse, but there are also further complications. Even with the move to community care, group and institutional care remain overall more important for older people (whether it is day-care, residential care or care till death) than for younger people. A related issue may be that much of this group and institutional care, especially in some urban localities, may itself be provided by black and ethnic minority staff, and particularly black and ethnic minority women. The presence of a multi-ethnic workforce does not guarantee that dominant policies and practices are changed; indeed it may even mean that in this context both black workers and white workers may, for rather different reasons, be very cautious in pursuing elder abuse. For the former, they may consider that predominantly white male hierarchies are unlikely to listen to them, and may even interpret any 'complaints' as a sign of worker incompetence; for the latter, they may wish to play safe to supposedly avoid charges of racism.

CONCLUDING COMMENTS

Child abuse and elder abuse are both similar and different; they need to be understood both as specific actions with their own characters and challenges, and within larger, more complex patterns. In rethinking theory and practice around elder abuse, feminist, pro-feminist and feminist-influenced perspectives continue to be especially powerful, just as they have been in rethinking child abuse.

First, both child abuse and elder abuse need to be contextualised within the web of wider social, political and economic relations that are themselves structured and pervaded by gendered power. Much remains to be done in connecting the question of gendered violence and abuse of older people to the more general gendered structural position of older people, and particularly older women, is society (compare Kosberg, 1988; Ogg and Munn-Giddings, 1993; Phillipson, Biggs and Kingston, 1995; Aitken and Griffin, 1996; Whittaker, 1996).

One partial way forward in the face of these difficult structural questions lies in 'Prevention, Prevention, Prevention', that is, changing these power relations in all spheres of life in the first place, just as it should be in placing children centrally in child protection. This means developing the politics of elder abuse just as much as that of child abuse (cf. Parton, 1985). While the perspective of children's rights, and indeed disability rights, has developed considerably in recent years in the UK and elsewhere, a comparable notion of 'older people's rights' or 'vulnerable elder protection rights', as in the Older Americans Act 1992 (Wolf, 1994: 12, cited in Ambache, 1997: 213) has not. *Grey Power* has been used as the name of the official journal of the British Pensioners and Trade Unions Associations, but the social movement of grey power has not generally transferred easily from North America to Europe.

Second, both child abuse and elder abuse are material and embodied experiences for all concerned: abuse is both on and constitutive of the body; it simultaneously constructs and 'destructs' bodies, and especially those that are relatively vulnerable. Thus, child abuse and elder abuse are to be understood not in isolation but as part of interconnected systems of violence, abuse and violating and abusive relations and relationships, yet still with specific and particular configurations of age/ageism, gender and other social divisions.

Third, child abuse and elder abuse are to be understood as forms of gendered violence performed by gendered agents, mainly men, sometimes women, on other gendered agents, mainly girls/women, sometimes boys/men, rather than as more abstract processes of abuse.

REFERENCES

Adams R (1996) *The Personal Social Services*, Longman, London.
Ahmad B (1989) Protecting black children from abuse, *Social Work Today*, 8 June.
Aitken L and Griffin G (1996) *Gender Issues in Elder Abuse*, Sage, London.
Ambache J (1997) Vulnerability and public responses, in Decalmer P and Glendenning F (eds) *The Mistreatment of Elderly People* (2nd edn), Sage, London.
Baker A A (1975) Granny Battering, *Modern Geriatrics*, **5**, 8: 20–24.
Bergström-Walan M-B (1997) Healing early sexual trauma in old age, in Hunt L, Marshall M and Rowlings C (eds) *Past Trauma in Late Life*, Jessica Kingsley, London.
Blythe R (1975) *Akenfield*, Penguin, Harmondsworth.
Bowker L, Arbitell M and McFerron J R (1988) On the relationship of wife beating and child abuse, in Ylló K and Bograd M (eds) *Feminist Perspectives on Wife Abuse*, Sage, Newbury Park, CA.
Butler R N and Lewis M I (1973) *Positive Psychological and Biomedical Approaches*, St Louis, Mosby, cited in Bytheway; *Ageism* (1995): 115.
Bytheway B (1995) *Ageism*, Open University Press, Milton Keynes, Buckingham.

Bytheway B and Johnson J (1990) On defining ageism, *Critical Social Policy*, **27**: 27—39.

Cloke C (1983) *Old Age Abuse in the Domestic Setting*, Age Concern, London.

Department of Health (1995) *Child Protection: Messages from Research*, HMSO, London.

Eastman M (1984) *Old Age Abuse*, Age Concern, Mitcham, Surrey.

Finkelhor D and Pillemer K (1988) Elder abuse: Its relationship to other forms of domestic violence, in Hotaling G T, Finkelhor D, Kirkpatrick J T and Straus M (eds) *Family Abuse and Its Consequences*, Sage, Newbury Park, CA.

Froggatt A (1985) *Adult Children and their Elderly Parents: A Web of Interdependent Roles and Relationships*, Paper at British Society of Gerontology Annual Conference, Mimeo, University of Bradford.

Froggatt A (1990) *Family Work with Elderly People*, Macmillan, London.

Glendenning F (1997) What is elder abuse and neglect? in Decalmer P and Glendenning F (eds) *The Mistreatment of Elderly People* (2nd edn), Sage, London.

Glendenning F and Delcalmer P (1997) Looking to the future, in Decalmer P and Glendenning F (eds) *The Mistreatment of Elderly People* (2nd edn), Sage, London

Grant L (1997) What the eyes don't see, *Guardian G2*, 20 May, 4.

Hearn J (1988) Child abuse: Violences and sexualities towards young people, *Sociology*, **22**, 4: 531–544.

Hearn J (1990) 'Child abuse' and men's violence, in Violence Against Children Study Group, *Taking Child Abuse Seriously*, Unwin Hyman, London.

Hearn J (1992) *Men in the Public Eye*, Routledge, London.

Hearn J (1995) Imaging the aging of men, in Featherstone M and Wernick A (eds) *Images of Aging: Cultural Representations of Later Life*, Routledge, London.

Hearn J (1998a) It's time for men to change, in Wild J (ed.) *Working with Men for Change*, Taylor and Francis, London.

Hearn J (1988b) *The Violences of Men: How Men Talk about and How Agencies Respond to Men's Violence to Known Women*, Sage, London.

Hearn J (1998c) The welfare of men? in Popay J, Hearn J and Edwards J (eds) *Men, Gender Divisions and Welfare*, Routledge, London.

Hearn J (1999) Men, social work and violence, in Christie A (ed.) *Men and Social Work*, Macmillan, London.

Holt M (1993) Elder sexual abuse in Britain: Preliminary findings, *Journal of Elder Abuse and Neglect*, **5**: 63–71.

Holt M (1994) Personal communication, cited in Pringle, K (1995) *Men, Masculinities and Social Welfare*, UCL Press, London.

Homer A C and Gilleard C (1990) Abuse of elderly people by their carers, *British Medical Journal*, **301**: 1359–1362.

Hornick J P, McDonald, L and Robertson, G B (1992) Elder abuse in Canada and the United States: Prevalence, legal and service issues, in Peters R DeV, McMahon R J and Quinsey V L (eds) *Aggression and Violence throughout the Life Span*, Sage, London.

Hugman R (1995) The implications of the term 'Elder Abuse' for problem definition and response in health and social welfare, *Journal of Social Policy*, **24**, 4, 493–507.

Hyder K (1996) Abuse and neglect terrorise the elderly, *Observer*, 3 November, 18.

Kalish R A (1979) The new ageism and the failure models: A polemic, *The Gerontologist*, **19**, 4, 398–402.

Kosberg J L (1988) Preventing elder abuse: Identification of high risk factors prior to placement decisions, *The Gerontologist*, **28**, 1: 43–50.

McCreadie C (1991) *Elder Abuse: an Exploratory Study*, Institute of Gerontology, London.

Macdonald B and Rich C (1983) *Look Me in the Eye: Old Women, Ageing and Ageism*, Women's Press, London.

Manthorpe J (1997) Developing social work practice in protection and assistance, in Decalmer P and Glendenning F (eds) *The Mistreatment of Elderly People* (2nd edn), Sage, London.

Miller R B and Dodder R A (1989) The abused–abuser dyad: Elder abuse in the State of Florida, in Filinson R and Ingman S R (eds) *Elder Abuse: Practice and Policy*, Human Sciences Press, New York.

Mullender A and Morley R (eds) (1994) *Children Living with Domestic Violence: Putting Men's Violence of Women on the Child Care Agenda*, Whiting and Birch, London.

Office of Population and Census Surveys (OPCS) (1985) *General Household Survey: Informal Carers*, Series THS No. 15, HMSO, London.

Ogg J and Munn-Giddings C (1993) Researching elder abuse, *Ageing and Society*, **13**: 389–413.

Parkin W and Hearn J (1989) Child abuse, social theory and everyday state practices, in Hudson J and Galaway B (eds) *The State as Parent. International Research Perspectives on Interventions with Young Persons* Kluwer, Dordrecht.

Parton C (1990) Women, gender oppression and child abuse, in Violence Against Children Study Group, *Taking Child Abuse Seriously*, Unwin Hyman, London.

Parton N (1985) *The Politics of Child Abuse*, Macmillan, London.

Penhale B (1993) The abuse of elderly people: Considerations for practice, *British Journal of Social Work*, **23**, 2: 95–112.

Phillipson C, Biggs S and Kingston P (1995) *Elder Abuse in Perspective*, Open University Press, Milton Keynes, Buckingham.

Pringle K (1995) *Men, Masculinities and Social Welfare*, UCL Press, London.

Pritchard J (1992) *The Abuse of Elderly People: A Handbook for Professionals*, Jessica Kingsley, London.

Pritchard, J (1996) *Working with Elder Abuse*, Jessica Kingsley, London.

Rathbone-McCuan E (1980) Elderly victims of family violence and neglect, *Social Casework*, May, 296–304.

Scott S (1997) The experiences of the survivors of ritual abuse, unpublished PhD thesis, University of Manchester.

SSI: Department of Health Social Services Inspectorate (1992) *Confronting Elder Abuse: an SSI London Region Survey*, HMSO, London.

SSI: Department of Health Social Services Inspectorate (1993) *No Longer Afraid: the Safeguard of Elderly People in Domestic Settings: Practice Guidelines*, HMSO, London.

SSI: Department of Health Social Services Inspectorate (1994a) *Abuse of Older People in Domestic Settings: a Report of two SSI Seminars*, HMSO, London.

SSI: Department of Health Social Services Inspectorate (1994b) *Putting People First*, the Third Annual Report of the Chief Inspector 1993/94, HMSO, London.

Stevenson O (1996) *Elder Protection in the Community: What Can We Learn from*

Child Protection?, Department of Health Social Services Inspectorate, London.

Thone R R (1992) *Women and Aging: Celebrating Ourselves*, Haworth Press, New York.

Whittaker T (1996) Violence, gender and elder abuse, in Fawcett B, Featherstone B, Hearn J and Toft C (eds) *Violence and Gender Relations: Theories and Interventions*, Sage, London.

Waters M (1989) Patriarchy and viriarchy, *Sociology*, **23**, 2, 193–211.

Wolf R S (1994) Responding to elder abuse in the USA, in Kingston P (ed.) *Proceedings of the First International Symposium on Elder Abuse*, Action on Elder Abuse, London.

Wolf R S and Pillemer K A (1989) *Helping Elderly Victims: The Reality of Elder Abuse*, Columbia University Press, New York.

III

ISSUES OF MULTIDISCIPLINARY AND INTER-AGENCY WORKING

7

DECISION-MAKING IN CASE CONFERENCES— MEETING WHOSE NEEDS?

Nancy Kelly and Judith Milner

INTRODUCTION

Child protection decisions are fundamentally concerned with the assessment of risk. A series of published inquiry reports into the deaths of children already known to child protection practitioners led to the establishment of government guidelines which regarded risk assessment in child protection practice as a discrete activity (Department of Health, 1988; Home Office, DOH, DES, Welsh Office, 1991). Checklists to do with 'dangerousness' were devised as a mechanism for facilitating effective decision-making and monitoring. The forum in which risk was to be assessed was the case conference; inter-agency exchange of information being viewed as central to improved decision quality (Lewis, Shemmings and Thoburn, 1992).

Despite this intention to improve the assessment of risk via good information flow, there remain approximately 120 notifications of child deaths or serious injury each year to the Department of Health (DOH, 1994). Additionally, data exist suggesting that there is a high level of non-fatal reabuse of children known to child protection agencies, estimates varying from 25–60% (Herrenkohl, Herrenkohl, Egolf and Seech 1979; Cleaver and Freeman, 1995; Farmer and Owen, 1995; Thoburn, Lewis and Shemmings, 1995). There exists, therefore, detailed documentation on risk assessment processes resulting in poor outcomes for children.

However, existing analyses (DOH, 1991; Hallett and Birchall, 1992; Reder, Duncan and Gray, 1993; James, 1994) have not been located at the level of conceptual analysis associated with decision-making

Children, Child Abuse and Child Protection. Placing Children Centrally, by The Violence Against Children Study Group.
© 1999 John Wiley & Sons Ltd.

research in real life contexts. This chapter explores established psychological explanations for risk-taking behaviour at individual and group level and demonstrates how a conceptual framework can be developed to understand the limits of the effectiveness of case conferences in improving decision quality.

THEORETICAL FRAMEWORK

The central role of the case conference in child protection decision-making demands that any theoretical perspective must have the potential to describe and explain not only group effects on an individual's performance in groups but also the individual's effect on group performances. The psychological concepts of 'framing' and 'groupthink' have been used in a wide variety of risk assessment contexts and therefore have considerable appeal as potential conceptualisations in child protection.

INDIVIDUAL DECISION-MAKING

How an individual 'frames' a problem, or is led to frame a problem, in the first place, may influence the direction of their decision. For Tversky and Kahneman (1981) a decision frame is concerned with the decision-maker's perception of the acts, outcomes and contingencies associated with a particular choice. Tversky and Kahneman suggest that people tend to avoid risks when the problem or outcomes are stated or perceived in terms of gains but tend to take greater risks if the same problem is stated or perceived in terms of losses. Early work involving decisions about financial speculation meant that the actual losses and gains involved were readily quantifiable yet in child protection practice the terms losses and gains have the potential for confusing rather than clarifying the situation. It is likely that, in any complex family situation, numerous and competing losses and gains can be identified by a decision-maker, and the long-term effects of child abuse cannot be easily quantified.

Nevertheless the distinction between two diametrically opposed ways of framing a decision context, one of losses or gains, may be of prime importance in understanding decision-making. In the context of risk assessment and management of potentially dangerous offenders in probation practice, Kemshall (1996) identifies how the same decision problem can be perceived by individual probation officers under two different frames; implicitly, one of losses and one of gains. In the losses frame, and more traditional social work frame, the probation officer perceives low risk of physical harm to others, is attempting to preserve a working relationship with the offender within which options of trust and fairness are crucial, and is concentrating on a rehabilitative function as the main focus for their work. This she refers to as 'client primacy'. The focus of probation officers' intentions is around avoiding losses for the offender, notably liberty. Probation officers, with a frame in terms of gains, place potential victims and harm to the public at the centre of their intentions, having an emerging notion of community safety as their context for risk assessment and management. The offender is still considered within this decision frame, yet the focus is on how a gain of public safety can be best achieved. The practical implication of holding either one frame or the other is likely to be reflected in very different assessments of risk and associated management plans for dealing with offenders. These two frames are integrated into how the probation officer sees herself or himself in their role and within the organisation. In child protection practice it is likely that the policy frame, that is the no order principle and partnership in the Children Act 1989, pushes child protection practitioners into adopting the losses frame. The Children Act itself is framed entirely in terms of avoiding losses, there being no notion of what constitutes significant well-being for a child, that is there is no explicit gains perspective, and 'drift' is built into child protection work.

GROUP DECISION-MAKING

Conventional wisdom about effective decision-making groups emphasises the desirability of group members working well together through an understanding of each other's roles, a commitment to a shared objective and an ability to reach a consensus which can be defended outside the group. Janis (1982) analysed American government policy groups with these qualities that were nevertheless responsible for spectacular fiascos and suggested that these groups developed a mind set he terms 'groupthink', which leads to the defective decision-making. Janis (1982) lists the 'symptoms' of the phenomenon as: shared rationalisations to support the first adequate alternative suggested by an influential group member; a lack of disagreement; a belief in unanimity and cohesiveness, direct pressure on dissenters and a high level of confidence in the group's decision. Several researchers in child protection practice have noted these 'symptoms' (DOH, 1990, Reder, Duncan and Gray, 1993). Perhaps the most notorious example of groupthink can be found in the Beckford Report (London Borough of Brent, 1985), where a cohesive group of social workers discounted information presented to the first case conference, by holding a subsequent meeting two weeks later at which they decided not to invite those professionals with whose views they did not agree.

Janis seems to suggest that once the 'symptoms' of groupthink have been identified, 'correctives' such as appointing a 'devil's advocate' or independent chairs of meeting will provide a remedy (Janis and Mann, 1977). These measures have been promoted in government guidelines on chairing case conferences and are recommended in a major child protection decision-making training pack (Lewis, Shemmings and Thoburn, 1992). Trainers have not, however, found it easy to apply these correctives (Lawson, Masson and Milner, 1995), suggesting that groupthink alone cannot supply an adequate framework for analysis. Paradoxically, if the group is subject to the symptoms of groupthink, then the group may effectively counteract any attempt at correctives.

These two strands of psychological theorising concern themselves predominantly with either group or individual effects on decision-making. Whyte (1989, 1991) proposes a model that attempts to integrate these ideas. His model outlines a process whereby problems that are initially framed as choices between unattractive options by an individual, which then get taken up by a group, can lead to high risk decision-making.

AN INTEGRATED MODEL OF DECISION-MAKING

Drawing upon Whyte's model, the integrated process can be simply described as follows. An individual frames a choice as one between unattractive options, both of which involve losses, and in order to avoid a certain loss chooses an alternative course of action that has the potential for either no loss or greater loss. Hence an individual has embarked upon a course of action that involves risk. The individual then presents information to a group and that group polarises around the individual's loss avoidance preferences. By the nature of group polarisation this means that the group embarks upon a riskier course of action than the individual would have done had s/he been working in isolation. As subsequent group meetings occur, the group will display a commitment to its initial decisions and course of action and will not re-evaluate the whole situation in terms of risk, but rather will focus on assessing the success of actions in relation to the original objectives. As time elapses the group becomes subject to the symptoms groupthink and therefore does not consider that its decisions and actions might be failing, nor will it consider abandoning its original plans. In fact the group will continue to commit further resources to the actions to try to ensure its success. This whole process means that the group is unwilling to accept that previous plans may be failing and shows a marked reluctance to accept that resources already committed may have been wasted. Ultimately the group exacerbates the risk-taking behaviour of an individual and group processes almost inevitably mean that initial decisions and courses of action are not reassessed. The group is in a position of high risk decision-making with the potential for a decision fiasco present. For a more detailed explanation of this model see Whyte (1989).

This then suggests that conventional wisdom about case conference efficacy in risk management may be inappropriate—two heads not necessarily being better than one (Whyte, 1991) and, as such, provides potentially a useful integrated underpinning for an analysis of child protection decision-making.

In order to test whether the psychological explanations outlined above do have the potential to explain child protection decision-making, research by the authors has been undertaken into well known notoriously bad decisions and into decisions where the social workers considered that the decisional quality was good.

Using an integrated psychological conceptual model as a framework for analysing decision-making in child protection practice holds the potential for a major difficulty: that being that the Children Act contains two important principles, the welfare of the child and the desirability of children remaining with their families. This conflation of potentially contradictory principles suggests that in practice it is likely to be extremely difficult for any practitioner to disentangle or disaggregate the losses and gains for family members involved in any single course of action.

THE RESEARCH

The research outlined here uses techniques of documentary analysis (Hakim, 1983, 1987; Forster, 1994), and was conducted in two stages. In the first stage of the research documentary analysis was carried out using the Report into the death of Tyra Henry. This analysis showed remarkable fit with the model, with evidence of all aspects of the influences described earlier on decision-making being present. The model then appeared to have value in illuminating the processes of demonstrably defective decision-making in relation to situations where the outcome for the children was death. (For a fuller discussion, see Kelly and Milner, 1996.)

The second stage of the research was concerned with investigating the utility of the model in relation to what was considered by practitioners to be effective decision-making. A subsequent analysis of 'live' decision processes was therefore designed to overcome the restricted perspective often described in decision-making research whereby the decisions that are analysed are either artificial or retrospective. Additionally the study hoped to use material where cases were ongoing; where group decisions would continue to be made; and where outcomes for children were not disastrous.

This second study analysed the ongoing documents of 'live' child protection cases and details of the five stages of the documentary analysis in relation to the cases are presented below.

Stage One: Access

A childcare agency in a nearby metropolitan authority was approached and a meeting with senior management staff was arranged to discuss the theoretical perspective outlined earlier. At that first meeting, managers demonstrated an understanding of the relevance of groupthink and group polarisation effects to their decision processes but they were considerably less clear about the implications of framing, asking for the concept to be explained in terms of their work experience. This was achieved by using their case examples in a modified version of a gains/losses matrix (Kahneman and Tversky, 1979, see Exhibit 7.1).

POSSIBLE LOSSES	POSSIBLE GAINS
	HOME
	CARE

Exhibit 7.1

This provided the opportunity to separate out the possible gains and losses to children and their families of two separate decisions: either leaving the child at home with the parents or admitting the child to public care.

The managers' verbal feedback suggested that this matrix enabled them to identify not only the information which they had actively selected previously to inform their decisions but also the information they had ignored. After lengthy discussions with senior management staff and members of the Area Child Protection Committee to establish the ethics of the research, the agency granted access to live case material. Both researchers were police checked before analysis of documents took place. In order to analyse a sequence of successive decisions; to have a sufficiently widespread type of cases to test the generic nature of the model; and to enable the identification of decisions possibly made in the domain of gains, the sample fulfilled the following criteria: that each case was ongoing, covered a minimum of three case conferences (preferably four or five); involved a range of types of abuse; and had outcomes which the professionals considered to be satisfactory.

The agency provided the minutes of case conferences and allied reports in respect of nine ongoing child protection cases from two social work teams. Each satisfied the previously outlined criteria. The principal training officer selected these two teams deliberately as she considered both teams to be adequately staffed with fully qualified, confident staff, well supported by their team leaders. Subsequent to the initial analysis, senior management selected documents from two further ongoing cases in other teams for the purpose of triangulation. One case was rejected at this stage as there had been allegations of widespread abuse within the family over a long period of time, and not all documents relating to the case could be made available. With the material provided for triangulation, the sample consisted of 10 cases with 58 documents presented for analysis.

Stage 2: Checking for Authenticity

Documents were examined under conditions of strict security at the agency's training centre. This onsite research meant that the researchers met regularly with relevant staff to check the genuineness and validity of the documents. This arrangement had the additional benefit of aiding reflexivity as the researchers established a purposeful dialogue with members of staff who commented on and made suggestions as to how the investigative technique could be improved.

Stage 3: Understanding the Documents

The matrix outlined (Exhibit 7.1) was used to analyse each document relating to each stage of the decision-making process, in order to establish whether the decisions had been taken in the domain of losses or gains. During this process, each matrix was tested with the team leader and the training officer, checking that there was a shared understanding of what was meant in the document and how it was displayed on the matrix. For example, a typical document would begin with a summary of the causes of concern:

> (social worker) told the meeting that it had always been [child 1] who had received injuries, mainly to the head, and there appeared to be a lack of protection at home for him.

This would be displayed on the matrix as a loss to the child (physical abuse).
Similarly:

> Mother has bonded with [child 2]. [Mother] has spent large amounts of time with her mother and father. They have given her considerable support and so she has not been the sole carer of [child 2]. While this may have clouded any assessment of her parenting skills it is felt that she would be able to cope with one child.

This would be displayed on the matrix as a gain to the mother (mother–child relationship). Additionally the potential loss to the child of the mother–child relationship would be entered onto the matrix.

A possible matrix relating to one document would be displayed as shown in Exhibit 7.2. This constituted a first attempt to disaggregate gains and losses to different family members although, within the documents, there was no evidence that the welfare of the child was considered separately from the family, despite this being the paramount consideration of these conferences (Inter-agency Child Protection Procedure Handbook Oct. 1994: 82).

Stage 4: Analysing the Data

The reflexive dialogue clarified persistent clusters and themes within documents about which there was a high level of agreement between the researchers and the researched. These corresponded with the themes in the model.

POSSIBLE LOSSES	POSSIBLE GAINS	
Physical injury, C1, C2 Sexual abuse, C1, C2 Nutrition, C2 Speech delay, C1	Parent–child relationship resources, C1, C2	HOME 2PF
Parent–child separation	Safety, C1, C2 Consistency of care, C1, C2	CARE

Exhibit 7.2

- Framing: 27 of 39 decisions in the cases were taken in the domain of losses. In three cases all the decisions were taken in the domain of losses and in one case all the decisions were taken in the domain of gains. In the remaining cases the decision frame fluctuated from case conference to case conference. In seven out of eight cases the initial decision was in the domain of losses.
- Losses to the children (total number of children 18): No attempt was made to categorise the seriousness of these losses but any loss that could be identified from the welfare checklist as outlined in the Children Act 1989 was included in the number; 85 potential and 90 actual losses were identified. The number of actual losses is greater than the number of potential losses because it includes losses that occurred prior to the initial case conference and which triggered that case conference. In six cases, the number of potential losses increased as the case progressed. In three cases, the number of actual losses increased as the case progressed. Although an increase in losses was spread among cases taken in both the domains of losses and gains, a significant increase in actual

losses occurred at a time when the decision-making was framed in the domain of losses. It seems then that the patterns and trends in decision-making with regard to domains of risk or caution may be more important than the actual numbers of losses and gains.

- Commitment of resources and escalation effects: Escalation was calculated each time a new resource item was committed at a case review. In total 141 items of resources were committed to plans. Escalation of commitment to risky behaviour occurred only 18 times. These numbers, in themselves, reflect only the fact that the themes are identifiable and cannot provide evidence or information with regard to patterns that may occur or how a sequence of events might unfold. Seven of the eight cases demonstrated an excellent fit with the model of high risk decision-making. The remaining case (the only one in which decisions were all taken in the domain of gains) would have been useful for purposes of comparison, however the situation was specific as a private fostering arrangement existed which provided immediate protection for the children. Such immediate protection was not available in any of the other cases. While the categories and themes can be explicitly revealed from statements in the documents and the sequence can be illustrated, it is apparent that in these real life ongoing decision-making situations, further elaboration of the identifiable themes is necessary to illustrate the model more convincingly. With regard to framing effects, one very particular sure loss was consistently avoided. In all cases it was the mother–child relationship. Indeed, at some point, every document commented upon the need to maintain the mother–child relationship even when a mother was actually requesting that the children be admitted to public care. This view was supported in discussions with management.

- Escalation effects: These were the easiest to identify in terms of the commitment of resources. Whyte's (1989) predictions about groups' unwillingness to abandon projects were supported by the frequent comments in the documents to do with self-justification. This took the form of comments about the care plan not having had time to work despite evidence of its failure to protect children. Risky behaviour was implicit throughout but proved difficult to quantify. Self-justification seemed to be accompanied by an increasing timespan between reviews, which holds the potential for compounding and accelerating risky behaviour. However, the measurement of this acceleration process presents difficulties.

- Group polarisation and groupthink symptoms: These were apparent as case reviews progressed, with the most notable symptoms being discounting and selecting information. These symptoms were often exacerbated as multi-agency attendance at conferences successively reduced. It seems that groupthink might be best considered as illustrative of high risk decision-making but the fact that it is evidenced so late in the decision sequence does not suggest it to be a practically useful diagnostic tool. Once groupthink can be identified it may be too entrenched for the group to consider reframing.

The categories described above provide substantial support for the existence of an identifiable structure of high risk decision-making and, furthermore, that complex real life decision contexts can usefully be analysed using the model. However, there are real problems concerning aggregated values. While this has implications for framing in general to which we return later, it is worth noting here that the reappearance of the alleged abuser invariably adds to the losses and gains in that the remaining family members will have lost or gained a relationship with one adult. In order to clarify the data a further matrix was developed which allowed the disaggregation of losses and gains for each family member (see Exhibit 7.3). Using this matrix meant that it was possible to see *who* gained and *who* lost at each decision point. The matrix had the added advantage in that it demonstrates how the clusters and themes in the text become translated into the matrix.

POTENTIAL LOSSES	ACTUAL LOSSES	POTENTIAL GAINS	ACTUAL GAINS	OTHER

PARTICIPANT A, B, C, ETC

Exhibit 7.3

Stage 5: Utilising the Data

A pertinent feature of documentary analysis is that the findings have some relevance and validity for the researched (Forster, 1994). As such, the results outlined above were presented to the agency's senior managers who replicated the method with two further cases, one involving sexual abuse and one a complicated case involving physical abuse and neglect. Their analysis confirmed the efficacy of the method and the findings of the main study. While it had been hoped to focus the final discussion on framing effects, the managers showed most interest in the acceleration of risky behaviour and resource commitment noted earlier. They identified a preoccupation with housing issues as a persistent theme in their own work. They viewed this as a good indicator that the case conference was running out of options and was experiencing 'stuckness'. That preoccupation with housing issues occurs earlier than symptoms of groupthink occur might suggest that the identification of reduced options in any real life decision context might be the most useful point at which project abandonment could be seriously considered and therefore the most useful indicator that the decision context might be reframed. It was interesting to note here that the team of senior managers could not recall a single instance where they, as chairs of case conferences, had been involved in reversing an initial course of action, yet the senior operations manager, who would be working in isolation and monitoring case conference decisions, had overturned three decisions over the past year, insisting that the children concerned be taken into public care. The case conference had clearly not effectively monitored risks to children, yet an individual overseeing cases was able to identify situations of potential high risk.

SUMMARY

This research has supplied evidence which provides support for the view that an integrated model of psychological explanations of decision-making can be usefully applied to explain an unfolding sequence of decision processes in a complex real life decision-making context. There was evidence that the case conference was subject to the influence of groupthink late in the decision proceedings, while individuals were subject to the framing effect in the domain of losses in the very early stages of decision-making. In this real decision context it is impossible to investigate fully the effectiveness of the group, in comparison with individual influences, since only the group can make the formal decision. However, it is clear from this analysis that the group is not able to counteract risky decision-making; to act as a safe-guard against individual risk-taking; or to institute reframing except when the group is subject to influences outside its control, that is the abuser ceasing to have access to the children or on the rare occasions when the senior operations manager, acting as an individual, decides to overrule the case conference decision.

As the research progressed, it became clear that the crucial determinant of the outcome, in terms of actual losses to the children, was the initial decision frame determined by the key case holder, who presented the case to the conference. Once the choices had been positioned in the direction of risk, the group then polarised around that and there was evidence of escalation of both resource commitment and risky behaviour. This was accompanied by a marked reduction in the number of perceived options available. Self-justification (by the individual case holder and the group) was employed to avoid project abandonment and the possibility of reforming. The case reviews did not then perform the function of re-evaluating risk.

An interesting finding was that the documents contained quite specific comments about children's welfare when the decision was taken in the domain of gains. When the decision was framed in the domain of losses, potential and actual losses were ignored, subsumed or obfuscated. This research found that aggregation was a means by which one family member's potential losses or gains (children's) could be subsumed to other family member's losses and gains (usually to the male abusers). This finding further illustrates the influence of the decision frame on the tendency to aggregate values. The implication of this is that decisions taken in the domain of losses are bound by severe constraints in every element of the process.

The research suggests that decision-making in child protection case conferences can be predicted from the initial decision frame that the case conference adopts. If the initial frame is in the domain of losses, then almost inevitably the case conference will embark irretrievably upon a sequence of decisions and course of action that is characterised by a successive narrowing of options, escalation of commitment and resources and self-justification culminating in the display of symptoms of groupthink. The research suggests that correctives applied once these symptoms are apparent will be ineffective. This is gloomy news for child protection practitioners already aware of the difficulties of protecting children within the context of preserving the mother–child relationship.

However, our most recent research which compares risk assessment and management in probation practice, from both a losses and a gains perspective, shows that holding a community safety view has the potential to increase the efficacy of the case conference. Where the case is framed in terms of public safety gains at conference level, the group makes detailed management plans with contingency arrangements that are proving beneficial to the offender, the family and the community. Ultimately what may be important for the case conference is a raised awareness of how the decision process is driven by its decision frame and group effects, and a subsequent awareness of how it might act to reframe a problem if its actions are not having sufficient desirable outcomes for the children. In this way the case conference can fulfil its original intention to monitor judgements and decisions and to better protect children.

REFERENCES

Cleaver H and Freeman P (1995) *Parental Perspectives in Cases of Suspected Child Abuse*, HMSO, London.

Department of Health (1988) *Protecting Children: a Guide for Social Workers Undertaking a Comprehensive Assessment*, HMSO, London.

Department of Health (1990) *The Care of Children: Principles and Practice in Regulations and Guidance*, HMSO, London.

Department of Health (1991) *Child Abuse: A Study of Inquiry Reports 1980–1989*, HMSO, London.

Department of Health (1994) *Study of Working Together 'Part 8' Reports*, ACPC Series, Report No. 1, HMSO, London.

Farmer E and Owen M (1995) *Child Protection Practice: Private Risks and Public Remedies—Decision Making, Intervention and Outcome in Child Protection Work*, HMSO, London.

Forster N (1994) The analysis of company documentation, in Cassell C and Symon G (eds) *Qualitative Methods in Organisational Research*, Sage, London.

Hakim C (1983) Research based on administrative records, *Sociological Review*, **31**, 3: 489–519.

Hakim C (1987) *Research Design*. Allen and Unwin, London.

Hallett C and Birchall E (1992) *Coordination and Child Protection: A Review of the Literature*, HMSO, London.

Herrenkohl R C, Herrenkohl E C, Egolf B and Seech M (1979) The repetition of child abuse: How frequently does it occur? *Child Abuse and Neglect*, **3**, 1: 67–72.

Home Office, Department of Health, Department of Education and Science, Welsh Office (1991) *Working Together under the Children Act 1989: a Guide to the Arrangements for Inter-agency Cooperation for the Protection of Children from Abuse*, HMSO, London.

Janis I L (1982) *Groupthink: Pshychological Studies of Policy Decisions and Fiascos*, Houghton Mifflin, Boston.

Janis I L and Mann L (1977) *Decision Making*, Free Press, New York.

Kahneman D and Tversky A (1979) Prospect theory: an analysis of decision under risk, *Econometrician*, **47**: 263–91.

Kelly N and Milner J (1996) Child protection decision making, *Child Abuse Review*, **5**: 91–102.

Kemshall H (1996) Risk assessment: Fuzzy thinking or decisions in action? *Probation Journal*, April, 2–7.

Lawson B, Masson H and Milner J (1995) There but for the Grace . . . ? Developing training for multidisciplinary managers following a local child death inquiry, *Child Abuse Review*, **4**: 340–350.

Lewis A, Shemmings D and Thoburn J (1992) *Participation in Practice—Involving Families in Child Protection: A Training Pack*, Social Work Development Unit, University of East Anglia, Norwich.

London Borough of Brent (1985) *A Child in Trust: the Report of the Panel of Inquiry into the Circumstances Surrounding the Death of Jasmine Beckford*, HMSO, London.

Reder P, Duncan S and Gray M (1993) *Beyond Blame: Child Abuse Tragedies Revisited*, Routledge, London.

Thoburn J, Lewis A and Shemmings D (1995) *Paternalism or Partnership? Family Involvement in the Child Protection Process*, HMSO, London.

Tversky A and Kahneman D (1981) The framing of decisions and the psychology of choice, *Science*, **211**: 453–458.

Whyte G (1989) Groupthink reconsidered, *Academy of Management Review*, **14**, 1: 40–56.

Whyte G (1991) Decision failures, why they occur and how to prevent them, *Academy of Management Review*, **5**, 3: 23–31.

8

SCHOOLS AND CHILD PROTECTION

Eric Blyth and Helen Cooper

INTRODUCTION

Conventional approaches to the role of teachers and the school system in child protection have tended to focus on a relatively narrow, albeit expanding, range of activities (e.g. Sage, 1993; DFEE, 1995b). This chapter extends analysis of this role to explore the contribution of schools as potential sites for abuse (between peers and between students and adults) and argues that this needs to be understood to gain a more complete understanding of the role of schools in child protection.

SCHOOLS, THE WELFARE NETWORK AND CHILD PROTECTION

The potential role of schools and school staff within the welfare network was recognised in the nineteenth century. Teachers were seen as having duties of care towards children in their charge over and above the mere imparting of academic knowledge and schools became a legitimate avenue for the provision of welfare. The 'fact' of compulsory education provided unrivalled access to the child population and unique opportunities for identifying and monitoring children experiencing disturbance and distress, including victims of abuse, while a child's absence could also indicate difficulties needing some form of intervention. (For a more detailed discussion of the contemporary role of schools in supporting 'vulnerable' children and families see Blyth and Milner, 1997, and Gilligan, 1998.)

Elucidation of the role of teachers in child protection has progressed beyond simplistic 'see and tell' prescriptions of recognising the 'signs'

Children, Child Abuse and Child Protection. Placing Children Centrally, by The Violence Against Children Study Group.
© 1999 John Wiley & Sons Ltd.

and referring on, to include: dealing with suspicions, disclosures or discovery; referral to a child protection agency and participating in the inter-agency response; involving parents; giving evidence, and prevention and promoting personal safety in the curriculum.

CONTRIBUTING TO AN INTER-AGENCY CHILD PROTECTION STRATEGY

A child protection issue can involve a member of the school staff in a lengthy process, as described by Blyth and Milner (1997). The first stage of this would be the disclosure or discovery of abuse, which would not necessarily be to, or by, a class teacher. Non-teaching classroom assistants, for example, are more likely to deal with children on a one-to-one basis or in small groups. Disclosure or discovery can occur at any time, making it difficult for a member of staff to prepare themselves to accept it and react in the most appropriate manner towards the child as well as remembering to follow specified child protection procedures.

Sufficiently comprehensive notes should be taken at the time, preferably contemporaneously, otherwise as soon as possible afterwards. It is important for this account to be as factual as possible, the DFEE advising that clear distinctions be made between 'fact, observation, allegation and opinion' (DFEE, 1995b: 8). It may well be necessary to compile a more formal report at a later stage. Therefore, this would be an appropriate time to look at the child's personal file. The advice from the DFEE is that the report should focus on the child's educational and behavioural progress and their relationships with peers and other family members. Blyth and Milner (1997) also suggest that reports could usefully contain information about any health concerns, family contact with the school and details of siblings, together with any views from colleagues.

Concern should be reported to the designated teacher for child protection who should gather as much further information as possible from other colleagues. School staff are sometimes wary of involving too many people for reasons of confidentiality, but such concerns also need to recognise the importance of building as comprehensive a picture as possible.

Referral to social services is usually made by telephone by the designated teacher. Many local authorities have specialist child protection teams to whom the first call should be made. They would advise on the action to be taken, based on the current referral and taking account of any other information they might have. In practice there could be difficulties at this stage, for example social services considering that insufficient information is being provided, and the school complaining about the inaccessibility of key social services staff.

Inter-agency co-operation is vital in planning how to take forward the abuse complaint, although Kelly and Milner in Chapter 7 of this volume question whether group decisions are necessarily better than individual ones. The designated teacher who regularly attends case conferences can become part of a group of 'professional acquaintances' who may collude, although it is more likely that a teacher for whom case conference attendance is an infrequent event would be outside any such group and their views might not find easy acceptance. Teachers may find that they are pressurised into agreeing with a group decision they are not happy with but do not have the confidence to challenge, as social workers are likely to be perceived as the 'experts' in child protection (Blyth and Milner, 1997). Teachers should feel confident about their contributions to the inter-agency strategy from their unique position of day-to-day contact with the child and also having a comparative knowledge of non-abused children. Of all 'front-line' professionals, teachers are the ones most likely to have the most detailed first-hand knowledge of individual children. They should, therefore, be able to ensure that core group meetings are held at times convenient to facilitate their contribution.

In addition, schools are well placed to inform parents, although many teachers are apprehensive about the outcome of a child protection investigation and fear that a good relationship with parents would be damaged. It is, therefore, more likely that the investigating social worker will contact the parents.

School staff need to be adequately trained for their child protection role. Local training provision means that designated teachers will usually have quite a comprehensive training covering all aspects of their role, although the needs of other staff within the school may not be met. Many schools request training for all staff—this seems most effective when ancillary staff can be included—but child protection training may not be a high priority in the light of all the other training needs to keep up to date with curriculum issues and other work. A one-hour slot at the end of the school day can do no more than start to raise awareness and give some basic information.

For young people experiencing adversity school frequently provides a major source of stability and support (e.g. Rutter, 1991). More specifically Romans, Martin, Anderson *et al.* (1995) note the value of schools in providing protection to young female survivors of sexual abuse from the long-term effects of abuse and traumatic family relationships.

THE HAPPIEST DAYS OF YOUR LIFE? FEAR, OPPRESSION AND SCHOOLING

The preceding summary provides an image of caring and concerned staff doing their best for vulnerable children. However, students' experiences of school are not necessarily positive ones. First, there is a considerable weight of evidence identifying the limited implementation of inter-agency co-operation and 'partnership' in child care (e.g. Audit Commission and HMI, 1992; Audit Commission, 1994; OFSTED, 1995, 1996; SSI and OFSTED, 1995; National Commission of Inquiry into the Prevention of Child Abuse, 1996; SSI, 1996), due largely to a combination of factors: the introduction of competition and market forces to public services; increasing pressures on budgets of local government agencies; and challenges to the very existence of some local government services.

Second, particular pressures on schools emanating from education reforms of the late 1980s and early 1990s mean that some of the most vulnerable children are those with whom schools are *least* likely to want to be bothered and whom they may seek to exclude, either formally or informally (Blyth and Milner, 1994).

Third, schools may institutionalise oppression and reinforce disadvantage, residential schools in particular displaying many of the characteristics of a 'total institution' (Goffman, 1961) which ensure the powerlessness and dependence of residents and encourage the circumstances under which children may be abused by staff (e.g. Westcott and Clément, 1992).

Measures which might be seen as protecting the interests of schoolchildren, such as the European Convention on Human Rights and the United Nations Convention on the Rights of the Child, have in fact had limited impact. While children have been undoubted beneficiaries of the European Convention (action taken under its provisions being instrumental in securing the abolition of corporal punishment in UK state schools), it formally recognises parental rights in respect of their children's education and not the rights of children *per se*, a trend emphasised in UK education legislation, and which affords little recognition of the possibility—and implications—of conflict between the rights of parents and those of their children.

While the UN Convention is more specifically focused on the *rights of children*, it is not enforceable in the same way as the European Convention, education provision in the UK resting uneasily with key provisions of the Convention. Despite having ratified the Convention the government did not consider the welfare of the child (Article 3) should explicitly underpin the Education Act 1993 (Lansdown, 1996). Consequently, decisions made concerning school choice and admissions, exclusion and special educational needs procedures are not required to have regard to the welfare of the child. Neither is there any legal entitlement for children to participate in these education decisions (Article 12) or to make their views about them known (Article 15). A clear example of the latter received national publicity in July 1997 when 15-year-old Sarah Briggs was permanently excluded from her Mansfield grammar school (although subsequently she was reinstated by school governors and the headteacher resigned) after refusing to apologise for complaining to her local newspaper about staff lateness and absenteeism and the school's failure to act on OFSTED criticisms of the school (Ward, 1997). As Lansdown (1996) poignantly notes, the ways in which children are often treated by adults in school provide poor examples of the much-vaunted values of 'citizenship' (responsibility, respect for others, democracy and human rights) and which the formal curriculum might ostensibly be trying to foster.

Although children themselves generally recognise the intrinsic value of education (O'Keeffe, 1994; Hughes and Lloyd, 1996) school nevertheless provides a major source of worry for many children, in particular the source of fears—and the frequent reality—of being bullied or picked on by peers and getting into trouble with teachers (Ghate and Daniels, 1997).

Bullying and Intimidation by Peers

Fear of being bullied and actually being bullied are not new phenomena either in wider society or in a school community. In a national survey 80% of young people considered bullying to be a problem (Roberts and Sachdev, 1996), and increasing awareness of bullying has sometimes made it seem as if there has been a huge increase in the occurrence of incidents (Olweus, 1978, 1993). Estimates of the prevalence of bullying range considerably. Olweus (1978), for example, citing a rate of 15%, while the DFE (1994) estimates a prevalence of 20%. (See also Helen Masson, Chapter 3 in this volume, discussing the particular issue of children and young people as perpetrators of sexual violence.)

Bullying has been used as meaning almost any distressing experience for children in school, from racist or sexist abuse to physical or sexual assault. It is hard to define without being overly simplistic or excessively detailed in providing lists of the types of behaviour involved. Children who are bullied often have little motivation to attend school and, when there, find it hard to concentrate and therefore may well be operating at considerably less than their full potential. In extreme circumstances bullying could represent 'significant harm' as defined by the Children Act 1989 where it may be appropriate to activate child protection procedures (DFEE, 1995b, para 34, p. 1).

Bullying is *almost* certainly a misuse of power and persistent in its nature. The amount of hurt to the victim is also a useful measure. Bullying comes in many forms—from a physical attack to subtle intimidation, the only manifestation of which may be either verbal or non-verbal. Where it is easy to spot a fight in the playground, it is much more difficult for a teacher to interpret the significance of non-verbal cues. The practice experience of one of the authors with children who have been bullied confirms Besag's (1989) conclusions that for many children intimidation and verbal bullying are harder to bear than physical assault.

Much serious bullying takes place outside the classroom, approximately 70% of in-school bullying taking place in the playground (DFE, 1994), the playground being twice as likely a site than the journey to and from school (Whitney and Smith, 1993). The reasons for this seem obvious. In a break from lessons children are keen to run about and 'let off steam' in a variety of ways. Supervision is minimal because of the low ratio of playground supervisors to students. This group of staff has limited opportunities for training and may have a low status in the eyes of other school staff, students and parents. Many playgrounds are neither safe nor suitable, being too large or too small and often with very little appropriate play equipment.

Abuse by Teachers

Although the particular characteristics of residential schools may encourage student abuse (Westcott and Clément, 1992), even a 'popular' primary school can provide an environment in which a determined abuser can subject children to systematic abuse over an extensive period. A report published by Cornwall County Council (1987) graphically demonstrates how a 'respected' primary headteacher was able to neutralise children's and staff resistance through the imposition of an oppressive management style. Abusers are known to seek employment, including teaching and other caring positions, which gives them access to vulnerable children and they either choose roles which are relatively unstructured and unsupervised, or situations where they are able to control and subjugate their working environment (e.g. Kirkwood, 1993; Cornwall County Council, 1994; Elson, 1996).

TEACHERS AS 'VICTIMS'

Paradoxically there is an emerging perception amongst teachers of themselves as potential and actual 'victims', arising in part from the expansion of their role in child protection, as well as their exposure to abuse and false allegations of abuse by students. Particular problems associated with their child protection role include: risks of intimidation and physical violence from parents following report to a child protection agency; damaging relations with the student and/or the student's family, and accusations of lying (Association of Teachers and Lecturers, 1995). Recent concerns expressed by teachers' professional associations indicate that the scope for this is now considered to extend to the courtroom with claims of teachers being 'victimised' by 'aggressive' defence lawyers (Rafferty, 1998).

The beleaguered position in which teachers perceive themselves to be is illustrated by the (unsubstantiated) assertion that: 'it has been proved that many children accuse teachers of abuse in an attempt to get help' (Association of Teachers and Lecturers, 1995: 3).

The concept of teachers as 'victims' is prompted by a view (contrary evidence notwithstanding) that the children's rights movement has 'gone too far'. The Children Act 1989 is seen as having:

- limited the range of sanctions available to teachers to discipline 'unruly' students (O'Leary, 1995), leading to their resorting to threats of strike action to prevent the return to school of violent or abusive students following a fixed term exclusion or reinstatement following a permanent exclusion
- increased opportunities for students 'to defy and undermine teachers who might support them' (Nash, 1996), and
- increased the vulnerability of teachers to allegations of abuse through its broad definitions of abuse (Association of Teachers and Lecturers, 1995), whilst providing teachers with no powers to protect themselves from malicious accusations (Sage, 1993: 29).

Teachers have depicted both an extensive range of abusive student behaviours to which they are subject—such as: verbal abuse; actual and threatened physical and sexual assault, harassment and damage to property, and false allegations of abuse (Association of Teachers and Lecturers, 1995; Malik, 1996)—and an increase in their prevalence (Sage, 1993; Association of Teachers and Lecturers, 1995; NASUWT, 1995).

A major problem in this kind of debate is the lack of unambiguous empirical evidence and it is difficult to find non-partisan corroboration.

Student exclusion for violent behaviour remains at a relatively low level and violence is not the principal cause for exclusion (DFE, 1993; OFSTED, 1996). However, the factors that impinge on official data are highlighted by arguments that teachers are more likely to report incidents of disruption and violence when they are frustrated and morale is low (Harris, Pearce and Johnstone, 1992), that pressures on schools to promote a positive image *constrain* the reporting of violence (Brook, 1993), and that stress and teacher demoralisation may increase the prevalence of abuse (Irvine, 1997). An attempt by the DFEE to conduct a survey of allegations of abuse made against teachers (DFEE, 1995a) was abandoned because of difficulties of obtaining comparable data from LEAs (DFEE, personal communication). Although a relatively small proportion of allegations against teachers result in successful prosecution (Preston, 1993, 1994; Cornwall County Council, 1994; DFEE, 1995b; NASUWT, 1995), dissatisfaction with school and agency investigation and disciplinary proceedings has been expressed by various interest groups (see, for example, *Independent on Sunday*, 1994; Association of Teachers and Lecturers, 1995; NASUWT, 1995), while difficulties of using children's evidence to mount a prosecution and secure a conviction have been noted (NCH: Action for Children, 1994).

In response to these 'threats' male teachers appear increasingly reluctant to work in primary schools (Charter, 1996) and professional associations have advised members to reduce all forms of avoidable physical contact with students, to refrain from administering medication and to ensure they do not find themselves alone with students (e.g. Sage, 1993; NASUWT, 1995), precautions that might well restrict teachers' opportunities to identify whether children are being abused by others and appropriately to deal with abuse.

MAKING SCHOOLS SAFER

Prescriptions for making schools safer require a clear vision of what needs to be achieved. They also need to recognise that schools do not operate in a vacuum and that there are tensions militating against progress—in particular the defensiveness displayed by overwhelmed teachers—which need to be moderated.

Policies on behaviour and anti-bullying, which have the potential to ensure that schools provide a welcoming environment conducive to teaching and learning (DFE, 1994), do not necessarily impact on the experienced reality of members of the school community, Kidscape claiming that only a third of the country's schools implement their anti-bullying policies, while 'the rest hide behind them' (Irvine, 1997). *Having* a policy is not the same as *implementing* it.

We consider that the concept of *inclusion* offers a way forward. Originally developed as a response to the *exclusion* of disabled children from mainstream education, *inclusion* is described as:

> a philosophy which views diversity of strengths, abilities and needs as natural and desirable, bringing to any community the opportunity to respond in ways which lead to learning and growth for the whole school community and giving each and every member a valued role. Inclusion requires striving for the optimal growth of all pupils in the most enabling environment by recognising individual strengths and needs. (The Council for Disabled Children, 1994, cited in Russell, 1995: 20)

School Behaviour and Anti-bullying Policies

Effective *whole* school behaviour and anti-bullying policies, owned by *all* members of the school community and not merely by a small number of senior managers, or those with designated welfare responsibilities, incorporate the philosophy of inclusive education, endorse the spirit of individual self-respect, respect for others, value individual differences and achieve an appropriate balance between individual rights and responsibilities towards others. Samson and Hart (1995), describing the development of school behaviour policies in Tameside, highlight the importance of the *process* by which such policies are developed, introduced and implemented in ensuring ownership by the entire school community. The process they describe consists of information gathering; feedback and identification of priorities; policy formulation and implementation, and evaluation. The involvement of different groups within the school is encouraged by: reports; parents' newsletters; the school prospectus; parents', staff, school council and governors' meetings; in-service training; assemblies and tutorial time. Finally, once a policy is in place and is implemented, it needs to be subject to regular review and evaluation to ensure that it is being applied consistently and fairly and that it is meeting its intended objectives.

Other emerging developments include peer counselling and mentoring, although the potential for such measures themselves to facilitate the abuse of power needs to be acknowledged. Older students may support and act as mentors to younger or 'vulnerable' students, for example those with 'special educational needs' and other disabilities, those who may be prone to bullying and those transferring from another school, especially at the primary/ secondary interface where fears about life in a larger school may accompany the transition from being among the oldest (and usually biggest) children in the school to becoming the youngest (and smallest).

Considering playground issues can also be a whole school activity. Children can be involved in looking at zoning the playground, learning new games and planting trees, shrubs and flowers, activities encouraging children to maintain a pleasanter environment by involving them in creating and shaping it.

Alongside improving the environment, there needs to be improvement in supervision. Teachers and lunchtime supervisors should be encouraged to initiate play, sometimes joining in rather than just adopting a surveillance role. Where training has been given particularly to lunchtime supervisors, it is noticeable that the playground has become a happier and more peaceful place.

Kelly (1992) has reviewed the particular difficulties for disabled children and those with 'special educational needs'. Their disability is likely both to place them at increased risk of abuse and to make the detection of abuse more difficult. Rieser (1995) also notes that the general boisterousness of some students may inhibit and intimidate others, in particular disabled students. Staff in these situations need to be more aware of the need to offer protection and to ensure that school is a safe place.

Preventive Teaching and the Role of the Curriculum

Potentially schools have a major role in preventing abuse through specific safety teaching, such as introducing children to the distinction between 'good' and 'bad' touches, 'secrets', 'say no to strangers' and paedophile awareness programmes, rights and responsibilities towards others and anti-bullying programmes (Sage, 1993; DFEE, 1995b; Rieser, 1995; Essex Child Protection Committee, 1997). In addition the curriculum can be used imaginatively, for example in integrating anti-violence work (Sudermann, Jaffe, Hastings *et al.*, 1994), teaching for 'responsible manhood' (Milner and Blyth, 1988), and involving Women's Aid groups on planning anti-violence work, particularly in conjunction with work on bullying and racism (Higgins, 1994). As Lansdown (1996) has intimated, many schools can do more to promote the concept of school as a safe environment for all students and staff.

Regenerating Teaching

None of these developments can succeed while the teaching profession remains beleaguered and demoralised. According to recent research, teaching (along with social work and the police) is not only seen as one of the most stressful jobs in the UK, but also as an occupation showing the greatest increase in perceived stress levels (a feature similarly shared with social work) (*Sunday Times*, 1997). The election of the Labour government in May 1997 with education ostensibly high on its agenda and a specific commitment to smaller class sizes, showed no obvious alleviation of pressures on teachers. Within days of his appointment the new Secretary of State for Education and Employment, David Blunkett (1997) stated 'we absolutely will not tolerate underperformance'. Failing schools have been publicly identified. New fast-track measures to dismiss 'incompetent' teachers are planned and knighthoods and other symbols of civic recognition have been awarded to those who excel.

The latter proposal arose in the context of evidence that the fortunes of schools failing to give pupils an acceptable standard of education can be reversed, as illustrated by the Ridings School, Halifax, which was temporarily closed in October 1996 because pupil safety could not be guaranteed. The idea of sending troubleshooting managers and teams into failing schools is a new and, to date, relatively infrequent occurrence, and there is a danger that attention will focus on individual rather than collective achievement. However, assuming that schools such as the Ridings can sustain progress, analysis of the process of regeneration will supplement what is already known about effective teaching and effective schools (Sammons, Hillman and Mortimore, 1995) and help to ensure that schools make a positive contribution to all members of their community and to the communities they serve.

REFERENCES

Association of Teachers and Lecturers (1995) *The Victims of Child Abuse: Both Adults and Children Suffer: Evidence from the Association of Teachers and Lecturers to the National Commission of Inquiry into the Prevention of Child Abuse*, ATL, London.

Audit Commission (1994) *Seen But Not Heard: Co-ordinating Community Child Health and Social Services for Children in Need*, HMSO, London.

Audit Commission and HMI (1992) *Getting in on the Act: Provision for Pupils with Special Educational Needs*, HMSO, London.

Besag V (1989) *Bullies and Victims in Schools*, Open University Press, Milton Keynes, Buckingham.

Blunkett D (1997) Time's up for schools that fail, *The Times*, 20 May, 22.

Blyth E and Milner J (1994) Exclusion from school and victim-blaming, *Oxford Review of Education*, **20**: 293–306.

Blyth E and Milner J (1997) *Social Work with Children: The Educational Perspective*, Addison-Wesley Longman, Harlow.

Brook S (1993) Quoted in Hirst A, Teachers may hush up attacks, *Huddersfield Daily Examiner*, 25 March, 7.

Charter D (1996) Male teachers are shunning primary schools, *The Times*, 31 July, 7.

Cornwall County Council (1987) *Child Abuse in Schools: Report of a Working Party on Child Abuse in Schools*, Cornwall County Council, Truro.

Cornwall County Council (1994) *The Principal Failing: A Case History Relating to Child Abuse by a Professional and a Review of Policy and Procedures*, Cornwall County Council, Truro.

Department for Education (1993) *A New Deal for 'Out of School' Pupils*, Press Release: 126/93, Department for Education, London.

Department for Education (1994) *Bullying: Don't Suffer in Silence. An Anti-bullying Pack for Schools*, Department for Education, London.

Department for Education and Employment (1995a) *Protecting Children from Abuse: The Role of the Education Service*, Draft Circular 10/95, Department for Education, London.

Department for Education and Employment (1995b) *Protecting Children from Abuse: The Role of the Education Service*, Draft Circular 10/95, Department for Education, London.

Elson T (1996) *Royd Edge School: An Overview Report*, Kirklees Metropolitan Council, Huddersfield.

Essex Child Protection Committee (1997) *Paedophile awareness programme for schools to be promoted at child protection conference*, press release, 11 September, Essex Child Protection Committee, Chelmsford.

Ghate D and Daniels A (1997) *Talking about My Generation: a Survey of 8–15 Year Olds Growing Up in the 1990s*, NSPCC, London.

Gilligan R (1998) The importance of schools and teachers in child welfare, *Child and Family Social Work*, **3**: 13–25.

Goffman E (1961) *Asylums*, Penguin, Harmondsworth.

Harris N with Pearce P and Johnstone S (1992) *The Legal Context of Teaching*, Harlow, Longman.

Higgins G (1994) Hammersmith Women's Aid Childwork Development Project, in Mullender A and Morley R (eds) *Children Living with Domestic Violence: Putting Men's Abuse of Women on the Child Care Agenda*, Whiting and Birch, London.

Hughes M and Lloyd E (1996) Young people: Stakeholders in the educational system, in Roberts H and Sachdev D (eds) *Young People's Social Attitudes: Having their Say—the Views of 12–19 year olds*, Barnardo's, Barkingside, Essex.

Independent on Sunday (1994) Fear and loathing in the classroom, 26 June, 20.

Irvine P (1997) Living in fear of the teacher, *Independent Education*, 12 June, 8–9.

Kelly L (1992) The connections between disability and child abuse: A review of the research evidence, *Child Abuse Review*, **1**: 157–167.

Kirkwood A (1993) *The Leicestershire Inquiry 1992*, Leicestershire County Council, Leicester.

Lansdown G (1996) Implementation of the UN Convention on the Rights of the Child in the UK, in John M (ed.) *Children in our Charge—the Child's Right to Resources*, Jessica Kingsley, London.

Malik R (1996) In silent fear of the pupils, *Guardian Education*, 5 November, 4.

Milner J and Blyth E (1988) *Coping with Child Sexual Abuse: a Guide for Teachers*, Longman, York.

Nash D (1996) Child monsters rule the roost, *Daily Mail* (letters), 8 December, 39.

NASUWT (1995) *Child Abuse Allegations against NASUWT Members*, NASUWT, Birmingham.

National Commission of Inquiry into the Prevention of Child Abuse (1996) *Childhood Matters*, The Stationery Office, London.

NCH: Action for Children (1994) *Messages from Children*, NCH: Action for Children, London.

OFSTED (1995) *Access, Achievement and Attendance in Secondary Schools*, OFSTED, London.

OFSTED (1996) *Exclusions from Secondary Schools 1995/6*. A report from the Office of Her Majesty's Chief Inspector of Schools, The Stationery Office, London.

O'Keeffe D (1994) *Truancy in English Secondary Schools*, HMSO, London.

O'Leary J (1995) Parents failing in duty to discipline, say head teachers, *The Times*, 31 May, 6.

Olweus D (1978) *Aggression in Schools: Bullies and Whipping Boys*, Hemisphere, Washington, DC.

Olweus D (1993) *Bullying at School: What we Know and What we can Do*, Basil Blackwell, Oxford.

Preston B (1993) Union tells teachers not to shout, *The Times*, 21 April, 5.

Preston B (1994) Teachers fall prey to flood of false sex abuse claims, *The Times*, 13 January, 9.

Rafferty F (1998) Protect teacher witnesses, *The Times Educational Supplement*, 6 March, 1.

Rieser R (1995) Developing a whole-school approach to inclusion: Making the most of the Code and the 1993 Act: A personal view, in National Children's Bureau *Schools Special Educational Needs Policies Pack: Discussion Papers III*, National Children's Bureau, London.

Roberts H and Sachdev D (1996) *Young People's Social Attitudes: Having their Say—the Views of 12–19 year olds*, Barnardo's, Barkingside, Essex.

Romans S, Martin J, Anderson J, O'Shea M and Mullen P (1995) Factors that mediate between child sexual abuse and adult psychological outcome, *Psychological Medicine*, **25**: 127–142.

Russell P (1995) Policy and diversity: Addressing values and principles when developing a school policy for children with special education needs, in National Children's Bureau *Schools Special Educational Needs Policies Pack: Discussion Papers I*, National Children's Bureau, London.

Rutter M (1991) Pathways from childhood to adult life: The role of schooling, *Pastoral Care in Education*, **9**, 3: 3–10.

Sage G (1993) *Child Abuse and the Children Act: A Critical Analysis of the Teacher's Role*, Association of Teachers and Lecturers Publications, London.

Sammons P, Hillman J and Mortimore P (1995) *Key Characteristics of Effective Schools: A Review of School Effectiveness Research*, OFSTED, London.

Samson A and Hart G (1995) A whole school approach to the management of pupil behaviour, in Farrell P (ed.) *Children with Emotional and Behavioural Difficulties: Strategies for Assessment and Intervention*, Falmer Press, London.

Social Services Inspectorate (1996) *Young Carers: Making a Start*, Department of Health, London.

Social Services Inspectorate and OFSTED (1995) *The Education of Children who are Looked After by Local Authorities*, Department of Health and OFSTED, London.

Sudermann M, Jaffe P G, Hastings E with Watson L, Greer G and Lehmann P (1994) *ASAP: A School Based Anti-violence Programme*, London Family Court Clinic, London, Ontario.

Sunday Times (1997) Stress Manager: Part 1: In the Workplace, 18 May.

Ward L (1997) Head is told to explain why girl was expelled, *The Independent*, 25 July, 3.

Westcott H and Clément M (1992) *NSPCC Experience of Child Abuse in Residential Care and Educational Placements: Results of a Survey*, NSPCC, London.

Whitney I and Smith P K (1993) A survey of the nature and extent of bullying in junior, middle and secondary schools, *Educational Research*, **35**: 2–25.

9

PRIMARY PREVENTION IN CHILD PROTECTION: THE ROLE OF THE HEALTH VISITOR

Suzanne Smith

The origins of health visiting can be located in Britain in 1867 with the emergence of the Manchester and Salford Ladies Sanitary Reform Association. The Association employed women to go from door to door offering advice about health and hygiene. Indeed, the existence of epidemics during that era demanded community action across the whole society to improve health. The task was not only to care for the individual but also to effect change throughout the neighbourhood by example and persuasion (Dingwall, 1976).

Formal training for health visitors was eventually introduced and, in the mid-1970s, some 25 years after the birth of the National Health Service, health visiting became part of its provision. Since then the nature of health visiting has been essentially proactive; no referral is required, no problem may have been presented and, consequently, coupled with the universal nature of the service, it is non-stigmatising. Health visiting concerns itself with prevention at all levels, but its essential, and to a large extent unique, function is that of the primary preventive role of the health visitor. The concept of primary, secondary and tertiary levels of prevention has its origins in the field of public health. As Fuller describes it:

> Primary prevention would prevent the emergence of a problem . . . secondary prevention would refer to working on a problem in its early stages . . . and tertiary prevention would limit the damaging effects of a problem already established. (Fuller, 1989: 9–13)

Children, Child Abuse and Child Protection. Placing Children Centrally, by The Violence Against Children Study Group.
© 1999 John Wiley & Sons Ltd.

Browne (1993) highlights the need for professionals involved with child protection to aim towards primary and secondary prevention rather than simply 'adequate control of the problem' at a tertiary level.

To place child protection within a health visiting context it is first necessary to consider the varying nature of child abuse from both historical and cultural perspectives. Child abuse is defined not only through how people behave towards children but also by how society reacts to those behaviours. This social reaction has varied as, through history, our notions of childhood have changed and therefore, child abuse is socially constructed (Parton, 1991). Gibbons, Gallagher, Bell and Gordon (1995) echo this point and state that child maltreatment is: 'a socially constructed phenomenon which reflects values and opinions of a particular culture at a particular time' (Gibbons *et al.*, cited in DOH, 1995: 15). The research also describes child abuse as a threshold of behaviour defined by official responses. Therefore, in order to be effective in trying to prevent child abuse, professionals should be striving to affect behaviour in relation to children.

Child Protection: Messages from Research (DOH, 1995) is explicit in the suggestion that services provided by child care agencies can lower the criticism and increase the warmth experienced by children whose parents feel some relief from the pressures upon them. The research calls for less preoccupation with abusive events and more concentration on the underlying processes. The preventive services of health visitors are highlighted within the research as being capable of offering support to children in need. The need to spend more time and resources on 'children in need' is currently the subject of much discussion within the field of child protection. Armstrong (1996) describes how nationally Area Child Protection Committees are trying to address themselves to 'the big debate'—how to balance child protection with family support. Health visitors are highlighted as being vital with regard to their primary preventive role, especially in terms of providing family support.

A review of the literature about prevention reveals that interventions which are designed to improve parental coping ability, parental self-esteem, parent–child interaction and the effects of social isolation, and which address issues such as power and control, violence and dependency, are essentially primary preventive in nature (Walker, 1996). A recent audit of the sort of interventions that fit this category revealed several hundred examples. These included sleep clinics for parents who find their children's sleep pattern difficult to manage but also to educate parents in what they can reasonably expect of their child; evening drop-in clinics for working parents who find slotting in attendance at day-time baby clinic a stressful experience; multidisciplinary teams that deal with parents who are finding their children difficult to cope with; parenting education programmes that provide crèche facilities to encourage attendance; domestic violence support groups intended to empower women experiencing violence from men they know by providing them with practical information as well as peer group support; public awareness campaigns and postnatal support groups (Leeds ACPC Prevention Working Party, 1996).

Health visiting interventions that are designed to impact upon parenting styles have long since been a feature of the profession. Stevenson, Bailey and Simpson (1988) acknowledge that interventions of this nature have a two-fold impact; both directly by improving parental coping skills and indirectly by raising parental self-esteem. However, studies of these interventions when compared to non-intervention controls have highlighted only modest effects.

One health visiting programme that is reported to evaluate well is the Child Development Programme (CDP) initiated by Professor Walter Barker at the Early Childhood Development Unit (ECDU), Bristol University. The CDP is based on a semi-structured strategy of home visiting which is intended to enhance a comprehensive range of parenting skills and awareness in child development (Barker, Anderson and Chalmers, 1992). The authors claim that the CDP is a successful health visitor intervention and describe how their research shows that rates of placement on the Child Protection Register are up to 41% lower with rates of physical abuse reduced by up to 50% in areas which adopt the CDP. They state this apparent success has come about not by placing a strong emphasis on actually avoiding abuse as such, but by focusing on parental conflict and self-esteem. The authors uphold the idea that the more confident the parent, the less likely they are to reach a point in the management of their children that threatens 'breaking point'.

The authors are explicit in their suggestion that empowering parents to gain control over their own lives will result in increased self-esteem and will remove their need to attempt to exercise control over individuals such as their offspring. In addition, gaining this control will render parents more capable of coping with the stresses of child-rearing and enable them to actually enjoy their children. This certainly seems to respond to the call from the Department of Health for concentration on the underlying processes of abuse rather than concentration on high-risk situations alone.

However, it could be argued that the validity of the research material evaluating the CDP is flawed because the ECDU, from whence the CDP originated, is also the main body which gathers the information, analyses the results and publishes the reports, albeit 'in collaboration' with the different health authorities. The lack of evaluation material from an entirely independent body serves to cast a shadow on the reliability of the ECDU studies.

The problems of evaluating preventive strategies in child protection are identified and reiterated by Gough (1993). Gough examined the literature (available up to 1992) which was concerned with the effectiveness of interventions designed to prevent or respond to abuse. Out of the 225 publications Gough found only a few that he felt could properly be classed as formal evaluations, many of the remainder being deemed to be methodologically limited. Armstrong (1996) describes how prevention involves building positive outcomes whilst at the same time avoiding the negative outcomes. She makes the point that measuring these gains may be impossible. Perhaps it would be more accurate to say that measuring the gains may not be 'impossible', but might involve time-consuming, expensive, qualitative, retrospective research. The National Health Service Management Executive (NHSME, 1993) strongly emphasised that dynamic primary health care depends on 'thorough and systemic research'. Mays and Pope (1995), who see qualitative approaches as an essential ingredient of health services research, echo this.

Despite this, however, the effectiveness of health visitors' primary preventive interventions is rarely the subject of such research. This lack of research has to be appreciated in the context of a market ideology in the NHS that increasingly demands that health visitors demonstrate the effectiveness of their interventions (Cowley, 1996). As a result of the market ideology and service provision governed by 'contracting', health visiting is now, more than ever, being assessed in terms of 'value for money'. This process is similar to that described by Adams and Horrocks in Chapter 10 of this volume that highlights how the police are forced, by recent legislation, to identify areas of priority crime where 'value for money' can be assessed. 'Value for Money' is recommended by the NHSME to be one of the 'cardinal principles' that should underpin the service provision from all community nurses. The reason given in its report 'New World, New Opportunities' (NHSME, 1993) is so that services can be effectively developed within the NHS structure.

The lack of demonstrable significant effects of health visitors' primary preventive interventions may be connected to the fact that health visitors feel inadequately supported in their role (Stevenson, Bailey and Simpson, 1988). The need for supervision in health visiting is one that has long been recognised by both health visitors and other agencies, particularly following the nationally publicised child abuse inquiries (DOH, 1991). Byrne (1994) suggests that effective supervision for health visitors would also fulfil the function of measuring quality and the monitoring of standards of practice. The issue of provision of adequate child protection supervision is a theme that runs throughout the latest guidance issued from the Department of Health (DOH, 1997a).

Clinically, health visitors are regarded as independent practitioners, but following the criticisms of child abuse inquiries, particularly those contained in the Beckford Report (London Borough of Brent, 1985), a more hierarchical supervision structure has evolved (Hudson, 1986). This form of hierarchical supervision can be questioned in terms of its appropriateness for health visitors and their child protection work, since the model which supervisors and managers adopt operates at a much more bureaucratic level than that of field social work staff (Dingwall, Eekelaar and Murray, 1983). Coupled with this, is the risk that supervision within a managerial hierarchy, divorced from fieldwork, will eventually fall into supervising procedures and not practice. Compliance with procedures will certainly serve to protect 'players in the system' should a tragedy occur, but will it serve any purpose in the day-to-day practice of those practitioners in their attempt to prevent the tragedy happening in the first instance?

Clinical supervision can be described as the means by which practising professionals engage each other in an exchange that enables them to focus on, and that facilitates the development of, professional skills (Butterworth and Faugier, 1992). It is not managerial oversight and should not be regarded as such.

Proctor (1988) has described the three functions of clinical supervision as: formative—the educative process of developing skills; restorative—supportive help for professionals working constantly with stress and distress; and normative—the managerial and quality control aspects of professional practice. These functions can be operated via different systems, for example, sessions with an expert supervisor from the same profession; sessions with a supervisor from a different discipline; peer supervision with people of a similar grade; group supervision and network supervision.

Many commentators have discussed the value of peer group support and supervision (see for example, Hallett and Birchall, 1992). Tower Hamlets Health Authority in 1989–90 (Byrne, 1994) piloted a study to explore supervision needs among community nurses and identified that the manager was not necessarily the most appropriate person to supervise health visitors in child protection; that the nurse manager's role is seen by the majority of field staff as restrictive and controlling. This study reflected the findings of the Kimberley Carlile report (DHSS, 1987) namely, that there is a clear distinction to be drawn between managerial and professional supervision. Professional supervision is seen to support the emotional aspects of child protection, allowing staff to explore such issues within a non-threatening environment. How far this concept of clinical supervision has been explored and developed in other areas is unclear, but hopefully it will succeed in fulfilling the very real need of supporting and developing health visiting practice and also serve to provide a means by which quality of practice can be measured and monitored.

The Audit Commission (1994) apparently applauds the idea of an integrated child care service with prevention at its root. However, the report *Seen But Not Heard* also describes the means of achieving this service as making health visiting more targeted and expanding the remit of social services. Buttigieg (1994) warns that such a plan would result in less proactive work by health visitors and thus, less primary prevention. The report also states that:

> After a universal visit from a health visitor . . . all further routine visiting
> . . . should be based on assessed need against agreed priorities in order
> to release resources for situations where there are clear needs. (Audit
> Commission, 1994: para. 118 p. 39)

Does a 'clear need' in child protection equate with 'high risk'? The implementation of this recommendation would inhibit health visitors, following the initial visit, from using their professional judgement in developing a plan of support in partnership with the parents.

Armstrong (1996) supports Buttigieg's reservations by highlighting how several ACPC annual reports reflect social services departments which are at full stretch and for whom effective prevention work is, frankly, an unachievable goal. Blyth and Waddell echo this point in Chapter 2 of this volume. Buttigieg emphasises how the value of health visitors with regard to prevention in child protection work is reiterated in report after report. Many ACPCs focus on the necessity of the health visitor service remaining universal, and as such non-stigmatising. These sentiments are an echo of the main themes of the DOH (1995) *Messages from Research* and have been more recently endorsed by the National Commission of Inquiry into the Prevention of Child Abuse (NSPCC, 1996).

The Gulbenkian Foundation (1995) warns of the dangers of targeting 'at risk' children alone and calls for anti-violence policies as a primary preventive measure. Identifying 'at risk' children and focusing on them at secondary and tertiary levels exposes some major problems: some children will be wrongly identified, while others will be missed; the targeted service would be stigmatising and would fail to place responsibility for creating a non-violent society on individuals (Newell, 1996). Thus, the statutory services are left with the responsibility and, therefore, the power. This directly contradicts the principle of partnership within the Children Act 1989 and supports Buttigieg (1994) in her argument against the targeting recommendations of the Audit Commission (1994).

There is, however, an argument that supports the targeting of primary preventive interventions. Gough (1993) raises the point that the efficacy of preventive interventions depends on the client group and one cannot assume that all such interventions can be applied indiscriminately. Stevenson, Bailey and Simpson (1988) reported a strong positive effect on attenders at a postnatal support group in London. However, only those attenders who were experiencing some adverse life events were found to report positive effects. Those attenders who were not experiencing such difficulties had worse outcomes than those in the control group. In addition, Affleck, Tennen, Rowe and Walker (1989), in their study of parents with children in special care units, found that extra support to those who were already coping might have been less beneficial and more disruptive.

If targeting is to be used it must be very specific and highly researched and not based on something as broad as, for example, social need. As Iwaniec (1995) emphasises, severely emotionally abused and neglected children sometimes have parents with affluent backgrounds, good material standards and a good education. She describes how, in these families, an almost 'clinical atmosphere' prohibits freedom of expression and play and the development of individuality. Iwaniec echoes Gibbons et al. (1995) when she describes the most worrying parent–child interaction as lacking 'warmth and approval' and the prevalence of negative attitudes. She adds 'sexual abuse frequently enters the picture as well'. Since emotional abuse is often disguised and hidden in suburban areas (Iwaniec, 1995), targeting strictly according to social need would miss these families altogether.

With the implementation of the NHS and Community Care Act 1990 came the introduction of the purchaser–provider separation and the market economy. The 1990 GP contract gives GPs a direct incentive to play a major role in child health surveillance where the quantity of routine screening and immunisation rates is a far more tangible measure than the less immediately evident benefits of primary prevention of child abuse. Bearing this in mind and recognising the fact that health visitors are now usually attached to a GP practice, the question one must ask is: Are health visitors really best placed to work at a primary level any more? Or have they too been caught up on the tertiary treadmill with case loads so high and staffing levels so low that targeting 'high risk' families for intervention is the best they can hope to manage? The National Commission of Inquiry into the Prevention of Child Abuse expresses concerns that:

> linking too closely with primary healthcare teams, the health visiting service may be losing its ability to become familiar with the problems and pressures within the communities. (NSPCC, 1996: para. 8.16: 93)

Orr describes how health visitors were removed from participation in community-centred initiatives by nursing management and policy-makers who emphasised the focus on primary health care teams. She points to the move in social policy towards community-based policies as being the time when health visitors were 'retreating into forms of service delivery which took them away from any identifiable role as health workers based in local areas' (Orr, 1985: 2). I would argue, that this retreat is still prevalent. In some areas health visitors are no more able to offer primary preventive service than their social service counterparts. In truth, many health visitors have become almost entirely clinic-based and one birth visit at home may be all that occurs in the first year of a child's life. Whilst I acknowledge that not all health visiting interventions which are designed to impact upon parenting styles need necessarily depend on home visits and that group work may seem an appropriate method of intervention in many circumstances, there is always the issue of the limitations of group attendance with regard to those parents who feel too disempowered to attend a group intended to help empower them!

At a proactive level, how can health visitors adequately identify 'need' if they do not home visit? At clinic? By the time a parent has got themselves to clinic and managed to get the health visitor's attention long enough and in sufficient privacy to express a concern which may require intervention, in many cases that problem is quite well established and the opportunity for primary prevention is fast disappearing.

The National Commission of Inquiry into the Prevention of Child Abuse is explicit in its call for protecting the public health role of the health visitor and acknowledges:

> the worrying decline in resources of staff and facilities for health visiting, which is considered by many, including the Commission, to be one of the most important of the non-stigmatising and universally available services. (NSPCC, 1996: 93)

Ironically, just as health visitors in the UK are under pressure to justify themselves, the United States of America is seeing a sudden growth in interest in the health visiting role; in particular its effect on child abuse.

Daro (1993) writes that the most promising approach to reducing the number of abuse and neglect cases is 'home visitation'. The US Advisory Board on Child Abuse and Neglect and the US Accounting Office (1992) has endorsed the idea of home visitation in the prevention of child abuse. Wolfe (1993) also highlights the benefits that could be gained by transforming a reactive child protection strategy into one that is proactive.

The National Commission of Inquiry into the Prevention of Child Abuse highlights how the retention of health visiting as a universal service is vital to the success of child protection strategies. It also emphasises how 'prevention is, itself, being prevented' and echoes Armstrong (1996) in recognising the difficulty for statutory services to shift to effective prevention work. Among the report's recommendations is the demand that 'effective child protection services must be maintained alongside improved family support provision'.

Logistically, there is a solid case for primary prevention on social, cultural, ethical, health and economic grounds. However, the widespread adoption/purchase of interventions that incorporate primary preventive strategies depends on the provision of much more clear evidence; evidence which highlights their effectiveness and thus, their cost-effectiveness. The need for this overrides the argument to continue to spend most of the £1 billion spent on child abuse and neglect on the consequences of failing to prevent it (NSPCC, 1996). The need for the type of rigorous research required is particularly vital to convince those who manage within the current market-driven culture of the National Health Service and those whose task it will be to dismantle the NHS internal market, to have permanently on their agenda the primary prevention of child abuse.

Within that agenda item must remain the role of the health visitor. Policy is needed to develop primary prevention within child protection work in health visiting practice. This requires reorganisation of resources to evaluate its effectiveness alongside the development of appropriate support mechanisms such as clinical supervision. This would reflect the Department of Health requirement for clinical governance and the call for quality and consistency in practice and service delivery (DOH, 1998).

The signals coming from the present government are promising. The draft consultation paper *Working Together to Safeguard Children: New Government Proposals for Inter-Agency Co-operation* (DOH, 1998) regards as positive the universal nature of health professionals and points out that: 'health professionals are often the first to be aware that families are experiencing difficulties looking after their children' (DOH, 1998: 23). The document places a great emphasis on the health service, and all other agencies involved in child protection, intervening with such families earlier to support children 'in need': 'rather than waiting until concerns about abuse mean that a S47 enquiry becomes necessary' (DOH, 1998: 21). The hope that such interventions will reduce the number of unnecessary child protection enquiries and achieve better outcomes for children and their families is explicit in the document.

These themes are echoed in the Government White Paper (England) *The New NHS: Modern, Dependable* (DOH 1997b) and the Green Paper *Our Healthier Nation* (DOH, 1997c). *Working Together to Safeguard Children* (DOH, 1997d) mentions the White Paper as emphasising the need for increasing partnerships and co-operation between all agencies, and a major focus is placed upon reducing inequalities in the health status of the population. The government has stated its commitment to improve family support, parenting initiatives and the overall quality of life for children (Home Office, 1998).

It seems that, on paper at least, the Government plans to address the problem of child abuse within a wider socio-economic and political context. However, fine words are easy to write and some aspects of these new papers are themselves a cause for concern. Primary Care Groups/Trusts may well be better placed to identify needs at a local level, but will the identification of child protection issues or the link between health needs and the primary prevention of child abuse come down to the experience, knowledge and interest of members on that particular trust board? Will all primary care groups/trusts have equal ability to place child protection within the wider context of children in need as the consultation paper requires?

Singer identifies some of the concerns about the management and representation of professionals' views within the Primary Care Group/Trust structure:

> There is obvious disharmony between the rhetoric used in the recent papers and the means likely to be provided to achieve the fine words. And it is mirrored by the disharmony in the planning and implementation of local services while apparently letting GPs make the running in the establishment of the new primary care groups and trusts. (Singer, 1998: 130)

The importance of community nurses, particularly health visitors, ensuring that their voices are heard within the new structure cannot be overstated. The ability of health services effectively to respond to the whole 'refocusing' debate could be compromised if the child protection experience and knowledge that community nurses possess is not adequately represented. The main positive point about the Government's proposals is that we are now in a better position than ever before to help shape policy and ensure that the primary prevention of child abuse is adequately addressed.

The model of Figure 9.1 is loosely based on Neuman's Systems Model (1989). Neuman highlights the need to evaluate intervention in terms of primary, secondary and tertiary prevention. This model (Figure 9.1) presents how different levels of prevention serve to protect the individual throughout their life. At the core is the child in a time line that extends to adulthood. The three levels of prevention, primary, secondary and tertiary, form flexible lines of defence. The lines of defence are flexible because positive experiences must be allowed to infiltrate to the core in order to protect the integrity of the core. The most primary line of defence is all-embracing and primary preventive interventions, thus affording early protection of the core. However, because the line of defence is not solid, some negative influences may permeate it. At this point a second layer can be formed by interventions which fulfil the secondary preventive level of intervention. Should further negative influences permeate then a tertiary layer can be formed. In addition, having established a secondary line of defence successfully, this may result in improved self-esteem and empower the core to further establish the primary line of defence against similar experiences perhaps later in life. The same also applies between the secondary and tertiary lines.

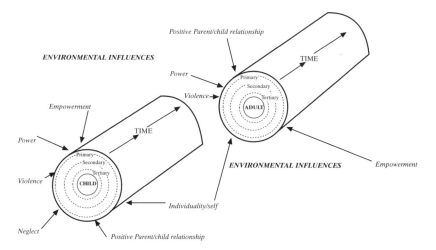

Figure 9.1: Protective prevention

Interventions that are tertiary in nature may, over time, feed into the primary line of defence as the child, through therapeutic intervention for example, learns to cope with its abuse, protect itself and, therefore, become better equipped to protect any children it goes on to have, or have contact with.

Because the lines of defence provide different levels of protection at different points in time, their co-existence is essential. The argument for primary prevention is not, therefore, to remove resources from the tertiary line of defence and place them all at the primary level, but rather to share the resources across all three levels in order for them to protect the core. The aim is that if successful primary preventive interventions can be sufficiently well established, there will eventually be less need for the secondary and tertiary interventions, although these should always remain available.

At present, primary preventive interventions in child protection are underresearched, undervalued and underresourced. The National Commission of Inquiry into the Prevention of Child Abuse (NSPCC, 1996) calls for commitment to prevention. This commitment must include recognition, support and funding for the health visitor's unique role in primary prevention. Such commitment must come not only from other agencies and managers within health, but initially and most crucially, from the health visitors themselves. Health visitors must examine the nature of their role and from where it has evolved if it is not to slip away altogether. Perhaps then, the unique collection of skills health visitors possess can be marketed with more vigour.

Reaffirming, strengthening and supporting the role of the health visitor in the primary prevention of child abuse may add to that balance between prevention and protection which is currently hotly debated in child protection. Perhaps the future holds a more credible realisation of S17 of the Children Act 1989 where the key agency in responding to children under five who are 'in need' may no longer be social services, but health. Perhaps we will see core groups for 'children in need' where the keyworker is the health visitor, ultimately resulting in less time being spent on tertiary interventions and with a Social Services Department more able to respond effectively at that level of prevention. Then perhaps, will health visitors be able to contribute more seriously to the concept of inter-agency co-operation in a much more meaningful way. They might then be in a position to help fulfil the aim that lies at the heart of the Children Act 1989: the need to strike a balance 'between protecting the innocent and weak and protection from unwarrantable interference, particularly from the state' (Parton, 1992: 112).

REFERENCES

Affleck T, Tennen H, Rowe J and Walker L (1989) Effects of formal support on mothers' adaptation to the hospital to home transition of high-risk infants: The benefits and costs of helping, *Child Development*, **60**: 488–501.

Armstrong H (1996) *Annual Reports of Area Child Protection Committees 1994/95*, DOH, London.

Audit Commission (1994) *Seen But Not Heard: Co-ordinating Community Child Health and Social Services for Children In Need*, HMSO, London.

Barker W E, Anderson R M and Chalmers C (1992) *Child Protection: The Impact of the Child Development Programme. Evaluation Document No. 14*, Early Childhood Development Unit, University of Bristol.

Browne (1993) Home visitation and child abuse: The British experience, *APSAC Advisor*, **4**: 11–31.

Butterworth C A and Faugier J (1992) *Clinical Supervision and Mentorship in Nursing*, Chapman and Hall, London.

Buttigieg M (1994) Measuring Success, *Health Visitor*, **67**, 9: 296.

Byrne C (1994) Devising a model health visitor supervision process, *Health Visitor*, **6**, 195–198.

Cowley S (1996) Reflecting on the Past: preparing for the next century, *Health Visitor*, **69**, 8: 313–315.

Daro D (1993) Home visitation and preventing child abuse, *The APSAC Advisor*, **4**.

Department of Health (1991) *Child Abuse: A Study of Inquiry Reports 1980–1989*, HMSO, London.

Department of Health (1995) *Child Protection: Messages from Research*, HMSO, London.

Department of Health (1997a) *Child Protection: Guidance for Senior Nurses, Health Visitors and Midwives and their Managers* (3rd edn), Stationery Office, London.

Department of Health (1997b) *The New NHS: Modern, Dependable*, Stationery Office, London.

Department of Health (1997c) *Our Healthier Nation*, Stationery Office, London.

Department of Health (1997) *Working Together to Safeguard Children: New Government Proposals for Inter-Agency Co-operation*, draft consultation paper, Department of Health, London.

Department of Health (1998) *A First Class Service*, Stationery Office, London.

DHSS (1987) *A Child In Mind: Protection of Children in a Responsible Society* (The Kimberley Carlile report), HMSO, London.

Dingwall R (1976) Collectivism, regionalism and feminism; health visiting and British social policy 1850–1975, *Journal of Social Policy*, **63**: 291–315.

Dingwall R, Eekelaar J and Murray T (1983) *The Protection of Children: State Intervention and Family Life*, Blackwell, Oxford.

Fuller R (1989) Problems and possibilities in studying preventive work, *Adoption and Fostering*, **13**: 9–13.

Gibbons J, Gallagher R, Bell C and Gordon D (1995) *Development After Physical Abuse In Early Childhood*, HMSO, London.

Gough D (1993) *Child Abuse Interventions: A Review of the Research Literature*, HMSO, London.

Gulbenkian Foundation Commission (1995) *Children and Violence: Report of the Gulbenkian Foundation Commission*, Calouste Gulbenkian Foundation, London.

Hallett C and Birchall E (1992) *Co-ordination and Child Protection: A Literature Review*, HMSO, London.

Home Office, Department of Health, Department of Education and Science, Welsh Office (1991) *Working Together Under the Children Act: A Guide to Arrangements for Inter-agency Co-operation for Protection of Children from Abuse*, HMSO, London.

Home Office (1998) *Supporting Families*, green paper, Stationery Office, London.

Hudson C (1986) cited in Hallett C and Birchall E (1992) *Co-ordination and Child Protection: A Review of the Literature*, HMSO, London.

Iwaniec D (1995) *The Emotionally Abused and Neglected Child*, John Wiley, Chichester.

Leeds ACPC Prevention Working Party (1996) *Audit of Preventive Interventions*, Leeds ACPC, Leeds.

Mays N and Pope C (1995) Rigour and qualitative research, *British Medical Journal*, **31**: 109–112.

National Society for the Prevention of Cruelty to Children (1996) *Childhood Matters: Report of the National Commission of Inquiry into the Prevention of Child Abuse*, HMSO, London.

Neuman B (1989) *The Neuman Systems Model: Application to Nursing Education and Practice* (2nd edn). Appleton and Lange, New York.

NHSME (1993) *New World New Opportunities: Nursing in Primary Health Care*, HMSO, London.

Newell P (1996) Children and violence: An individual responsibility, *Health Visitor*, **2**: 56–57.

Orr J (1985) The community dimension, in Luker K and Orr J (eds) *Health Visiting*, Blackwell Scientific, Oxford.

Parton N (1991) *Governing the Family: Child Care, Child Protection and The State*, Macmillan, Basingstoke.

Parton N (1992) Contemporary politics of child protection, *Journal of Social Welfare and Family Law*, **2**: 100–113.

Proctor B (1988) Supervision: A co-operative exercise in accountability, in Marken M and Payne M (eds) *Enabling and Ensuring*, Leicester National Youth Bureau/Council for Education and Training in Youth and Community Work, Leicester.

Singer R (1998) Opportunity knocks, *Community Practitioner*, **71**, 4: 130.

Stevenson J, Bailey V and Simpson J (1988) Feasible intervention in families with parenting difficulties: A primary preventive perspective on child abuse; cited in Browne K, Davis C and Stratton P (eds) *Early Prediction and Prevention of Child Abuse*, John Wiley, Chichester.

Walker S (1996) *The Role of the Health Visitor in the Primary Prevention of Child Abuse*, unpublished MA dissertation, University of Huddersfield.

Wolfe D (1993) Child abuse prevention: Blending research and practice, *Child Abuse Review*, **2**, 1, 153–165.

10

THE LOCATION OF CHILD PROTECTION IN RELATION TO THE CURRENT EMPHASIS ON CORE POLICING

Cath Adams and Christine Horrocks

INTRODUCTION

The NSPCC report on the prevention of child abuse, *Childhood Matters* (NSPCC, 1996) maintained that nearly all forms of child abuse could be prevented provided the will to do so was there. The Commission set up to produce this report adopted a wide definition of child abuse:

> Child abuse consists of anything which individuals, institutions or processes do or fail to do which directly or indirectly harms children or damages their prospects of safe and healthy development into adulthood. (NSPCC, 1996: 120)

One institution that has a role to play in preventing child abuse has been neglected in the literature. This chapter will therefore look closely at the role of the police in child protection, accepting the view that institutions and processes have their part to play in the critical issue of protecting children within an inter-agency perspective. The views offered will draw upon the professional experience of one of the authors who, until recently, held the position of Detective Inspector in charge of three Domestic Violence and Child Abuse Units in the West Yorkshire Police (DV and CPUS).

The 1990s have been marked by smoother working relationships than previously between police and other professionals, most notably

Children, Child Abuse and Child Protection. Placing Children Centrally, by The Violence Against Children Study Group.
© 1999 John Wiley & Sons Ltd.

social workers involved in child protection. Saunders, Jackson and Thomas (1996) suggested that in order for police and social services to work together effectively two things were required. First, there must be an extensive change in attitude on the part of practitioners in each of the agencies and second, this had to be supported by the context within which child protection work was undertaken. We will therefore primarily look at the way in which the police response to child abuse has evolved, considering the relationship between the police and other agencies. We will then contextualise the setting up of specialist units (DV and CPUS) within the West Yorkshire Metropolitan Area.

By making visible the priorities of today's police service we intend to facilitate an appreciation of the current climate that exists in relation to the core functions of the police and how this might impact upon child protection work. We will present the argument that the police response to child protection may currently be at risk of coming full circle. The initial priority of evidence gathering and prosecution, with scant attention given to the paramountcy of the child's interests, which was present in the 1970s, may be in danger of re-emerging. This re-emergence, we contest, will be a consequence of recent legislation forcing the police to target its efforts into both public and politically identified areas of priority crime where 'value for money' can be measured. We will also consider the further issue of the feminisation of child protection work within the police, drawing into question the position of child protection, not only in relation to core policing and political and public priorities, but in its location within the police organisational culture.

POLICING AND CHILD PROTECTION: AN EVOLVING PROCESS

In order to understand the current police response to the complex problem of child abuse it is important to acknowledge that the police service as a whole, in line with other agencies, has significantly improved its knowledge and understanding. However, for the police, as with other agencies, these improvements have mainly been in response to external pressure in the form of public and political concerns. The police service in the early 1970s was in some difficulty in respect of its policing style, for example, traditional foot patrol versus the 'Panda' car and the concept of 'hard' as opposed to 'soft' policing. Increasing social tensions led to violence on the streets such as the Brixton riots in 1981. As a result of these events the police came under close scrutiny with the subsequent judicial inquiry placing great emphasis on the ideology of policing by the *consent* of the public and working in *partnership* with communities and other agencies:

> Provision must be made for the police to be involved, like other important agencies, in community development and planning. The social functions of the police—in handling the problems of the elderly, domestic disputes and juveniles, for example—are important to the social health of the community. (Scarman, 1981: 6.9)

This then required a 'softer' approach with an appreciation of the impact of social factors within society and subsequently how these might affect how the police do their job. Such changes did not, however, come easily in particular areas. During the early 1970s there had been an appalling naïveté and ignorance regarding the specific issue of abuse and patterns of offending in relation to both children and women. Kelly (1994) talks convincingly of the 'interconnectedness' of domestic violence and child abuse. Historically, the helping professions, including the police, have reacted unsympathetically and ineffectively to women in need of assistance when experiencing domestic violence, often 'blaming' them for 'provoking' the violence (Mullender and Morley, 1994: 8). The policing process resulting from such attitudes was exposed in 1982 with the screening of a TV 'fly on the wall' documentary about the Thames Valley Police's callous handling of a woman reporting rape (BBC 1, 'Police' documentary, February 1982). In addition there had been damaging corruption scandals within the police service. For example one of these scandals revealed that officers of the obscene publications squad confiscated pornographic films only to show them on the squad's projector at regular Friday evening 'stag' parties (Reiner, 1992: 79). Therefore a level of ignorance regarding abuse is compounded by a particular set of attitudes within the police situated within the male culture of the service. Scraton has asserted that the police had 'a culture of values which revolves around white, masculine respectability' (Scraton, 1985: 20). It can also be argued that the police culture was pervaded by gendered relations where women, and potentially children by their relational position, were disempowered and subjugated.

Compounding these gendered cultural barriers to change were tensions which to some extent were a manifestation of the stereotypical views held by police and social workers in respect of each other's roles and responsibilities in society (see, e.g., Thomas, 1986). Many police officers took the view that social workers were 'woolly minded do-gooders' who were reluctant to use their authority, instead finding excuses and justification for offenders. The police had distinct concerns about social workers' 'rule of optimism' (see Corby, 1993: 32) which were supported when the Panel of Inquiry which investigated the death of Jasmine Beckford concluded:

> Social workers were too ready to believe the best of parents or even to overidentify with their perspective, so that lies were not seen through and evasive actions not circumvented. (London Borough of Brent, 1985: 106)

The notion of inter-agency sharing of information was at this time unthinkable—the police being very clear about their role: to investigate crime, gather evidence and put the offender before a court. Conversely, social workers, in the eyes of the police, knew little about the law or the concept of evidence. Police involvement in respect of the investigation of child abuse was restricted to, and often a consequence of, extreme cases where maltreatment through neglect or physical abuse resulted in the death of a child (Parton, 1985). These emotive cases, purely from an evidential perspective, were relatively easy to investigate. However, with hindsight, the police demanded to be involved much earlier, before tragedy struck rather than as a consequence of such tragedies. This insistence on early involvement in all cases relates understandably to police responsibility for crime (Evidence, 1977, HC329-11) and is reiterated by Wedlake (1978) emphasising the duty of the police to deal with assaults on children. In contrast to this investigative view Otway (1996) explains that in the early 1970s social workers, via casework, provided more therapeutic interventions, thus leaving the police marginalised. This therapeutic orientation has its roots in the conceptualisation of the 'battered child' as a medical-social problem. The emphasis for social workers was not whether or not a crime had been committed but one of establishing relationships and working with families to alleviate distress. Here then are two, if not opposed, then very different points of reference in relation to child abuse. One is investigative and concerned with the pursuit of evidence; the other more mindful of therapeutic and relational issues. Saunders et al., referring to the conceptualisation of social services and police involvement in child protection, maintain that there was 'a dichotomy between treatment therapeutic objectives and investigative legal objectives' (Saunders, Jackson and Thomas, 1996: 88). Such differing objectives did not engender any real level of co-operation or indeed accommodation.

In the aftermath of the violent and untimely death of 7-year-old Maria Colwell in 1973 the public demanded to know what went wrong and sought assurances that such tragedies would not happen again. In the subsequent report (Secretary of State for Social Services, 1974) both the police and social workers were criticised for failing to pass on relevant information. With the aim of ensuring the avoidance of such tragedies the Department of Health and Social Security issued the 'Non-accidental injury to children' circular (DHSS, 1974) that advised the implementation of Area Review Committees (ARC) which later became Area Child Protection Committees (Home Office, DOH, DES, Welsh Office, 1991). The inclusion of paediatricians, general practitioners, health visitors and social workers on these committees was considered crucial. Nevertheless, there was no specific role at that time for the police other than a senior police officer being invited to attend meetings. However, professionals suspecting ill treatment were advised to inform the police of such cases. A further circular (DHSS, 1976) was to recommend the inclusion of a senior police officer on all ARCs and at case conferences. Perhaps police misgivings about not previously being involved in the process were addressed when the document stressed the need for good communication and a need to enforce criminal law.

Nevertheless, up to the mid-1980s, there had been 35 public inquiries concerning the deaths of children at the hands of their parents or carers. A significant issue was that social workers were seen as too trusting of parents, and therefore failing to secure the well-being of the child and to use the statutory authority entrusted to them. These inquiries also pointed toward failures in inter-agency and inter-professional co-ordination and co-operation (Hallett and Birchall, 1992). There was an acceptance of the need to rethink the management of child abuse not only at an individual case level but also at the inter-agency and agency level. Saunders, Jackson and Thomas (1996) call this period an 'uneasy alliance' which continued until 1987.

THE SETTING UP OF CHILD PROTECTION UNITS

In 1988 the Home Office issued guidance to the police in England and Wales. It stated that:

> The success of the police intervention, however, is not to be measured in terms of prosecutions which are brought, but of the protection which their actions bring to children at risk. (Home Office, 1988: 10)

This is a distinct shift from the notion of evidence gathering toward a more child-centred approach. Conroy, Fielding and Tunstill (1990) questioned the simplistic interpretation of police as controllers and social workers as carers, maintaining that this does not reflect the complexity of the work. They propose that the police need to become more aware of welfare considerations and that social workers should accept the need for control. Therefore the Home Office (1988) guidance paved the way for the police to accommodate a more welfare-oriented position. At this time the number of reported cases of child abuse, especially child sexual abuse, showed a significant increase (we do not intend to make further comment upon the actual 'discovery' of child abuse, merely to acknowledge its increased attention). Concern was also being expressed regarding police investigative procedures when interviewing children who had been victims of abuse (Vizard, Bentovim and Tranter, 1987) and the overall insensitive treatment of children within the judicial system. This growing disquiet with the police and the joint-investigative response to child abuse drew more specific media attention with events in Cleveland and the ensuing inquiry which suggested a total breakdown between the police and local SSDs and associated medical professionals (see Butler-Sloss, 1988). Waterhouse and Carnie (1990), examining the response to inter-familial child sexual abuse, found differences in the way sexual abuse was defined by police and social workers. They also found that communication between agencies was impeded by competing professional objectives.

The Cleveland Report (Butler-Sloss, 1988) recommended the establishment of multidisciplinary *specialist* assessment teams which would have an approved medical practitioner, a senior social worker and a police officer. Although to date this model has not materialised, a number of Child Protection Units are now in operation in police forces throughout the country. The NSPCC Commission (1996) believes that the standard of police work has improved, 'particularly those in child protection units . . . partly as a result of training' (NSPCC, 1996: 98). The training of police officers in the 1970s was centred on learning legal definitions and powers of arrest. No direct insight into the roles and responsibilities of social workers would have been given, nor indeed were any sociological or psychological concepts imparted, the training therefore failing to provide any real insight into the more diverse and subjective aspects of victim care. The function of the police was to protect life and property and to detect crime, with the generally held belief being that the best deterrent to crime was the likelihood of detection followed by the certainty of conviction. Policing in the 1990s operates on a less simplistic vision and requires more than a dogmatic use of statutory authority. These objectives aimed at the certainty of conviction contrast with the idea of measuring success in child protection terms, clearly highlighting a change in emphasis and the importance of building up a specialist knowledge base.

The effects of this change of emphasis had been evident as early as 1985 when, in response to both national and local concerns, primarily from women's groups, the West Yorkshire Police formed two specialist units of women officers to deal specifically with women (not child abuse) who had been subjected to rape or domestic violence (Major Crime Support Unit—Policewomen's Section). These units were later to evolve into specialist child protection units in the wake of the Cleveland affair. The Implementation Plan (July, 1985, Section 3b) which preceded the setting up of these units in West Yorkshire stressed the need for training incorporating inter-agency collaboration and co-ordination:

> All selected officers will attend a two weeks residential course . . . and will continue to receive on the job inter-agency training locally. It is anticipated that joint training will evolve with other agencies.

The Implementation Plan identified the following terms of reference, which again reflect the aim of inter-agency working:

1. To undertake the total investigation of all cases of child abuse referred to them from police officers or the caring agencies, or other source.
2. To develop and maintain effective communication and consultation with other caring agencies in particular in respect of the investigation of child abuse.
3. To develop and practise inter-agency working and joint planning, interviews and investigation of child abuse.
4. To participate in joint training programmes with other agencies.
5. To attend case conferences where appropriate.

Here, then, would be the change in attitude and context that Saunders, Jackson and Thomas (1996) spoke of with not only joint training in the specific area of child protection but also effective communication, consultation, joint planning and investigation of child abuse. Nevertheless, Weeks emphasises the reality that both work from a different 'standpoint':

> It used to be the case that Social Services and the police worked separately on child abuse cases whatever form it took. It was traditionally a 'them and us' group. Today they work closely together but from different standpoints. Social Services continue to support families and protect the child, the Child Protection Unit has a remit to collect evidence for court appearances. (Weeks, 1997: 20)

While accepting the existence of differing standpoints it is to be hoped that the Child Protection Units can do more than fulfil their evidence-gathering remit. In their research focusing on specialist police units undertaking the investigation of child abuse, Lloyd and Burman (1996) found that some police officers still expressed concern in relation to social workers 'dragging their feet' when informing them about cases. This was countered by social workers who thought that the police sometimes moved too quickly once they were informed of a suspected case of child abuse. Nevertheless, police working in specialist child protection units were much more positive in their evaluations than those officers working with less formalised arrangements.

The Department of Health (1995) issued a guide to policy-makers, managers and practitioners on the principle of working in partnership with family members in all cases where this does not counteract the provision of adequate protection. Believing that a more co-operative working relationship is likely to lead to better safeguarding of the child's welfare, Humphreys' (1996) research (not undertaken in West Yorkshire) noted a marked difference in the way parents viewed the police response when dealing with child abuse. Those who had experienced the specialist unit were very positive in their comments, while parents who had experienced a more 'fragmented' response, where officers outside the unit were involved in the investigation, were unable to make any positive comments about the police response and some offered extremely negative comments, relaying an intense dissatisfaction. Recent research would therefore point toward the positive outcomes of specialist child protection units and the need to accept that child abuse requires specialist skills and knowledge from all professionals involved. Although difficulties still prevail, these are viewed as not insurmountable with CPUs making a leap forward in securing a more sensitive and pertinent response to child abuse. However, it should be mentioned that there has been a move toward a system of tenure, where officers serve only for a limited period of time in specialist units, thus diluting the continuity and knowledge base of the CPUs.

FEMINISATION OF CHILD PROTECTION IN THE POLICE

The first Major Crime Support Unit (MCSU) in West Yorkshire was set up in 1985, in the same year the Equal Opportunities Act came into being, followed a year later with the Sex Discrimination Act—in theory male and female officers were to be treated equally. However, from the perspective of the women officers working within the MCSU, who were supervised by a male Detective Inspector, this ground-breaking work brought to the fore not new, but ongoing, prejudicial treatment of women officers.

The women officers in the MCSUs brought their specialist skills of tenacity, patience and sensitivity to this work, with the result of providing a more appropriate and effective service to victims of domestic violence and sexual assault. A major breakthrough was the appointment of female police surgeons and the provision of victim examination suites. A tension developed between the more mainstream officers and officers in the MCSUs, who were predominantly female. This tension had its basis in differing viewpoints on how to deal with victims, with the more sensitive approach of the MCSUs being seen as moving too far away from the police's more customary male-oriented approach.

Sampson (1991) confronts such tensions by saying that although it is acknowledged that the occupational culture of the police 'is a rich repository of both racist and sexist prejudice', gender issues are 'completely neglected' in discussions of police–social work relations (Holdaway, 1986; Thomas, 1986). This omission would be reflected in the attitudes of male police officers to the more enlightened approach of specialist units that were predominantly staffed by women officers. Reiner has commented that, 'the police world remains aggressively a man's world' (Reiner, 1985: 216). Sampson goes on to assert that the occupational 'world' of the police reproduces expectations, and structures work practices, requiring 'masculine qualities' and 'masculine traits' from which male officers can obtain status. The investigation of child abuse is an area of police work that does not necessarily require such 'masculine traits', therefore the gaining of status may be diminished and as such the work becomes undervalued and misunderstood.

Jones (1986) made a salient point when she observed that, although theoretically women officers have been fully integrated with their male counterparts, the role of women officers is 'ambiguous'. Prior to their integration women officers were recognised specialists in traditional 'policewomen's work', working often with victims of domestic violence and sexual offences. This specialism, Jones maintains, 'in some senses might compensate for the general lack of equality with their male counterparts' (Jones, 1986: 129). With the removal of segregated deployment patterns for male and female officers one might have expected the perception of particular police tasks as 'women's work' to diminish. However, research by Brown, Maidment and Bull (1993) showed that women police officers tended to be deployed in low frequency, labour-intensive specialist tasks such as supporting victims of sex abuse or rape. This was supported by Anderson, Brown and Cambell (1993) who found that women police officers more often dealt with victims of sexual offences and young offenders. Funnelle (1992) found that in the West Yorkshire Police women constables were more likely to be asked to deal with victims of sexual offences and with young offenders.

Differential deployment patterns have a two-fold effect; they limit the amount and type of experience women officers are able to gain and this has a consequential effect on job satisfaction and promotional prospects (Jones, 1986). Furthermore, this feminisation of particular policing tasks may have the potential to diminish the organisational priority of such work. If the prevailing culture of the police were 'masculine' it would be unwise to overlook the repercussions of gendered power differentials.

POLICING AT THE CORE

A further crucial issue to heed is the prevailing political context within which child protection inter-agency work is evolving. Since 1993 there have been a succession of ministerial statements and government publications directed at improving police efficiency and effectiveness, with the White Paper on Police Reform of that year followed by the Police and Magistrates' Court Act, 1994. In line with other public services the emphasis was placed on greater managerial accountability linked to performance measures and the development of performance indicators designed to provide evidence to the tax-paying public of efficiencies or inefficiencies in service delivery. It is this application of performance indicators that may prove to be problematic for the police when considered in light of the various demands made upon them. Loveday (1996) claims that for the government the primary task for the police is one of 'crime fighting', believing that this basic tenet has been 'progressively over-shadowed' by non-crime demands on police time. This frustration was expressed in the White Paper on Police Reform:

> The main job of the police is to catch criminals. In a typical day, only 18% of calls to the police are about crime and only about 40% of police officers' time is spent dealing with crime. (Home Office, 1993: para. 2.3)

A belief that the police were failing to target core activity, that of fighting crime, indicated a need to establish clear and 'right objectives'. These objectives, identified jointly by government and the local community, would provide such direction, the 1993 White Paper on Police Reform being very clear in its main focus:

> The government believes that reductions in the levels of crime against the person and property and improved protection of the public must be the top priority of police work. (Home Office, 1993: para. 7.4)

The Police and Magistrates' Court Act 1994 gave the Home Secretary the powers to identify and set objectives for all police forces in England and Wales. The Home Secretary's power to set objectives was underpinned by the requirement placed on local police authorities (LPA) to develop local policing plans. However, while the LPA would be able to set local objectives and performance targets, these would be expected to be in line with those set by the Home Secretary which focus on crime-fighting activities. These objectives include a reduction in violent crime and an increase in the detection of burglaries. There is the requirement for the police to uphold the law, to bring to justice those who break the law, while at the same time providing 'value for money'. It is clear then that government interest is toward crime reduction, particularly that which is measurable. Therefore a core indicator of police effectiveness, not only for the government and the police but also for the media and the public, would be crime rates.

The Audit Commission has also provided support for this approach, suggesting that the police be 'proactive' in order to help stem the growth in crime (Audit Commission, 1993). This is to be achieved by a clarification of the role of the police and by concentrating more on core policing, which the Commission identifies to be the prevention and investigation of crime. By 'hiving off' police work which is viewed as 'service or caring functions' the police can concentrate their activities and resources to core crime fighting (Audit Commission, 1993). Child abuse is a crime against the person and by its nature would be situated within a discourse of violent crime, so it would seem logical to assume that child protection is part of the police's core function. Nevertheless it should be acknowledged that measuring the outcomes of this work is notoriously difficult. If the focus of policing is once again to engender objectives that concentrate on prosecution with the added accent on accountability, there is a need to ensure that the advances that have been made do not recede. This cautionary observation relates not only to attitudes on inter-agency collaboration and co-operation but also to the enlightened handling of child protection as a whole. The police have perceivably become more 'caring' in their attitude toward child protection issues so it would surely have detrimental effects to return to a much criticised, purely investigative role.

THE ROLE OF THE POLICE AND ACCOUNTABILITY

Having previously made direct reference to the issue of accountability and the way in which police objectives are set, we will move on to raise our concerns regarding the setting of these objectives and the effect on child protection work within the police. West Yorkshire Police serves approximately 2.1 million people and around 5200 police officers and 2100 support staff (Local Authority Policing Plan, 1997) police the area. The West Yorkshire Police Authority in its 1997–1998 Policing Plan listed what it saw as its priorities, which were: combating drugs misuse, increasing community safety, tackling priority crime, and creating a more effective working relationship with the public. Each of these identified priorities carries with it a range of objectives, yet in the Policing Plan none are specifically related to children and the more particular issue of child abuse. It is interesting to note that combating drugs misuse is first on the agenda and this is deemed to have been in response to an assessment of local policing priorities and needs. Those living in the community were consulted but it is hard to see how the needs of children who are potential victims of child abuse can have been served by this consultation. Young people were involved in this consultation but *how* might they openly broach the issue of child abuse as a policing issue? Child abuse is often a 'hidden' crime, not one that individuals will openly acknowledge as a feature of their more prevalent concerns.

While responding to community needs is a vital aspect of contemporary policing there is a need to be mindful that those without a significant voice, in this instance children, should also be able to rely on a prioritised position. If policing objectives are to be set in line with public opinion and political priorities, which it might be argued are a consequence of public opinion, there is a real need to ensure that child protection does not become less of a concern. In the past child protection strategies have been reactive rather than proactive; there is a need to be aware that while child protection may not appear to be high in the public priorities; statistics (Table 10.1) from the West Yorkshire, Domestic Violence and Child Protection Units testify to its continuing presence.

Table 10.1 shows a significant rise in child abuse referrals with the numbers more than doubling between 1989 and 1995. This rise was not supported by a similar rise in the total recorded crime in West Yorkshire over the same period, with the figures remaining fairly static. However, there has been a significant national increase in violent crime of 9% (Rufford, 1997). Nevertheless this is no way comparable to the more than two-fold increase in child abuse referrals.

Table 10.1:   Child abuse statistics, West Yorkshire Police 1989–1995

	1989	1990	1991	1992	1993	1994	1995
No further action	2443	3281	2879	3125	3582	4995	4711
Caution	191	266	201	188	161	178	152
Court	474	433	290	177	79	174	156
Outstanding	23	63	511	1459	1929	1891	2143
Total CPU Referrals	3131	4043	3800	4949	5751	6237	7162
Total Recorded Crime (West Yorkshire)	N/A	228080	289197	301220	299870	288890	283125

(Adapted from Policing Plan for West Yorkshire 1997–1998 and West Yorkshire Police, Child Abuse statistics, produced by the Domestic Violence and Child Protection Units 1993–1995.)

A further point to consider is that the 'clear-up' rate has fallen, with fewer individuals being prosecuted and cautioned in later years. There may be differing explanations of such changes. However, it could be optimistically argued that the overall increase in referrals is due to the visibility of the CPUs and the specialist skills and knowledge of those working with them. This visibility would provide children, parents, carers, relatives, and others with a point of contact within the police and establish a police acceptance of the discrete nature of child protection work. Additionally, the increase may be a characteristic of improved working relations with other agencies.

The reduction in 'clear-up' rates may be attributable to a change in emphasis; with the police being less single minded in their pursuit of prosecutions and more attentive to the paramountcy of the child's needs. Nevertheless, there are alternative explanations which would need to be considered, one being that the increase in cases outstanding would necessarily be reflected in a reduction in the 'clear-up' rate, therefore suggesting only cautious optimism. Another might be the considerable difficulty involved in pursuing criminal proceedings in relation to child abuse (Wattam, 1997). The increase in the number of cases outstanding may be accredited to the CPUs' inability to handle the rise in recorded incidence of child abuse. However, again a more positive interpretation may be that the rise is a consequence of increased communication and co-ordination, which all take time and additional work.

Whatever interpretation is imposed on the statistics presented it is undeniable that child abuse referrals have risen substantially and thus require a concerted and vigilant response. There is no desire to minimalise this rise; therefore, while the CPUs themselves may have had an effect on referrals, such a substantial rise is alarming. An additional worry is the reduction in 'clear-up' rates in light of the current refocusing of police work in terms of 'value for money' and performance measures. If child protection units do not perform to some kind of cost benefit criteria will they become expendable and a return be made to a more 'fragmented' response?

CHALLENGES TO THE POLICE IN CHILD PROTECTION

The challenge facing the police is one that will need to ensure that the perceivably more child-centred and co-operative climate in child protection is not pervaded by the current emphasis on 'crime-busting' objectives. While fully agreeing with the view that child abuse can be a criminal offence requiring the full punitive power of the law, there is a need not to lose sight of the interests of the child as paramount and to afford this a prioritised position. Performance measures and public opinion, while being useful tools in the quest for an efficient and viable public service, should not be allowed to set the whole agenda.

Some outcomes are essentially non-specific; arguably child protection work falls in this category. The work is highly specialised and time-consuming and it would be careless to underestimate the effects in child protection terms. While it may be too early to make any resounding judgements as to the success of inter-agency working and the role of the police in such work a cautious optimism may be permissible in relation to the effectiveness of CPUs. The notion of 'hiving off' the more caring aspects of police work is one that the police should consider carefully. It has been a long and uphill task moving toward inter-agency co-operation. The introduction of yet another agency or functionary may have detrimental effects not only in regard to the handling of the investigation of child abuse but in terms of the outcomes for children and families, which may once again result in the police being marginalised within the child protection process. Finally a further challenge would be to face up to the gendering of child protection work within the police. There is a need to provide an organisational response that is not only to the advantage of women officers but one that ensures that the primary function of CPUs, in providing a sensitive and appropriate response to child abuse, remains paramount.

REFERENCES

Anderson R, Brown J and Cambell E (1993) *Aspects of Discrimination within the Police Service in England and Wales*, Home Office Police Research Group, London.

Audit Commission (1993) *Helping with Enquiries*, Police Paper, No. 12, London, HMSO, London.

Brown J M, Maidment A and Bull R (1993) Appropriate skill–task matching or gender bias in deployment of male and female officers? *Policing and Society*, **3**: 121–136.

Butler-Sloss, Right Honourable Lord Justice (1988) *Report of the Inquiry into Child Abuse in Cleveland*, HMSO, London.

Conroy S, Fielding N and Tunstill J (1990) *Investigating Child Sexual Abuse*, Police Foundation, London.

Corby B (1993) *Child Abuse: Towards a Knowledge Base*, Open University Press, Milton Keynes, Buckingham.

Department of Health (1995) *The Challenge of Partnership in Child Protection*, HMSO, London.

Department of Health and Social Security (1974) *Non-Accidental Injury to Children*, LASSL, (74) (13), DHSS, London.

Department of Health and Social Security (1976) *Non-Accidental Injury to Children: The Police and Case Conferences*, LASSL: (76) (26), DHSS, London.

Funnelle R (1992) *Sex Discrimination in the Police Service*, PRSU Award Scheme.

Hallett C and Birchall E (1992) *Coordination and Child Protection: A Review of the Literature*, HMSO, London.

Holdaway S (1986) Police and social work relations—problems and possibilities, *British Journal of Social Work*, **16**: 137–160.

Home Office (1988) *The Investigation of Child Abuse*, Circular 52/1988, Home Office, London.

Home Office, Department of Health, Department of Education and Science, Welsh Office (1991) *Working Together Under the Children Act 1989: A Guide to the Arrangements for Inter-agency Cooperation for the Protection of Children from Abuse*, HMSO, London.

Home Office (1993) *Police Reform: A Police Service for the Twenty-First Century*, Cm 2281, HMSO, London.

Humphreys C (1996) Exploring new territory: Police organizational responses to child sexual abuse, *Child Abuse Review*, **20**: 337–344.

Jones S (1986) *Police Women and Equality*, Macmillan, Basingstoke.

Kelly L (1994) The interconnectedness of domestic violence and child abuse, in Mullender A and Morley R (eds) *Children Living with Domestic Violence*, Whiting and Birch, London.

Lloyd S and Burman M (1996) Specialist police units and the joint investigation of child abuse, *Child Abuse Review*, **5**: 4–17.

London Borough of Brent (1985) *A Child in Trust: the Report of the Panel of Inquiry into the Circumstances Surrounding the Death of Jasmine Beckford*, HMSO, London.

Loveday B (1996) Crime at the core, in Leishman F, Loveday B, Savage S P (eds) *Core Issues in Policing*, Longman, Harlow.

Mullender A and Morley R (eds) (1994) *Children Living with Domestic Violence*, Whiting and Birch, London.

NSPCC (1996) *Childhood Matters, Report of the National Commission of Inquiry into the Prevention of Child Abuse*, HMSO, London.

Otway O (1996) Social work with children and families, in Parton N (ed.) *Social Theory, Social Change and Social Work*, Routledge, London.

Parton N (1985) *The Politics of Child Abuse*, Macmillan, London.

Reiner R (1985) *The Politics of the Police*, Harvester, Brighton.

Reiner R (1992) *The Politics of the Police* (2nd edn), Harvester, Brighton.

Rufford N (1997) Sharp rise in violence tests Straw, *Sunday Times*, 10 August, 5.

Sampson A (1991) Gender issues in inter-agency relations, in Abbott P and Wallace C (eds) *Gender Power and Sexuality*, Macmillan, Basingstoke.

Saunders R, Jackson S and Thomas N (1996) Police and child protection management, *Policing and Society*, **6**: 87–100.

Scarman, Lord (1981) *The Brixton Disorders*, Report of the Inquiry, HMSO, London.

Scraton P (1985) *The State of the Police*, Pluto, London.

Thomas T (1986) *Police and Social Workers*, Gower, Aldershot.

Vizard E, Bentovim A and Tranter M (1987) Interviewing sexually abused children, *Adoption and Fostering*, **11**: 202–211.

Waterhouse L and Carnie J (1990) *Child Sexual Abuse: The Professional Challenge to Social Work and Police*, Report to Social Work Services Group, Scottish Office, Edinburgh.

Wattam C (1997) Is the criminalisation of child harm and injury in the interests of the child? *Children and Society*, **11**: 97–107.

Wedlake M (1978) A police view of the present position, in A. W. Franklin (ed.) *Child Abuse: Prediction, Prevention and Follow Up*, Churchill Livingstone, Edinburgh.

Weeks J (1997) Suffer the little children, *Police Review*, March, 20–1.

West Yorkshire Police (1985) Implementation Plan for Major Crime Support Units—Policewomen's Section, West Yorkshire Police, Wakefield.

West Yorkshire Police (1997) Local Authority Policing Plan, West Yorkshire Police, Wakefield.

IV

AN OVERVIEW OF THE RESIDENTIAL CARE SYSTEM

11

'BEING THERE': RESIDENTIAL CARE OF CHILDREN AND YOUNG PEOPLE

Christine Horrocks and Kate Karban

INTRODUCTION

The situation of children and young people in residential care has increasingly been brought to the notice of the public through the attention paid to 'scandals' and abuse, and also through the longer term consequences of care in relation to the difficulties faced by young people leaving care.

The context for this chapter is the positioning of residential care within the child care and protection systems. Within this the notion of good enough parenting for children and young people, who, for various reasons, are unable to live within their families of origin, on a permanent or temporary basis, will be explored. A key feature will be the inclusion of the views of young people, drawing on research material derived from 'leaving care' interviews recently implemented in one local authority. Notwithstanding the critique of care that will be offered, a theme throughout the chapter will be the endorsement of the value of residential care as one element in an integrated child welfare strategy. Similarly, by considering the social and historical context of residential care, our intention is to understand the pressures and constraints within which many highly motivated staff work. Underlying these issues will be a recognition of the complex dynamics that operate within organisations and institutions which reflect wider societal inequalities based on 'race', gender, heterosexuality, class and age.

The chapter begins by reviewing the current profile of children who

Children, Child Abuse and Child Protection. Placing Children Centrally, by The Violence Against Children Study Group.
© 1999 John Wiley & Sons Ltd.

are 'looked after' and may be placed in residential care. We then consider the wider context of child care policy and provision before turning to the realities of residential care and the extent to which children and young people's needs are met. This is followed by a section that will focus on the views of young people themselves in relation to themes of *freedom*, *understanding* and *being there*. The conclusion considers the notion of 'good enough' care, taking into account the views of young people previously discussed, and the current circumstances in which 'care' is delivered and some thoughts concerning the future for residential child care services are outlined.

THE PROFILE OF YOUNG PEOPLE WHO ARE LOOKED AFTER AND IN RESIDENTIAL CARE

There has been a significant decline in the numbers of children and young people who are placed in a residential setting, with currently less than 8000 living in local authority residential homes in England (Utting, 1991, 1997; Berridge, 1997). The changing profile is also one of older children being placed in residential care, where it has been estimated that 70% are over 13 years of age (Utting, 1991; Triseliotis, Borland, Hill and Lambert, 1995). Rowe, Hundleby and Garnett (1989) found that three times as many residential placements were created for adolescents as opposed to foster placements, although some young people will have experience of both foster and residential care. The emphasis on adolescence is also significant in that, while the majority of young people progress through this period of change and transition without undue difficulty (Coleman and Hendry, 1990; Rutter, 1990), those in need of social work services, in particular those who are accommodated, frequently experience a range of emotional and/or behavioural difficulties (Packman and Hall, 1995), requiring highly skilled and sensitive attention and support. The Warner Report (1992) identified that 64% of children living in local authority children's homes had serious and specific problems of emotional or behavioural disturbance. Bullock, Little and Spencer (1993) also maintain that young people placed in residential settings are often felt to be increasingly those with serious problems. Triseliotis *et al.* (1995) also found that 35% of girls as compared to 4% of boys in care had been sexually abused in the past.

At first sight the reasons for young people becoming 'looked after' are varied, including experiences of serious abuse, family conflict or an inability (or indeed an unwillingness) of families to care for them. Adolescents can also be remanded into care in court proceedings following offences, although offending behaviour as a contributory factor in bringing about intervention is a significantly higher factor for boys (58%) than girls (37%) (Triseliotis *et al.* 1995). However, there may also be a shared level of vulnerability amongst young people in care in that they have been identified as coming disproportionately from households who live in poverty and are headed by a lone parent (Bebbington and Miles, 1989).

The overall picture of the young people placed in residential settings is therefore one that suggests a high level of disadvantage and vulnerability. The question of what is necessary to ameliorate the effects of previous experience and/or abuse, as well as the provision of an appropriate setting to receive young people who have been deemed in need of care apart from their families, challenges the historical understanding of residential care as a refuge of last resort. In order to understand the notion of 'parenting' in relation to the often troubled and disadvantaged children and young people requiring care, it is necessary to consider the wider context of child care policy and frameworks within which residential care is located.

THE WIDER CONTEXT—CHILD CARE AND PROTECTION

In locating residential child care within the broader range of services for children and families, several different but interrelated themes can be identified.

The Socio-historical Perspective

In many respects residential services for children and young people continue to be viewed as an inferior alternative to foster care for those unable to live within their own families. This legacy relates to an association with the negative images of large-scale institutions, as well as more recent disturbing incidents of abuse and neglect. Added to this is a belief in the value of 'family life' and a view that the twentieth-century (Eurocentric and heterosexual) nuclear family unit is the preferred and most effective location for child-rearing, although the relative effectiveness of foster care *vis-à-vis* residential care is not unequivocal (Berridge, 1997). The gendered division of labour in residential care, with its implications for pay and status, has also been highlighted (Aymer, 1992; NISW, 1995). The prevailing ethos of masculinity within the service is discussed elsewhere in this section.

The Rights of Children and Young People and their Families within the Context of the Children Act

Within the framework of the Children Act, guidance and regulations for residential care set out the expectations placed upon local authorities and other agencies providing residential services for children. They incorporate the principle that: 'the institutional needs of the Home should never be allowed to dominate the lives of children and staff' (Department of Health, 1991: 2), and require that an individual care plan is drawn up for each child. Each establishment is required to have a statement of purpose and functions, complaints and representations procedures must also be in place and available to the child, parent or other carers. These developments have taken place in the wider context of the debate on children's rights (Franklin, 1986; Fox-Harding, 1996) and the growth of user-led initiatives such as NAYPIC and the Who Cares? Trust.

Local Authority Funding, Community Care and the Purchaser–Provider Divide

Residential child care cannot be understood outside of its location within a complex system of funding and organisational realities. Reductions in local authority funding have led to reorganisation and financial restrictions in the provision of social services. While attempts to do away with residential child care services altogether have not been implemented widely (Berridge and Cliffe, 1991), there has been a move towards fewer places in the public sector with a corresponding growth in private care. The moves towards the purchaser–provider split have also contributed to this process, leading to an emphasis on assessment, care management and quality assurance within statutory child care services and a 'devaluation of direct care provider skills' (Braye and Preston Shoot, 1995: 59).

A review of the funding of local authority social services (Schorr, 1992) concluded that social services are 'chronically' underfunded and that the priority afforded to child abuse investigations and assessments leaves fewer resources for preventive work with families. Such findings might also suggest that there are insufficient levels of funding for services for children who are 'looked after' in general, and residential care in particular.

Current Debates on Child Care and Child Protection

Evidence on the outcomes of residential child care in terms of the longer term sequelae suggests that, for a number of reasons, many young people do not have the maximum opportunity to realise their full potential. Indeed some of them are subjected to further abuse. Arguably, some young people can be seen not only to fail to benefit from the experience but also to decrease rather than increase their life chances, making it necessary to enquire into the balance between *protection*, that is accommodating young people away from their families, and the need to provide a *compensatory* experience. This is also highlighted by the low priority given to treatment *vis-à-vis* investigation and prevention (Saunders, Jackson and Thomas, 1996). Thus, the emphasis is placed on investigation at the expense of providing a more holistic service that encompasses prevention and a range of therapeutic services. Similarly, Parton (1997) comments on the tension between child welfare and child protection, where the latter is the dominant concern, relating this to the notion of accountability, and the public inquiries which have forcibly brought about changes in policy and practices. He refers to the need to 're-balance' approaches between family support and child protection in order to offer an 'integrated' child care system. If concerns are polarised between child welfare and child protection where does this leave children who are looked after, particularly those in residential care?

Residential services thus occupy an uneasy position in the overall scheme of child welfare policy. They represent a historical legacy of an undervalued but financially costly resource for local authorities under pressure to reduce their role as service providers, yet they do not feature highly in the priorities of child protection investigation and assessment. Despite this, however, the views of young people, while at times justifiably critical, also point to ways in which a high-quality residential service may be a valuable and desirable option. Before moving on to consider these, it is important to explore some of the evidence concerning the reality of residential care.

THE REALITIES OF RESIDENTIAL CARE

There are two key issues that have been highlighted in any recent discussion of residential child care. One of these concerns the series of 'scandals' relating to the physical and sexual abuse of children and young people by staff within residential settings while the other relates to the consequences of care in terms of the difficulties faced by young people on moving towards independence. Taken together it would not be surprising if there was considerable resistance to the idea of placing children in residential care and a sense that the consequences could not possibly be worse than those in which the child was currently living.

The evidence concerning the lives of young people after care is considerable and well documented. In terms of education and occupation/employment, a number of studies have demonstrated that young people who are 'looked after' achieve lower standards and qualifications in school than their counterparts (Jackson, 1989; Department of Health and OFSTED, 1995), linked to higher risk of unemployment and/or employment in low-paid manual unskilled work (Stein, 1990; Cheung and Heath, 1994; Biehal, Clayden, Stein and Wade, 1995). Young people who have been 'looked after' are expected to leave 'care' before the age of 18 but frequently fail to secure and maintain suitable accommodation, having high levels of homelessness and instability (Centrepoint, 1994; Biehal et al., 1995). There is also the question of early pregnancy which, while not necessarily problematic, requires young women, frequently as lone mothers, to take on the responsibilities of parenthood at a significantly younger age than their peers (Biehal et al., 1995).

This 'legacy of care' (Stein, 1997) results in further disadvantage for the lives of young people and is the aftermath of living in residential and or foster care as well as of pre-care experiences. In addition to the issue of 'compensating' for previous disadvantage, the abuse experienced by some young people while being 'looked after' raises equally serious and disturbing concerns.

Berridge and Brodie (1996) looked at three recent reports that focused on crises that had occurred in residential child care (Staffordshire, Ty Mawr, Leicestershire). Their analysis identified shared themes in terms of management style and unclear policy objectives as well as staffing issues and social isolation. They also point to the significance of masculinity and the effects of 'macho' forms of leadership. Others have also commented on issues of power and gender (Stein, 1992; Jones 1993; Pringle, 1993).

Such an analysis suggests that it is not sufficient to rely on an understanding of isolated incidents, poor management and/or recruitment of inappropriate staff in explaining such incidents. Instead, such crises represent one end of a continuum through which power and oppression are mediated for young people in need of care. If this is so, residential care requires a radical transformation within which the needs of young people are addressed and their voices heard and which contain genuine opportunities for development within a safe environment. Such a move will require that particular attention be paid to issues of gender and sexuality and that all aspects of residential care are scrutinised in terms of power, inequality and oppression and action taken to overturn the prevailing culture of 'care'.

An important element in shifting the reality of care is the need for staff who feel supported and confident in their ability to offer an appropriate service to young people. Evidence suggests that residential staff often feel ill-equipped to respond appropriately to the difficulties young people may experience (Hatfield, Herrington and Mahomad, 1996) and that support from field social workers and fieldwork managers is limited, as is that from child psychiatrists and psychologists.

The absence of training and support from external sources can also be seen as playing a part in causing incidents of abuse. As a result of the Utting review (1991), funding, via the Residential Child Care Initiative, has contributed to an increase in the number of qualified senior staff in residential homes but the short-term nature of the initiative has limited the possibilities for making serious inroads into attaining a predominately qualified workforce. Women continue to be underrepresented at management level while being less likely to have access to training; the opportunities for black workers are similarly limited with important consequences for young mixed race people who are over-represented in the care population.

The tangible reality of residential care for young people in terms of its outcomes and the day-to-day experience of care can therefore be seen as closely locked into wider systems of power and inequality where, at best, staff are often also unsupported and ill-equipped to carry out a difficulty task requring a high level of skill and support. At worst the inadequacy of systems to ensure safety and high-quality care increases the likelihood of abuse and maltreatment.

YOUNG PEOPLE'S VIEWS ON CARE

Listening to young people would seem the most obvious place to start when evaluating the quality of care offered to young people in residential care. We have recently been involved in an initiative to introduce Leaving Care interviews in one local authority, for young people who have been looked after, drawing on the Gulbenkein Foundation Report, *One Scandal Too Many*. Among the report's recommendations was that:

there should be an 'exit interview', at which the child or young person would be invited to comment, if s/he wished, on the placement and its successes, any problems, etc. (Gulbenkein Foundation, 1993: 208)

The emphasis in these interviews was that the local authority should increase its understanding of young people's views regarding the services provided, as well as their providing an opportunity to raise any concerns about safety and/or abuse. Many young people, whatever their placement, made reference to one or more of three fundamental concepts: 'being there', 'understanding' and 'freedom'. An important qualification to these comments is, however, the baseline expectations of young people who may set their sights low in evaluating the standards of care they receive.

The concept of 'being there' is drawn from young people's expressed need for carers to have time to listen and just be with the young person:

R ... [children's home] helped me most. Staff were always there when you needed someone to talk to. Didn't just send you to your room when anything was wrong [all the others used to] they'd sit you down and talk to you.

[The] children's home was the best because they always seemed to be there for me and like when I didn't go to school they didn't bawl at me, they just sat me down and talked about it. I enjoyed every minute of being at there it was just a bit far away from home for me. It were like a group of us going through the same thing—made it feel a lot better knowing it weren't just me.

The necessity to have someone there when you need them feeds into the 'understanding' that young people valued; it would be hard to conceive of understanding without having the time to talk and be with young people and an acceptance of the young person's own unique situation/biography:

Yes, my second foster parents were OK. They understood your problems, would talk things through with them. They were kind, they didn't hit me. They were a lot better than I thought they would be.

The Children's Home [D ...] was the best. They didn't pressurise you into doing something you didn't want to do—like trying to be good at exams or comparing me to other children.

The last issue that seemed to be important, regardless of the type of placement, was a degree of freedom. The experiences of these young people relate to the period of adolescence when a devolved level of freedom is to be expected and necessary if young people are to develop the skills they require if they are successfully to make the transition from 'care':

> In B . . . [community home] you could cook—staff trusted you and if you said I need this and want to make toast and scrambled eggs they'd leave you to cook your own.

> She [foster parent] made me feel more safe, she were old but she knew more things, let me have me own life—she used to go to local every night and I stopped in at home by myself—I enjoyed it. Used to stop in if I had the chance.

Comments made by young people regarding residential care raised issues concerning freedom and control. Three young people expressed views that raise real alarm bells in relation to the 'corrupting' influence of some residential placements:

> B . . . [community residential home] was OK because I could do what I wanted to, basically anything.

> Foster parents were better than R . . . [community residential home] because I didn't fit in. I don't steal or do drugs and they did and I wouldn't go with them so there was always trouble.

> D . . . [community residential home] and my last foster parents helped most.

> AU . . . [assessment unit] was bad—it was full of drug users an car thieves an I got into these while I was there because of peer pressure an because I felt like an outsider [originally from another town].

These young people's accounts clearly demonstrate how problems can develop. One young person recognises the lack of control, another feels the pressure to become involved and resists—with 'trouble' being the result. Finally we are confronted with the consequences where a young person succumbs to such pressure. Further contact told of persistent offending which continued until the birth of her first child.

From these brief observations it can be discerned that the needs and experiences of young people in residential care can differ markedly. While one young person finds the experience to be that of understanding and affinity, another highlights the distinct dangers that are often believed to prevail within the residential sector. Such accounts raise the issue of ensuring quality services for young people in residential care and the further consideration of how this might be achieved. A crucial aspect of these views is that residential care is not dismissed *per se*, a point also made by Utting, who found that many young people endorsed the advantages and benefits of life in a residential home as compared with foster care (Utting, 1991: 15).

WHAT IS 'GOOD ENOUGH' CARE?

What then represents the notion of good enough care for this group of sometimes troubled and troublesome young people? To what extent, if at all, can their needs be met in residential settings? These are the questions that need to be addressed if there is to be a future for quality residential child care services.

As we have already suggested, there is often a considerable gap between what is needed and what is on offer. Any way forward needs to take into account the views of young people, the needs of staff, and the location of residential services within the spectrum of child care services overall, and can be considered through three levels of intervention.

At the first level we need to address the needs of young people as expressed by themselves. From the material already referred to, it is possible to see their needs as not unrepresentative of any group of young people seeking a clear and responsive framework of support and care as they move towards adulthood, summed up by the concepts of 'being there', 'understanding' and 'freedom'. As many parents will understand, this is not always easy and requires a flexible and sensitive response as a threshold for standards of care.

It is also vital to consider a second level, that of the particular needs of young people who are 'looked after', many of whom are already disadvantaged and distressed by their experiences before entering care. This raises the issue of a compensatory experience and the need to provide appropriate treatment and/or support for young people to assist with any difficulties they might be experiencing relating to past experiences of abuse or distress. In terms of 'state parenting' there is clearly an expectation that resources and expertise should be mobilised to ease distress and improve future life chances. The underlying principle here is again the same as that of any *reasonable parent* who, where necessary, 'goes beyond what would normally be done' (Parker, Ward, Jackson *et al.*, 1991: 63).

Third, it is important that the care experience itself offers a positive opportunity for development rather than creating further disadvantage. The question of stigma and prejudice towards young people in residential care must be confronted and safeguards against further abuse must be in place; at the same time it is important to consider the effect of residential care on a young person's sense of self-esteem and self-efficacy, and steps must be taken to provide positive and validating experiences.

In considering these three levels it is clear that experience of parenting and 'common-sense' views of what is required in looking after young people, while helpful in providing a benchmark in terms of commitment, are insufficient criteria for staff recruitment and training. The historical legacy of residential child care work as an extension of parenting seriously downgrades (and feminises) the skills required in providing high-quality compensatory care, which is then reflected in the status, pay and working conditions of the staff concerned.

The provision of high-quality care requires a high level of skill and commitment to meet the particular needs of this group of young people. It is essential that staff are well supported and equipped to offer a compensatory experience within a safe living environment. In particular, skills and experience of working with young people who have a history of disadvantage, together with a willingness to engage with young people in building confidence and participation, are required. Managing the tension between control and safety is an essential element within this approach and, from the comments above, one which, handled respectfully, is welcomed by the young people themselves. In this respect the comments here are echoed in the words of the Utting report (1997) where young people and others commented on the importance of the delicate 'balancing judgement' required (Utting, 1997: 121).

Only if safety can be guaranteed and safeguards are in place to prevent abuse can the other essential ingredient of care and welfare be provided; that is, the need to promote the development of young people in residential care. This relates closely to the concepts of 'understanding' and 'being there' which were earlier identified with regard to the views of the young people contained within the 'leaving care' interviews.

The delivery of such a service depends fundamentally on the valency of residential care within child welfare services and, related to this, the priority and resourcing made available. Within the current climate this is, in itself, a difficult objective, where a vicious circle is perpetuated through the value accorded to residential services, the resources available for staff support and training and the incentives for highly skilled and motivated staff to enter and remain within the sector, a circle also infused with societal inequalities and oppression in terms of race, gender and sexuality. This circle can only be broken if a direct challenge is made to existing power structures and values from a perspective that places the needs of young people at the heart of service planning and delivery.

REFERENCES

Aymer C (1992) Women in residential work: Dilemmas and ambiguities, in Langan M and Day L (eds) *Women, Oppression and Social Work, Issues in Anti-Discriminatory Practice*, Routledge, London.

Bebbington A and Miles J (1989) The background of children who enter local authority care, *British Journal of Social Work*, **19**: 349–368.

Berridge D (1997) *Foster Care—A Research Review*, The Stationery Office, London.

Berridge D and Brodie I (1996) Residential child care in England and Wales, the Inquiries and after, in Hill M and Aldgate J (eds) *Child Welfare Services, Developments in Law, Policy, Practice and Research*, Jessica Kingsley, London.

Berridge D and Cliffe D (1991) *Closing Children's Homes, an End to Residential Care?* National Children's Bureau, London.

Biehal N, Clayden J, Stein M and Wade J (1995) *Moving On, Young People and Leaving Care Schemes*, HMSO, London.

Braye S and Preston-Shoot M (1995) *Empowering Practice in Social Care*, Open University Press, Milton Keynes, Buckingham.

Bullock R, Little M and Spencer M (1993) *Residential Care for Children: A Review of the Research*, HMSO, London.

Centrepoint (1994) *A Word From The Street*, Community Care, Reed Business Publishing, London.

Cheung S Y and Heath A (1994) After care: The education and occupation of adults who have been in care, *Oxford Review of Education*, **20**: 361–374.

Coleman J C and Hendry L (1990) *The Nature of Adolescence*, Routledge/Chapman and Hall, London.

Department of Health (1991) *The Children Act 1989: Guidance and Regulations, Vol. 4, Residential Care*, HMSO, London.

Department of Health Social Services Inspectorate and Office for Standards in Education (1995) *The Education of Children Who Are Looked After by Local Authorities*, DOH and OFSTED, London.

Fox-Harding L (1996) Recent developments in 'children's right': Liberation for whom? *Child and Family Social Work*, **1**: 141–150.

Franklin B (1986) *The Rights of Children*, Blackwell, Oxford.

Gulbenkian Foundation (1993) *One Scandal Too Many . . . the case for comprehensive protection for children in all settings*, Calouste Gulbenkian Foundation, London.

Hatfield B, Herrington R and Mahomad H (1996) Staff looking after children in local authority residential units, *Journal of Adolescence*, **19**: 127–139.

Jackson S (1989) Residential care and education, *Children and Society* **4**: 335–350.

Jones J (1993) Child abuse: Developing a framework for understanding power relationships in practice, in Ferguson H, Gilligan R and Torode R (eds) *Surviving Childhood Adversity, Issues for Policy and Practice*, Routledge, London.

National Institute for Social Work, NISW (1995) *Working in the Social Services*, National Institute for Social Work Research Unit, London.

Packman J and Hall C (1995) *Draft Report on the Implementation of Section 20 of the Children Act, 1989*, Dartington Social Research Unit, Dartington.

Parker R, Ward H, Jackson S, Aldgate J and Wedge P (1991) *Assessing Outcomes in Child Care*, HMSO, London.

Parton N (ed.) (1997) *Child Protection and Family Support*, Routledge, London.

Pringle K (1993) Child sexual abuse perpetrated by welfare personnel and the problem of men, *Critical Social Policy*, **36**: 4–20.

Rowe J, Hundleby M and Garnett L (1989) *Child Care Now*, British Agencies for Adoption and Fostering, London.

Rutter M (1990) Changing patterns of psychiatric disorders during adolescence, in Bancroft J and Reinisch D M (eds) *Adolescence and Puberty*, Oxford University Press, New York.

Saunders R, Jackson S and Thomas N (1996) The balance of prevention, investigation and treatment in the management of child protection services, *Child Abuse and Neglect*, **20**: 899–907.

Schorr A (1992) *The Personal Social Services: An Outside View*, Joseph Rowntree Foundation, York.

Stein M (1990) *Living Out Of Care*, Barnardo's, Barkingside, Essex.

Stein M (1992) *The Abuses and Uses of Residential Child Care*, Conference Paper: Surviving Childhood Adversity, Trinity College, Dublin.

Stein M (1997) *What Works in Leaving Care?* Barnardo's, Barkingside, Essex.

Triseliotis J, Borland M, Hill M and Lambert L (1995) *Teenagers and the Social Work Services*, HMSO, London.

Utting W (1991) *Children in the Public Care*, HMSO, London.

Utting W (1997) *People Like Us: The Report of the Review of the Safeguards for Children Living Away from Home*, The Stationery Office, London.

Warner N (1992) *Choosing with Care—The Report of the Committee of Inquiry into the Selection, Development and Management of Staff in Children's Homes*, HMSO, London.

12

SEXUALITY, SEXUAL ABUSE AND CHILDREN'S HOMES—OPPRESSION OR PROTECTION?

Lorraine Green and Wendy Parkin

INTRODUCTION

The absence of research and theorising around residential care and issues of sexuality and sexual abuse has been noted by a number of American and English commentators (White, 1987; Parkin, 1989; Bloom, 1992; Bullock, Little and Milham, 1993). What literature exists consists mostly of inquiry reports (e.g. Warner, 1992), academic analyses of inquiry reports (Brannan, Jones and Murch, 1993; Pringle, 1993) and isolated small-scale research focused on certain aspects of sexuality (McMillen, 1991; Jesson, 1993).

Official inquiries following the aftermath of scandals regarding workers' sexual and physical abuse of children have been conducted within a 'judicial' framework and have tended to look at concrete, material issues such as lack of training, poor recruitment and management practices, and the care culture, subsequently suggesting improved general training and more resources as the solution (Warner, 1992; Berridge and Brodie, 1996). These inquiries have, however, neglected to consider issues of gender (Pringle, 1993) and how they may contribute to the sexual abuse of children by workers or peers. Small-scale research has tended to look at compartmentalised, selective aspects of sexuality, such as prostitution (Jesson, 1993; O'Neill, 1994, 1995) and same-sex sexual behaviour (McMillen, 1991), and has mainly focused on the effects of punitive staff responses.

This chapter looks more widely than the previous literature at how

Children, Child Abuse and Child Protection. Placing Children Centrally, by The Violence Against Children Study Group.
© 1999 John Wiley & Sons Ltd.

sexuality and sexual abuse issues are linked. It also considers the effects of the children's pasts and the immediate physical environment, having particular ramifications within residential settings. The word sexuality is also used to describe not only the occurrence of specific behaviours perceived to be sexual but also attitudes, feelings and beliefs around these. This chapter is therefore concerned with looking at how sexual behaviour is construed and constructed as well as how it may be enacted within this specific context. The word children will be used to describe both the children and the young people researched as the children's ages ranged from 8 to 17 with the majority being between 13 and 16. The word children will also be used preferentially because, although there are many different words used to describe older children, such as adolescents, young people, youth, these words are often used in an unqualified and *ad hoc* manner and are rarely defined or easy to define clearly (Coleman, 1993).

The findings in this chapter emanate from qualitative research conducted between 1994 and 1996. This involved ethnographic fieldwork in two children's homes situated in different local authorities, and a large number of non-ethnographic interviews. The findings of this research are also reported in terms of predominant, majority themes and there is no numerical analysis or statistical representation contained within the text.

The ethnographic studies encompassed participant observation of staff and children, formal interviews, and analysis of agency documents such as logbooks and care plans. Most of the interviews conducted within the ethnographies were with staff and social workers. Formally interviewing the children was dropped because they often seemed to give inaccurate accounts in formal interviews if their accounts were cross-triangulated (Robson, 1993) with a range of other ethnographic information, such as that gained from observation, from informal conversation with them and their peers, and from information from staff and logbooks. This may have been because the children associated the notion of interviews with 'oppressive' police and child protection interviews. These seemingly inaccurate accounts may also link with the hypothesis that children are more 'moralistic' about themselves and less so regarding their peers when being interviewed about sexual behaviour (Moore and Rosenthal, 1993).

In addition, a wide range of non-ethnographic interviews with external/internal managers, residential and other agency workers and ex-residents was also conducted. These were one-off interviews with previously unknown residents who had no connection with the ethnographic settings. Of the non-ethnographic residential respondents the majority of residential workers were assessed via contact with social work students from three different universities. The ex-residents were contacted via voluntary organisations and social services contacts.

Overall, 103 interviews, including both ethnographic and non-ethnographic, took place. Because a minority of the respondents were interviewed in small groups or couples, the number of respondents interviewed totalled 110. Of these, 65 were residential or ex-residential workers and managers, 5 were external managers, 7 were social workers, 9 were children in care, 15 were ex-residents and 9 constituted 'other' personnel. These 'other' respondents did not fit into any of the above categories but had extensive relevant experience of, or knowledge about, residents or ex-residents. They included HIV workers who had conducted sexuality work with children in homes, and workers with prostitutes and rent boys, many of whom had care backgrounds. The majority of these 'other' respondents were accessed via snowball sampling.

Data were accessed from over 100 settings and over 15 local authorities and voluntary organisations regarding contemporary and past experiences. The data utilised here are post the 1989 Children Act unless otherwise stated. The majority of settings were provided by local authorities.

Initially the young people's, residential staff's and external managers' sexual behaviour, or behaviour relating to sexuality, will be illustrated in terms of dominant themes. These themes will demonstrate the socially constructed nature of both gender and childhood and the pervasive effect these social constructions have on sexual beliefs and behaviour. They will then be theoretically located in terms of other influences including the institutionalised nature of the settings, compounded by seemingly asexualised and agendered organisational responses (Hearn and Parkin, 1987, 1995; Hearn, Sheppard, Tancred Sheriff and Burrell, 1989) and public/private dichotomies (Pateman, 1989).

THE CHILDREN'S SEXUAL KNOWLEDGE, ATTITUDES AND BEHAVIOUR

As regards the children's sexual knowledge this was often extremely poor in relation to both the mechanics of sex and sexually transmitted diseases and pregnancy:

> I think [the children] appear to be knowledgeable but they're not. They know all the sexual terminology and the slang and the sexual practices.

And they will have watched porn videos and will almost invariably have had sex. (residential worker)

The boys had no knowledge at all about contraception. The girls knew a bit more but not much. The boys knew about condoms but hardly any of them knew how to put one on right. They didn't know anything about sexually transmitted diseases and how you could catch them. Their role according to the knowledge they had was simply around fucking and babies and spunk. That was their vocabulary and it was really quite frightening. (HIV/AIDS worker)

This resulted in the potential for, and the actuality of contracting, sexually transmitted diseases as well as unwanted pregnancies.

Many of the young people also possessed sexist and homophobic gendered attitudes towards sexuality. This would frequently result in young men seeing their female peers as inferior and as objectified conquests:

Sex was absolutely nothing to do with feelings, love and emotions. It was something that made me feel good, my thing . . . the conquest was probably the most important thing looking back. The lads used to compare notes about how far we'd got with particular people, you just went from one to another. (male ex-resident)

The lads were generally really nasty about the girls they went with and used to say things to each other like 'fucking hell why you going out with her, she's a real dog, she wears glasses'. (residential worker)

Conversely, the young women, although often engaging in multiple sexual contacts, would be looking for love and a steady male partner via these sexual experiences. Because of this they often would excuse, condone or even exacerbate male sexual and physical exploitation of their female peers, thus justifying the sexual double standard. The following is an extract from a conversation between the researcher and a 15-year-old female resident:

She's just a slag, her, sleeping with anybody and it ain't fucking on sleeping with Rita's boyfriend. So we had to sort her out.
(Q)   What about Jim, nobody forced him to have sex with her?
(A)   You can't blame the boys, if it's offered to them on a plate they'll take it won't they?

Many of the young women also traded in sex for either physical affection or material commodities but because of fear of gaining a 'bad' sexual reputation they would rarely personally admit this. This following extract is derived from an interview between the researcher and a male ex-resident:

> One young girl had been sexually abused. She'd lost her little finger because she wouldn't give her stepfather a blow job and he'd chopped it off. I became very attracted to her physically and she was extremely sexually learned. She used to say—I'll give you a blow job for a packet of fags and I don't think I ever refused.
> (Q) Did she get anything out of sex with you?
> (A) Yes because of her fags.
> (Q) Did she get anything else out of it?
> (A) No not at all.

The females were also often wary of carrying or using contraception for fear they would be labelled 'slags' who had pre-empted a sexual encounter. They therefore often succumbed to male advances involving unprotected sex. These findings relate closely to school-based studies of working-class young women and the power the label 'slag' has in curtailing and dictating their behaviour (e.g., Lees, 1993).

The children's harassment of males they perceived as 'queers' was also linked to notions of gender and not always to actual sexual behaviour or a homosexual identity. The male residents were more virulently homophobic than the females but were less likely to be prepared to talk about, or admit, this during discussion:

> If a boy was effeminate, if he had a high voice, if he didn't like rough and tumble, if he didn't kind of associate with the girls, the lads would say he's queer without exploring with him whether he was or whether he wasn't. It was just like a labelling thing. (residential manager)

The following extract is from a conversation between a 19-year-old female ex-resident and the researcher:

> One lad turned gay in care because he didn't really like girls and then he started selling himself. (ex-resident)
> (Q) What did you and the other kids think about him?
> (A) Don't know.
> (Q) Did you think him being gay was all right or not?
> (A) Thought it was all right.
> (Q) Did the lads in care think it was all right?
> (A) No, they spat at him, brayed him and beat him up and cig burned his arse.

Because of the lack of affection both the young men and the young women received in these settings (discussed in more detail in the section on institutionalisation below) sexual needs would often become blurred and undifferentiated from other needs and 'quick fix' sex would thus be used to try and fulfil other needs:

You never knew who was sleeping with who and I did it because it were
going on, as simple as that. It was all I had to give or thought I had to
give at the time. I think a lot of kids did it for that because they needed
somebody, whether it was for five minutes or the whole night ... and
that was the only way we had with each other. (female ex-resident)

Both the males and females were also at risk from potential abuse from
either outsiders or exploitative workers, because of their desire for
affection and the fact that their main contacts were limited to people
within the homes or to members of outside, marginalised, criminal
subcultures such as prostitutes, pimps and drug dealers.

A lot of it's by force because the pimps black or white make you think
they love you. Then they force you into prostitution and then you've got
no choice and you can't get out. (female ex-resident)

The following is an excerpt from an interview between the researcher
and a residential worker:

(Q)   What do the girls see prostitution as?
(A)   He wouldn't do it if he didn't love me. It's because he thinks
      I'm so special that he lets me do it with other people, and it's
      only because he loves me that he hits me. And I find it really
      hard because twelve months earlier I've had the same bloke tell a
      different girl the same thing.

There was also a lot of peer pressure to become involved in
prostitution:

A lot of kids get into it because of peer pressure, lots of people are doing
it and tell you it's alright, and because of a flat and all the things you get.
And care messes you up. (ex-resident)

The research provided accounts of paedophile workers who would
often attempt to get the children to consent to sexual activities through
grooming tactics that involved material rewards and affection, and
through terrorisation techniques. The two residential workers cited
below are both talking about paedophile workers who have since been
prosecuted:

He had certain boys that were his little favourites and he used to get them
expensive presents but at the same time if the boys had not pleased him
he would denigrate them ... I once went abseiling with him and he'd
give them hugs when they had abseiled down a big rock but then he
would tell them to go back up there. And they used to say 'oh no' and
then he'd turn nasty with them. He was playing with the kids on the

rope and they were quite high up. I said 'don't do that' and I was terrified for them. And he was saying 'it'll be alright, it'll teach them who's boss'.

This kid told me how the manager used to run the unit when he had been there before by waking kids up, keeping them awake all night and making them sit in front of a door, freezing cold, with just their boxer shorts on.

This potential for abuse was compounded by the fact that many residents had been previously sexually abused within their families, and they either could not differentiate between abusive and non-abusive sexual behaviour, or they accepted fleeting sexual encounters because that was the only way they knew of procuring affection.

The following is an extract from an interview with a 15-year-old female resident:

> I didn't really go out with lads before but with being abused and stuff I started to sleep around.
>
> (Q) Are you saying you being abused had something to do with you sleeping around?
>
> (A) Yeah, I thought it was right. And because my parents and no one else had ever loved me that was my only way of showing love.

The young people's vulnerability and low self-esteem were also exacerbated by their past experience of the care system which had involved stigmatisation, objectification and multiple moves to different settings with little consultation or participation.

> I've been in care for two and a half years and not once has anyone suggested I have any say in where I go to live. They've moved me about all over the place. And kids in care just get treated like objects and kicked from pillar to post and back again. And then they just move us somewhere else where they can forget about us for six to eight months. (female resident, 15)

STAFF ATTITUDES AND RESPONSES

The grassroots residential workers had little support, training, or guidelines to help them deal with sexuality issues. The only clear but often informally instituted guideline in most homes was that sex was prohibited within the building. Staff responses to sexuality were therefore in the main dictated by ignorance, fear, embarrassment and the staff's own moral values, including their views around gender and sexuality.

> Mary had make-up on and last summer we were going out. And she just walked out of the bedroom and Mark [staff] looked at her and said 'where do you think you're going—the red light district?' And he wasn't joking he was being serious. And before when I've been dressed up he's just grunted at me and said I look cheap. (resident, 17)

> I hear them [the other staff] using derogatory slang like 'pouf'—nonchalantly in conversation like they aren't even aware they are saying it and it's not a good impression to give children—it's like saying the word's acceptable. Also with this project we've worked with there was supposed to be some lesbians working in it and a lot of the older members of staff would say 'fucking lesbians corrupting our girls'. (female residential worker)

Staff who disclosed they had been sexually abused as children, particularly those who had received no counselling for this, were also observed to be less likely to be able to respond to the needs of children with sexual abuse histories.

The most common staff response to sexuality issues was denial and invisibilisation:

> I don't think children's homes deal with sexuality. They just push it to one side and they don't do anything about abuse at all. With regard to getting to know about sexuality you have to find out yourself and all they tend to do about things like prostitution is to tell you not to do it again and make you feel dirty and try and watch you. (ex-resident, 17)

> The staff I saw did not seem to respond to the children's sexual behaviour at all. It was as if they had put blinkers on and were saying this is not happening. (residential worker)

Many staff were also punitive with regard to preventing or stopping sexual activity occurring in the building and rarely did any discussion around sexuality or relationships accompany the physical separation of children engaged in sexual activities. When staff did respond to sexuality issues, they frequently did so in a reactive, technical and gendered manner which tended to implicate only females.

> Issues of sexuality were mainly that you didn't do it on the premises. There would be advice of sorts in terms of contraception and family planning and staff would go with the young people down to the family planning clinic. But it was always female staff with girls, boys never got sent down or asked to go. (residential worker)

Men often both saw themselves and were seen by women as not having any responsibility for dealing with sexuality issues, which they conceptualised as a purely female phenomenon, as illustrated by the following extract from an interview with a male residential worker:

(Q) If you talked about various children their sexuality must have cropped up at some time?

(A) Certainly female sexuality was not something I was ever involved in. I wouldn't have expected to be involved. It was handled by the female staff and seen as women's business.

This situation not only resulted in a failure to challenge the sexist and misogynistic behaviour of many male residents and some male workers, it also obscured the fact that young males as well as females could be subject to sexual victimisation.

The lack of male worker involvement in sexuality issues was further exacerbated by a commonly voiced male fear surrounding potential fictitious allegations of abuse from female residents, although such allegations were extremely rare. Organisational guidelines also often stipulated this:

One night after all the other staff had gone home, unbeknownst to me one of the girls got drunk and I was told she was ill in the toilet. So I went in there and she looked as if she was unconscious . . . and she only had this really flimsy top on and bed shorts on. I thought I can't leave her there but if I touch her I might be in bother. And I know it's not very fair but I had to knock two of the other girls up in the early hours of the morning and ask them to carry her to bed. (male residential worker)

Staff also tended to use euphemisms such as 'be careful' when talking to the children about sexuality, which were sometimes misunderstood. Also the language staff used to converse in about sexuality was often different from that used by the children and hence misinterpreted by them. An example occurred when one of the young females who was taking the contraceptive pill had a stomach bug which could have reduced its effectiveness. The staff member she was talking to explained this and advised her to use a sheath. The only problem was that she did not know what a sheath was and subsequently asked the researcher.

Grassroots staff were also influenced by the wider social con-struction and naturalisation of childhood (Aries, 1962) and children's sexuality (Evans, 1994). Children have been increasingly socially represented as being at either end of a dichotomous pole and con-structed as either 'little angels' or 'little devils' (Warner, 1994). They have been seen as innocents needing to be protected from evil and corruption, yet at the same time as inherently corruptible and cor-rupting in themselves (Evans, 1994). Therefore many staff in resi-dential care felt that discussing sexuality would lead to a rampant and uncontrollable sexuality being unleashed in the children, for which they would subsequently bear the blame, and thus they avoided dealing with sexual issues. They would also justify not talking to younger children about sexuality on the lines that they would be seen as corrupting them and that they were too young to be given the information.

MANAGERIALISM AND SEXUALITY

> It's just this big hidden area. If you can imagine social services as this big pan, there's renting and prostitution and all that sort of thing in there. And [the managers] just try and keep it at the bottom so nobody can see it, but occasionally it pops up and they push it back down. If we were prepared to use education and therapeutic intervention we could maybe move it from the bottom of the pan to the top and then stop it . . . But they won't do it because of politics and fear the papers would get hold of it and know they had a problem. (HIV/AIDS manager)

Managerially, little attention was formally paid to sexuality issues within these homes. Policies, guidelines, directives and training around sexuality were a rarity within most organisations researched. Where policies did exist, they were either not known about by residential staff, or were contradictory, ambiguous or inoperable. Similarly, what little training around sexuality and sexual abuse issues was offered to residential workers was piecemeal, optional and rarely geared to the needs of the job, for example generalised HIV and AIDS training.

In terms of informal managerial intervention there were initial attempts to deny the existence of sexuality or, reactively, to hide and obscure it. Pregnant teenagers would be moved into their own accommodation as a way of denying that pregnancy occurred whilst in care. Young females or males involved in prostitution would often be incarcerated in secure units or just moved to another setting with little or no therapeutic intervention. Teenagers approaching leaving care, who were involved in prostitution, would often be left by staff to their own devices, as they could soon be placed in their own accommodation.

Managerial intervention, like the children's and staff's behaviour, was also informed by an often covert and unacknowledged gender subtext. This was visible when the rationale for condoning lack of male involvement in sexuality issues was analysed.

> We used to have this checklist of things you would tell the workers not to do. Men not going into the girls' rooms was one and another one was not going into a car with a resident on your own . . . the main reason given to me by senior male managers eight years ago was because if a man was accused of something it might ruin his career. But the fact that

women might be accused of things or might be raped by a 17-year-old male resident didn't enter into it. (external female manager)

Managerial practices, however, extended further than denying the sexual needs and activities of teenagers in residential care through a lack of formal agenda setting and through informal minimisation and concealment processes. Often the research findings mirrored the findings of the inquiries in that they showed managers had a tendency to cover up and fail to properly investigate instances of sexual exploitation and abuse. Some workers talked about making complaints to management of child sexual abuse by workers or others. Many of these complaints were subsequently ignored or minimised, despite the existence of internal complaints procedures.

A guy who had done temping in residential care spoke to the newspapers about the girls in one home being picked up by their pimps at 9 a.m. and dropped back at the children's home early in the morning. Now social services say they have solved the problem but they haven't, they've just moved the girls out to another area. (HIV/AIDS worker)

There were two occasions I put in a complaint whilst I was working there but they was totally ignored. (residential worker)

The police told me the director had been really sly and had tried to quash all the complaints without any adverse publicity. (residential worker)

Other staff spoke of managers doing minimal investigations in order to avoid paying out large amounts of financial compensation.

There was one bloke who was sexually abusing kids in his care and there was a lot of kids. What [the managers] could have done was a massive backtracking investigation to check every person who had been in that person's care but they didn't do that because they could have had 50 kids claiming criminal compensation from the authority. (HIV/AIDS manager)

Although not all senior managers neglected issues of sexual abuse and exploitation, cover-ups, whitewashes and minimisation were frequent occurrences. This inability or unpreparedness of managers to deal adequately with sexuality and sexual abuse issues appeared to be linked to the perceived need to prevent scandals, protect organisational reputations and careers, and save money. These, in turn, were linked to the denial of the possibility of sexuality occurring within the public realm of organisations (Hearn and Parkin, 1987, 1995) and the masculine and linear goal orientation of the public sphere (Lupton, 1992; Vanstone, 1995).

SITUATING THE CONTEXT: CHILDREN'S HOMES AS TOTAL INSTITUTIONS?

Many residential homes are becoming increasingly smaller, with homes accommodating 10 or fewer children being seen as desirable (Langan and Day, 1992). Many are also geographically located within, rather than segregated from, local communities. Correspondingly it has been suggested that institutionalisation or 'total institutions' (Goffman, 1961) are no longer useful concepts to apply to children's homes (Berridge, 1994; the Bonnington Report, 1984; Berridge and Brodie, 1998).

Although Goffman's work on 'total institutions' was concerned primarily with large, isolated asylums and prisons operating in America in the 1950s and 1960s it does, however, appear to still be highly relevant to contemporary children's homes (see also Blyth and Cooper, Chapter 8 in this volume, regarding its relevance to schools) and to how sexuality is perceived, enacted and responded to by staff and residents within these settings. Goffman also employs an 'ideal type' typology to analyse total institutions, involving a loose constellation of features. This means that not every single feature identified by Goffman needs to be evident to posit a setting as a 'total institution'.

Although physically located within communities, unlike Goffman's institutions, many children's homes were not integrated within the communities in terms of being a part of that community. Therefore Goffman's collapse of normally geographically differentiated domains of the family, work or education, and leisure, into one domain was evident. Isolation, both in terms of links with the community and organisationally, was therefore a common finding. Children had few links with other people in the community other than marginalised sub-groups such as drug users, prostitutes or other children in care. School attendance was rare, confirming other research findings (for a review see Blyth and Jessop, in press). Contact with families was sporadic and sometimes non-existent and contact and quality of relationships with social workers varied considerably. The young people talked about 'living in a goldfish bowl' or a 'world within a world' where they were cut off from wider society, and staff talked about having few links with the wider organisation.

The settings were still overwhelmingly concerned with notions of containment rather than care and development. Staff and social workers referred to children's homes as 'dumping grounds' characterised by the often mentioned staff colloquialism of 'heads for beds'. In many authorities staff reported that the only obligatory training course was a control and restraint one, typifying the notion of containment. In terms of managerial action, staff talked about external managers implicitly condoning abusive regimes.

> I believe the managers are only concerned with there being as little trouble as possible in their units. The first unit I worked in was abusive and the manager used 'pindown' type methods. The kids were so petrified they either didn't put a foot wrong or they did a runner. In other units the kids would be breaking windows and stuff. So because our unit was costing less money and appeared to have fewer problems it became the role model for the other units. Noises were being made about how it was run but they were swept under the carpet. (residential worker)

Units were disproportionately characterised by an emphasis on control and surveillance. This could be physical through locks on doors, cupboards and fridges, or frequently used restraint practices, or psychological, through regular scrutiny and lack of privacy. Many children spoke of being under continual scrutiny with all their movements and actions being noted in logbooks. In one home the night worker spoke of children's bedrooms being checked by entering them every hour. Managers spoke of homes being good or bad for surveillance purposes.

The homes were also often regimented and rigid, treating children 'uniformly' as Goffman described, through, for example, the majority of children's homes having fixed mealtimes and lack of choice or options for food. In some homes all children would be punished, for example by switching off the television, for the misdemeanour of one child. More subtly there would frequently be removal of responsibilities, with repeated examples from staff and residents of the lack of preparation for independence, as this would interfere with the regimented routine.

There was also observation and reporting of separate and divisive staff/children's cultures as outlined by Goffman. Negative views of residents by staff were reinforced by children's files containing many negative comments which could be described as 'discreditable facts'. The behaviour of the children was frequently described as 'disturbed', 'inherent' or as 'individual deviance' rather than as being at least partially attributable to these divisive cultures. In one instance when children kicked at doors when locked in a room for a substantial period the behaviour was perceived at 'naughtiness' rather than a result of the situation.

The children also had a culture which perceived staff as punitive and controlling and in which they developed their own forms of resistance, space and privacy as well as a form of hierarchy known as the 'top dog' system. This involved one or a small number of children exercising considerable power over the other children and some staff via use of physical and psychological manipulatory and intimidatory techniques. Often, as well as the 'top dog' system, a reverse child counter-culture existed where rejection of societal and institutional norms, criminality, excessive drink and drug use and colonisation outwards towards marginalised and stigmatised community groups was the norm. Although this culture involved much antagonism towards staff, it was in many ways also abusive, as children still abused each other sexually, psychologically and physically. Children not conforming would be likely to be subjected to punitive strategies and exclusion from the group and ex-residents talked of a 'dog eat dog' or 'pack mentality' pervading.

Although, in Goffman's view, there is little penetration between the two cultures, there is evidence from this research and the Castle Hill enquiry (Brannon, Jones and Murch, 1993) of the way the 'top dog' system could be used by staff in order to abuse kids by giving them privileges and persuading them to prime and groom other children for sexual abuse. Staff would also use the 'top dog' system to use children to exercise control over other children:

> If you wanted to nip out for a fag you would say to the top dog 'can you keep an eye on the others?' I had no idea at the time of the threat or intimidation I was putting them under. (ex-residential worker)

Institutionalised practices including the 'top dog' system could also be strengthened or further abused by predominantly male paedophile workers within the settings, who could prey on and exacerbate the isolation of the settings and the children's need for attention and affection to groom them for sexual abuse. Paedophiles in positions of hierarchical, organisational power also sometimes terrorised, humiliated and threatened non-abusive staff with loss of their jobs if they complained. The following worker and the children in the home were unrelentingly terrorised by the unit manager but it was only in retrospect that the worker discovered the manager had also been sexually abusing the children:

> When I started standing up for my rights and the way he treated the kids he kept on saying things like I wasn't pulling my weight in the group and it was him and his clique onto me and they kept on saying I was aggressive. And they had me doing jobs like cleaning out the gutter and picking up litter and making me hoover the house four or five times a day ... Another worker who complained, he made

derogatory sexual remarks to and told all the other workers about an affair he had found out he was having with a female member of staff. (residential worker)

The link between institutionalisation and sexuality has represented a neglected issue in Goffman's analysis as well as later modifications to parts of his analysis (e.g. Cohen and Taylor, 1971; Prior, 1995). However, Wardhaugh and Wilding (1993) and Crossmaker (1991) show how institutionalisation in a range of residential settings can contribute to abusive regimes which include sexual abuse.

In this particular research the manner in which the settings operated as 'total institutions' affected how sexuality and sexual abuse issues were dealt with, and perceived, in multifarious ways. The comparatively closed nature of the settings meant that both staff and children were often relatively isolated from the wider community and the larger organisation, and they therefore felt powerless to complain about sexual abuse.

The divisive staff and child cultures also resulted in children rarely confiding in staff, and staff often behaving punitively and insensitively towards the children, concentrating almost exclusively on control and surveillance issues within the building:

My main view regarding promiscuity and prostitution is that we should make our girls be aware and be careful. But other than that I don't have any feelings on it . . . with prostitution it's up to them as long as they avoid pregnancy and diseases. (residential worker)

When I first starting working there one lad and a girl disappeared. I hadn't even noticed but this other member of staff shot up the stairs. He stopped it, separated them and made then come back downstairs. (residential worker)

This section on institutionalisation draws attention to forms of power which manifest themselves through particular organisational processes. These give staff power over children and engender certain child responses, some resistant, to this exercise of power. This can be further illustrated by the observation that resistance on the part of the children varied, with establishments being seen as less institutionalised having the least negative behaviours on the part of the children. Another issue is that many of the staff were simultaneously powerful and powerless, with them holding considerable power over the children but in turn being subjected to similar institutionalised processes as the children, or being manipulated by managers or paedophiles.

CONCLUSION

This chapter illustrates how children in residential care perceive and behave in relation to sexuality and how vulnerable they are to sexual exploitation and abuse from peers and adults both within and outside the settings. It also outlines a number of factors which exacerbate and influence their vulnerability. These include previous abusive family and 'in care' experiences, gendered staff and child beliefs around sexuality, and the institutionalisation of the settings. Managerial responses informed by organisational constraints and ideologies and managers' 'common sense', socially constructed notions of gender and sexuality, including how such issues are perceived within organisations, are also relevant.

Policy and practice implications suggest the need for independent monitoring of both staff and managers, and for children and staff to have formal external organisational avenues of complaint or advocates. It also appears to be necessary for both staff and managers to receive obligatory and challenging training on gender and its links with sexuality and sexual abuse issues. This needs to be instigated in conjunction with a great deal more support for residential staff to help them deal with the children in a more therapeutic and less punitive and controlling manner. However, given that children have few sexual or other rights in our society as a whole (Franklin, 1986; Evans, 1994), that children's homes are low-status, 'last resort' placements predominantly for adolescents with behavioural difficulties from materially deprived families (Aymer, 1992; Bebbington and Miles, 1989), and that gender, although socially constructed, is naturalised by the majority population (Rorty, 1997), it seems that significant improvements in the situation of children in residential care will be difficult to operationalise without major societal shifts regarding the nature of gender and children's relatively powerless positioning in mainstream society.

REFERENCES

Aries P (1962) *Centuries of Childhood*, Jonathan Cape, London.
Aymer C (1992) Woman in residential work: Dilemmas and ambiguities, in Langan M and Day L (eds) *Women, Oppression and Social Work: Issues for Anti-Discriminatory Practice*, Routledge, London.
Bebbington A and Miles J (1989) The background of children who enter local authority care, *British Journal of Social Work*, **19**: 349–368.
Berridge D (1994) Foster and residential care reassessed: A research perspective, *Children and Society*, **8**(2): 132–150.
Berridge D and Brodie I (1996) Residential child care in England and Wales: The inquiries and after, in Hill M and Aldgate J (eds) *Child Welfare*

Services: Developments in Law Policy, Practice and Research, Jessica Kingsley, London.

Berridge D and Brodie I (1998) *Children's Homes Revisited,* Jessica Kingsley, London.

Bloom R (1992) When staff members sexually abuse children in their care, *Child Welfare,* **71**(2): 131–145.

Blyth E and Jessop D (in press) Doing better: Improving the educational experiences of looked after children and young people, in Blyth E and Milner J (eds) *Improving School Attendance,* Routledge, London.

Bonnington Report (1984) *Residential Care: The Next Ten Years,* The Social Care Associations Publications, Surbiton, Surrey.

Brannan C, Jones J and Murch J (1993) Lessons from a residential school enquiry: Reflections on the Castle Hill Report, *Child Abuse Review,* **2**: 271–275.

Bullock R, Little M and Milham S (1993) *Residential Care of Children: A Review of the Research,* HMSO, London.

Cohen S and Taylor J (1971) *Psychological Survival: The Experience of Long-Term Imprisonment,* Penguin, Harmondsworth.

Coleman J (1993) Understanding adolescence today: A review, *Children and Society,* **7**(2): 137–147.

Crossmaker M (1991) Behind locked doors: Institutional sexual abuse, *Sexuality and Disability,* **9**(3): 201–219.

Evans D (1994) Falling angels? The material construction of children as sexual citizens, *International Journal of Children's Rights,* **2**: 1–33.

Finkelhor D (1986) *A Sourcebook on Child Sexual Abuse,* Sage, London.

Franklin B (ed.) (1986) *The Rights of Children,* Basil Blackwell, Oxford.

Goffman E (1961) *Asylums,* Penguin, Harmondsworth.

Hearn J and Parkin W (1987) *'Sex at Work': The Power and Paradox of Organisation Sexuality,* St. Martin's Press, New York.

Hearn J and Parkin W (1995) *'Sex at Work': The Power and Paradox of Organisation Sexuality* (revised edn), St. Martin's Press, New York.

Hearn J, Sheppard D, Tancred Sheriff P and Burrell G (eds) (1989) *The Sexuality of Organization,* Sage, London.

Jackson S (1987) *The Education of Children in Care,* School of Applied Social Studies, University of Bristol, Bristol.

Jesson J (1993) Understanding adolescent female prostitution: A literature review, *British Journal of Social Work,* **23**: 517–530.

Langan M and Day L (1992) (eds) *Women, Oppression and Social Work: Issues for Anti-Discriminatory Practice,* Routledge, London.

Lees S (1993) *Sugar and Spice: Sexuality and Adolescent Girls,* Hutchison, London.

Lupton C (1992) Feminism, managerialism and performance measurement, in Langan M and Day L (eds) *Women, Oppression and Social Work,* Routledge, London.

McMillen C (1991) Sexual identity issues related to homosexuality in the residential treatment of adolescents, *Residential Treatment for Children and Youth,* **9**(2): 5–21.

Moore S and Rosenthal D (1993) *Sexuality in Adolescence,* Routledge, London.

O'Neill M (1994) *Feminising Theory/Theorising Sex: Researching the Needs of Young People In Care Sexualities in Social Context,* British Sociological Association Annual Conference, University of Central Lancashire, 28–31 March.

O'Neill M (1995) Juvenile prostitution: The experience of young women in residential care, *Childright,* January: 14–16.

Parkin W (1989) Private experiences in the public domain: Sexuality and residential care organisations, in Hearn *et al.* (1989).

Pateman C (1989) *The Disorder of Women*, Polity Press, Cambridge.

Pringle K (1993) Gender politics, *Community Care*, 4 March: 16–17.

Prior P (1995) Surviving psychiatric institutionalisation: A case study, *Sociology of Health and Illness*, **17**(5): 651–667.

Robson C (1993) *Real World Research*, Blackwell, Oxford.

Rorty R (1997) Feminism, ideology and deconstruction: A pragmatist view, in Zizek S (ed.) *Mapping Ideology*, Verso, London.

Seidler V (1994) *Unreasonable Men: Masculinity and Social Theory*, Routledge, London.

Stacey M and Davies C (1983) *Divisions of Labour in Child Health Care: Final Report to SSRG* (December), University of Warwick, Coventry.

Vanstone M (1995) Managerialism and the ethics of management, in Hugman R and Smith D (eds) *Ethical Issues in Social Work*, Routledge, London.

Wardhaugh J and Wilding P (1995) Towards an explanation of the corruption of care, *Critical Social Policy*, **13**(37): 4–32.

Warner N (1992) *Choosing with Care: Report of Inquiry into the Selection, Development and Management of Staff in Children's Homes*, chaired by Norman Warner, HMSO, London.

Warner M (1994) *Managing Monsters: Six Myths of Our Time*, Vintage, London.

White K (1987) Residential care for adolescents: Residents, carers and sexual issues, in Horobin G (ed.) *Sex, Gender and Care Work, Research Highlights in Social Work*, vol. 15, Jessica Kingsley, New York and London.

13

PREVENTING INSTITUTIONAL ABUSE: AN EXPLORATION OF CHILDREN'S RIGHTS, NEEDS AND PARTICIPATION IN RESIDENTIAL CARE

Jenny Myers, Teresa O'Neill and Jocelyn Jones

INTRODUCTION

The public inquiry into the institutional abuse of children in residential care in North Wales and North West England, and the Utting Report (DOH, 1997) into the provision of safeguards for children who live away from home, expose, yet again, how the child protection system has failed to protect children in residential care.

The organisation of the institutional care of children, particularly in the public and voluntary sectors, continues in the main to be run on traditional paternalistic lines with hierarchical systems of management. Although recommendations are important, there is a danger that they will not in themselves prevent institutional abuse unless there is a change in the fundamental philosophy of how residential care is managed. The authors argue that a move towards a children's rights model of care, one that places children centrally in the system that endeavours to protect, may be a positive move to reduce the risk of institutional abuse.

This chapter draws on recent literature from institutional abuse

Children, Child Abuse and Child Protection. Placing Children Centrally, by The Violence Against Children Study Group.
© 1999 John Wiley & Sons Ltd.

inquiries and lessons learnt, to analyse whether recommendations made can actually protect children in residential care. It then examines some of the principles that are fundamental to a model of residential care based on a children's rights philosophy. The importance of a clear philosophy in residential care has been highlighted in a number of inquiries, and a recent study found the strongest relationship with the quality of care provided by a home was the extent to which managers and staff were clear about their purpose, theoretical approach and methods of work (Berridge and Brodie, 1998).

The chapter concludes with some recommendations for practice based on children's participation that could help reduce the likelihood of institutional abuse happening in the future.

INSTITUTIONAL ABUSE

The last two decades have seen a notable change in the way residential care is organised, the numbers of children accommodated and the nature of their problems (DOH, 1991a; Aymer, 1992; Madge, 1994; Gooch, 1996; Parkin and Green, 1997). Barter (1997) expands on these changes by discussing the increasing concern that children who have frequently been abused are being placed with those who have abused. This highlights the complex issues involved in the management and organisation of the care of children who are both perpetrators and victims. Despite these fundamental changes and the analysis of lessons learnt from recent inquiries into institutional abuse, residential care continues, in the main, to be managed on traditional hierarchical lines that do not take account of or address these changes.

Stein (1993) suggests that a conceptual exploration of the different forms of abuse in residential care is assisted by a recognition of four forms of abuse: *sanctioned* (forms of abuse that were not hidden or secret, but practised openly), *institutional* (the chronic failure to assist children developmentally, emotionally or educationally), and *systematic* and *individual abuse* (the organised physical, sexual and emotional abuse of children by individuals or members of staff). This recognises the impact of the wider inequalities of power on children in residential care as well as individual policy and practice. For the purposes of this chapter the term *institutional abuse* will include all of these forms of abuse.

The public tribunal currently being undertaken into children's homes in North Wales and the North West of England is the latest in a series of inquiries dealing with aspects of institutional abuse (in the widest sense). One suspects that it may draw similar conclusions to those made in previous inquires by Levy and Kahan (1991), Williams and McCreadie (1992) and Kirkwood (1993), all of which made a host of recommendations which have impacted on the delivery of residential services in this country. This chapter does not seek to discuss these recommendations in great detail as others have done (Berridge and Brodie, 1996), or indeed to further debate the definition as to what is and is not institutional abuse. Rather its aim is to show how participatory models might be used not only as a measure of the risk of institutional abuse but also as a means of prevention.

INSPECTION

The first major theme is the length of time over which the abuse (sanctioned, institutional, individual and systematic) continued. There are many possible explanations for this, of which the first is the failure of the inspection process to identify or listen to those who raised concerns. If the inspection systems had been working effectively then abusive regimes such as 'Pindown' would not have continued for so many years. Yet as Stein (1993) suggests, through their conceptual definition of abuse, abusive practices such as regression therapy as a form of treatment were openly sanctioned. Cawson (1997) shows that some individuals convicted of abuse in residential care had no previous criminal or disciplinary records and were highly regarded by their own management and other professionals. She argues that we need to consider the 'underlying causes' of abuse as well as ensuring an effective inspection process. The response by the Department of Health and many local authorities has been to tighten the regulation and inspection process (DOH, 1991b,c, 1992a,b, 1994) rather than to address these 'underlying causes'.

The Utting Report (DOH, 1997) demonstrates that, despite previous reports and guidance, there are still many loopholes, omissions and inconsistencies in the inspection system. For example, there are wide differences according to the type of service provided and it is possible for some smaller residential homes and schools to evade registration and inspection altogether. This is alarming considering that one of the significant changes in the organisation of children's residential care is a move towards a provision of service outside the statutory and voluntary sectors to small specialist private homes, which often provide care for the most difficult, challenging and hence vulnerable children.

Another form of professional investigation to remain popular is that of the statutory or 'rota' visit that a residential home receives from an appointed person (Children's Home Regulations, Regulation 22). As Cawson (1997) noted, current requirements are still inconsistent and there is wide variation in the appointment and practice of those charged with responsibility to visit. The rota visit provided much evidence for the 'Pindown' inquiry (Levy and Kahan, 1991) which found that the welfare of the child took a secondary place to the state of the buildings.

Both the Utting (DOH, 1991a) and Warner (DOH, 1992b) reports recommended that guidance should be prepared on rota visits, in particular on unannounced and night visits. The inspection into children's homes in Leicestershire that followed the conviction of Frank Beck commented on the fact that an inspection cannot guarantee that the abuse of children is not taking place. It can only provide a forum for children, staff and parents to report any concerns and to evaluate whether the department has established the policies and procedures that are likely to preclude abuse.

There is a danger of failing to recognise a significant weakness in the inspection process, and that is the notion of 'powerlessness'. A contributing factor to the existence of institutional abuse in the past was the relative powerlessness of not only the children living in the home, but also of the staff employed to work there. Residential staff were and in the main still are, underpaid, undervalued, and often unqualified. Morrison (1996) refers to the mirroring of behaviours and the unconscious process by which the dynamics of the children worked with are reproduced in the staff group. Children who are survivors of institutional abuse may remain powerless, silent victims, especially when the staff who are there to ensure their protection are also feeling powerless. The onslaught of inquiries, lowering of professional status, morale and unsure job prospects reduce the chances of staff being able to act positively. Parkin and Green (1997) emphasise the particular difficulties of powerlessness facing women staff in residential care.

The assumption that it is easy for both workers and children to report concerns and take action is a false one. The public tribunal currently under way in North Wales continues to support this. As Jones and Myers (1997) discussed, previous literature on abuse has frequently referred to themes of secrecy, powerlessness, denial, control and the hidden nature of sexual abuse (Summit, 1983; Finkelhor and Browne, 1986). Recent inquiries into institutional abuse have continued to observe how these themes are woven into the residential environment. Stein (1993) suggests that it is essential to understand the complex interaction of different indicators of powerlessness. This includes the directly exploitative relationships between mainly male adults and children (in both sanctioned and systematic forms of abuse) and more indirectly through dis-empowering structures, policies and practices in institutional abuse.

The question remains: would the current inspection systems and processes make the chances of concerns being heard and abuse identified more likely? The importance of having independent visitors and others with access to the homes, but who are not likely to be caught up in professionally accommodating behaviour within an abusive residential regime, is crucial. However, if an institution has an abusive culture then inspection alone is unlikely to prevent further abuse taking place.

CONTROL, CONTAINMENT AND THE DEVELOPMENT OF ABUSIVE CULTURES

All the inquiries reveal how a number of abusive, controlling, but highly organised regimes were able to function within the residential establishments. These helped sustain the possibility of abuse over long periods of time and ensured that a continuing supply of victims was recruited and drawn into the network of abuse. The Castle Hill report (Brannon, Jones and Murch 1993) demonstrates how such a regime was managed and maintained. It is therefore worrying that one of the recent initiatives by those involved in residential care is the increasing focus on the control and restraint of children. Indeed, as Kent noted in the parallel inquiry into safeguards in residential care in Scotland, 'there exists a sterile climate where bullying, threatening behaviour and verbal abuse are tolerated, the emphasis being on what children and staff are doing wrong rather than right' (Mitchell, 1997: 3).

Parkin and Green (1997: 76) found in their recent research into residential child care establishments that *'the issue of control and containment took precedence over care'* and the abusive culture became the norm. They indicated a high level of emphasis on surveillance and discipline and little evidence of caring for children or meeting their need for support and therapeutic help. They conclude that this has serious consequences for both adults and children, who end up feeling dehumanised and institutionalised. The process strips away individual identity and any sense of autonomy, leading to an increased helplessness and vulnerability to abuse. Utting (DOH, 1997) suggested that there is still much abuse in residential care that is on a 'mundane level, casual and opportunistic and supports their findings . . . by careless people and uncaring regimes' (p. 7). He concludes that it will take much more than regulation to cure such ills. All the inquiries suggest that one of the keys to preventing the development of an abusive culture is clear leadership and management at every level.

MANAGEMENT

Previous inquiries (Levy and Kahan, 1991; Williams and McCreadie, 1992; Kirkwood, 1993) exposed how the overall organisation of residential services lacked clarity and purpose. The homes were seen as a last resort for a variety of children with highly complex and differing needs and problems. In addition, they were isolated socially and geographically from the local community or the children's own locality, staffed by a number of inexperienced unqualified staff and frequently managed by a highly 'charismatic' officer in charge.

Bloom (1994) discusses the limitations of some of the recommendations made in the inquiries, particularly in relation to the recruitment and selection of employees. As the Leicestershire inquiry highlighted, the plausibility of the charismatic personality convinced many an interview panel, and other professionals, as to their suitability for the position (Kirkwood, 1993).

Pressley and Holmes (1996) argue that residential child care establishments still do not have clear management structures but rely heavily on the charismatic, autocratic leadership styles that continue to dominate the organisation of residential care. Although they acknowledge the importance of 'charisma' in the development of many 'pioneering' homes, they feel that the need for managers who are able to communicate effectively and from a distance is essential. Jones (1994, 1995), using Weber's typology of authority, has discussed this further, arguing that it is the combination of charismatic and traditional authority that creates the opportunity for abuse. She warns of the dangers of an over-reliance on the legal-rational regulation of institutions when abusive regimes are frequently managed by traditional, quasi-feudal, patriarchal and charismatic authority figures. This implies that the bureaucratic processes, the guidance, regulations and procedures designed to reduce the risk of institutional abuse in the future, will not offer adequate protection if more is not known about the operation of different management cultures in the residential care of children.

By identifying some of the persistent themes from previous inquiries (difficulty of regulating residential care and the inspection process, the notion of powerlessness and the combination of unclear, poor or highly charismatic management) it becomes possible to suggest a prevention strategy to reduce the risk of abuse of children in residential care that addresses these key themes. Stein (1993) discusses a number of foundations to prevention that include the need to recognise the positive value of residential care and the importance of having a sound legislative framework that encourages partnership and participation. Stein sees the exploration of empowerment as having the potential to inform a policy and practice framework which is not only complementary to the Children Act 1989, but which restores a belief in residential care as having a positive contribution to make. A model of practice that places children's needs and rights centrally is worthy of exploration, as Stein warns of practice that rejects needs in favour of rights or becomes so pathologising that it reduces young people in residential care to 'receptacles of professionally defined needs' (Stein, 1993: 243).

CHILDREN'S RIGHTS, NEEDS AND PARTICIPATION

The ratification by the Conservative government in 1991 of the United Nations Convention on the Rights of the Child and the passing of the Children Act 1989 are both recent measures that have been taken to safeguard children's welfare, placing special emphasis on the child's right to protection from abuse and exploitation. However, the term 'children's rights' is open to several interpretations. It is important to be clear about the use of the term. The most common explanations relate to either legal or moral rights, which according to Franklin (1995) 'support and inform one another' and which Joseph (1995) narrows down to call the liberationist (the right to more independence) and protectionist (the right to welfare and protection) ideologies. The authors of this chapter favour the protectionist approach as it concentrates on meeting children's needs and not just the fulfilment of rights. However, it is unlikely that children's needs will be effectively identified and met unless there is a recognition of and commitment to children's rights. We argue that where and how the emphasis is placed on children's needs and rights and on their participation in the process designed to protect them is crucial.

As Barter (1997) explains, adopting a children's rights perspective is not about encouraging children to reject order, or leaving residential workers with no authority or control. A child has a right to a safe and secure environment and therefore requires clear boundaries and to know that staff have the authority to ensure that not only are these set, but that they will respond appropriately when required.

Barter suggests that residential workers need to represent a legitimate authority to children, capable of protecting them from abuse, rather than powerless to do anything about it. This implies a leader-ship role, but is useless without the endorsement of an informed man-agement. Managing a residential home from a children's rights perspective is likely to be a difficult and complex task. If you empower the child it must not be at the expense of further dis-empowering staff. Both groups need to be enabled to function in a way that ensures value, rights and self-respect. As the Children's Support Force for Residential Care (1995) state in their report:

> A positive balanced ethos towards rights and empowerment carries with it the need to develop both self-control and external controls for indi-viduals and the group. Working together, managers, staff and children need to strive for an ethos, structure and daily living environment that provides positive opportunities whilst at the same time creates bound-aries around what is acceptable. (DOH, Children's Support Force for Residential Care, 1995: 48)

Smith (1997) gives a valuable account of developments that have helped emphasise the place of children's rights in residential care. Tra-ditionally it was accepted that planning for children in residential care was based on decision-making that reflected adult perceptions of their needs. This left enormous power in the hands of adults and contributed to the ability of abusers to maintain dominance and control and prevent disclosure of abuse (Levy and Kahan, 1991; Kirkwood, 1993). Steps that have been introduced to try and counteract this have included the cre-ation of Children's Rights Officers, the possibility of a Minister and or a Commissioner for Children's Rights, and the Utting Report (DOH, 1997).

Though the notion of children's rights has become more influential in recent social work practice and in the activities of those who provide residential care for children, there is still a long way to go. Smith (1997) suggests that there has been too much concentration on functional approaches to 'getting the job done' competently rather than on the skills required in caring for disturbed and complex children. This con-centration on increasing the 'professionalism' of residential staff will not in itself reduce the risk of abuse or ensure that children's rights are met. As Kellmer-Pringle (1974) discussed, children have basic needs which must be met to enable healthy physical, cognitive, emotional and social development, yet the Utting report (DOH, 1997) exposed, even in the 1990s, a scandalous neglect of children's basic and educative needs. If staff in residential care are not able to recognise and provide these basic needs, along with affection, support, boundaries, and respect for individuality to ensure their healthy development, then children's rights are likely to be neglected. The authors argue that there is a strong interrelationship between rights and needs which merits further exploration.

CHILDREN'S RIGHTS AND NEEDS

There continues to be considerable diversity in the roles and function of residential homes that accommodate and provide care for children and young people who are unable to live with their families. Society is ambivalent about children in residential care, particularly if they are adolescents and the children themselves are aware of the negative public stereotypes about children in 'care'. As we have already seen, the vulnerability of such children and young people resulting from adverse or stressful experiences may be compounded by their separation from family and further abuse or neglect in residential care. Many institutions have no clear statement as to their purpose, which limits opportunities for children to be placed in the homes most likely to be able to meet their needs. Moreover such an *ad hoc* approach frequently leads to an inappropriate combination of children in individual homes, and staff lack information about the needs and background circumstances of the children and young people and explanations for their behaviour. Staff groups have no coherent strategy or methods of working with the children and there is frequently poor liaison with other agencies and specialist services, leaving the institutions socially isolated (see Berridge and Brodie, 1998). All too often this results in a definition of children's needs and interests that is fragmented and incomplete and, crucially, excludes the children themselves from participation in the process. This, then, is the context in which institutional abuse can begin to occur. The rest of this chapter will seek to address how children's rights, needs and participation might be used as a method for regulating and preventing institutional abuse.

A children's rights perspective is one that 'emphasises the importance of the child's own viewpoint and wishes' (Fox-Harding, 1991: 155). The child is seen as the subject, rather than the object, of others' decisions and actions about their needs and interests.

Although the discourses of 'rights' and 'needs' are discrete there is, as already suggested, a strong interrelationship. The Articles in the UN Convention on the Rights of the Child that concern all children are grouped around four themes: survival, development, protection and participation. Rights may be seen as entitlements to have needs met and the UN Convention on the Rights of the Child refers to 'provision' rights, that is children have a right to be provided with the physical, social and psychological environment that will promote positive health and development outcomes as well as 'protection' and 'participation' rights. It has been suggested that attending to children's rights is of particular importance when children are in public care, and a relationship between poor quality of care and a failure to protect children's rights has been observed (Kahan, 1994).

It has been argued that a 'rights discourse can include needs and risks; needs or risk discourses can also include rights . . . a needs or risk discourse can include child advocacy and children's agency, just as a rights discourse can maintain adult power and question children's agency' (Hill and Tisdall, 1997: 254). However, the power relationship suggested by a 'needs' perspective is fundamentally different from that of a 'rights' perspective:

> A right implies a legitimate claim that derives from a respected status as person or citizen. In contrast a need can all too readily be seen as a personal deficiency associated with negative status . . . the idea of need implies a compassionate basis for action but in practice may mask decisions which are intended to make life easier for adults as with respect to some placements of children in hospital or secure accommodation. (Hill and Tisdall, 1997: 63)

This highlights the longstanding concern with regard to the considerable power held by adults making decisions for children about what is in children's best interests on the basis of their perceptions of need, rather than on the basis of identified need. Such decisions may represent a response to the child's presenting behaviour rather than to the needs of the 'whole' person. The exclusion of children and young people from the process of identification of their own needs and interests will inevitably result in the implementation of policies and practices designed to meet needs which are paternalistic, potentially oppressive and treat children as 'passive recipients'. This practice, which is unlikely to achieve positive outcomes for the children and young people, will perpetuate the unequal power relationships between adults and children which contribute to the climate of institutional abuse (Jones, 1994).

There is considerable evidence, some of which has already been examined, about the universal and basic physical and non-physical needs that can be seen as common to all children if they are to achieve positive outcomes. Yet children will experience childhood differently on the basis of a range of factors such as their class, gender, race, religion and sexuality and some needs will be experienced by children or groups of children arising from their age, stage of development or adverse experiences. Children with needs arising from ill-health or disability are described as having 'special needs' and legislation requires the provision of services to 'children in need'. Children require these needs to be met by parents or primary carers, drawing on specialist help where necessary. The increasing concerns about the failure of residential care to replace the commitment of parents to meeting the needs of their children, to protect them from abuse and to promote their development, have been described. As a response to these concerns, measures have been developed and implemented to provide an ongoing assessment of how far positive outcomes are achieved for individual children. Ward (1995) proposes seven dimensions of development with the aim of raising standards of care: health, education, identity, family and social relationships, emotional and behavioural development, social presentation, and self-care skills. As the measures are related to children's long-term development, they can be used to monitor outcomes following children through moves within and outside care or accommodation. While the focus is on outcomes for individual children, the link with the quality of their experiences introduces accountability: children will only achieve positive outcomes if they have received a high level of care. How far this system of assessment will improve the quality of outcomes for children and young people in residential care has yet to become clear. It is argued that the effectiveness of the assessment is likely to be significantly influenced by the degree to which the subject children and young people are provided with information and assisted and supported to be full and active participants in defining and prioritising their needs.

PARTICIPATION

A fundamental element of a children's rights perspective which emphasises a child's own viewpoint and wishes is their right to participation, that is to be actively involved or share in decision-making in matters of concern to them. The statutory framework provided by the UN Convention on the Rights of the Child and the Children Act 1989 in England and Wales has enhanced the participation of children in some services and matters of concern to them. However, beyond the Children Act there is no legal framework for children's right to participate in decisions of concern to them so they continue to be deprived of the right to participate in decisions about their education, even in the decision to exclude them from school, and their views remain marginal in other critical issues.

The debate about children's right to participation has been examined in detail elsewhere and will not be rehearsed here (see Cloke and

Davies, 1995; Franklin, 1995; Sinclair, 1996) although it is important to summarise some of the arguments in favour of, and to acknowledge some of the objections to, participation rights for children.

Archard (1993) suggests that how people are valued is determined by the rights accorded to them. The participation of children in decisions on matters that affect them is recognition that children are individuals who have views of their own, and is an acknowledgement of their status and worth. Children and young people have knowledge and experience that can and should contribute to debate and decision-making. Such decisions are more likely to be based on accurate and complete information about their needs. In turn children will have greater commitment to implementing decisions and plans when they have been involved, and the decisions are more likely to have positive outcomes. Lansdown suggests that participation 'is a simple and self-evidently worthy principle which would, if taken seriously, have a revolutionary impact on the nature of adult/child relationships. Without it children are denied the most basic of principles—to be accepted as people in their own right' (Lansdown, 1995: 30). Kahan (1994) observed the positive effect of encouraging participation for individual children and for the quality of care in the institutions in which they were living;

> Participation of children and young people is fundamental not only to openness in the daily life of an establishment, but also to their acceptance of the necessary structure and 'rules of the house' . . . young people respond to being involved even in matters as delicate as staff selection. When they are involved . . . staff will gain much greater commitment to what is decided because the children themselves have had a hand in it. This can also be a very effective way of ensuring that the establishment is child-centred and not, as sometimes happens, run for the convenience of the organisation or the staff. (Kahan, 1994: 317–318)

Participation enhances children's sense of responsibility and self-confidence, an issue of particular concern for children in residential care. The more they are encouraged to participate the better prepared they will be to exercise increasing responsibility effectively, both in the residential unit and more widely in all aspects of their lives.

Perhaps the factor that most strongly supports the argument in favour of children's right to participation, in the context of preventing institutional abuse is the relationship between participation and protection. It has been demonstrated that the right of children to participate is closely linked to their rights to protection from abuse and exploitation. The failure to listen to the views and wishes of children has been shown to be an important element in the continuation over long periods of time of abusive cultures in residential care (Berridge and Brodie, 1996; DOH, 1997).

Yet for all these compelling arguments in support of children's participation, there continues to be resistance to the implementation of children's rights in practice. Hill and Tisdall suggest that 'taking children's rights to participate seriously can be difficult to operationalise . . . because children's participation can threaten adult hegemony and established practice' (Hill and Tisdall, 1997: 35–36). This has been confirmed by Berridge and Brodie (1998) who found staff in children's homes who claimed that they were disadvantaged by the emphasis on children's rights and children 'knowing too much' while at the same time suggesting that children having 'more voice' was a positive development. This reveals confusion about the issues among residential staff that can prevent the implementation of positive practice, which would be of benefit to both children and staff. Sinclair (1996) found resistance to encouraging participation by children on the grounds that they should not be allowed to have their own way. However, she has suggested that such a view is a misrepresentation of the meaning of participation. Lansdown (1998: 222) agreed with this analysis and cites the comment of Sir William Utting that 'such loose attributions are made by adults grasping for excuses for welshing on their responsibilities to children'.

The issues that lie behind such resistance relate to the power relationships between adults and children that must be openly explored and questioned. The powerlessness of staff generally in residential institutions described by Morrison (1996) in his use of the 'Professional Accommodation Syndrome', and the particular difficulties of the powerlessness of women described by Parkin and Green (1997), mirror the powerlessness of the children they care for. The implementation of a strong framework of participation that would strengthen and empower the children, would also empower the staff caring for them.

Despite the resistance and continuing ambivalence, children's rights to participation have gradually gained ground although it is still clear that talking about participation is much easier and less costly than its implementation. Utting (DOH, 1997) reported that children were frequently prevented from participating in decisions being made about them, particularly in reviews, because they were poorly prepared and inadequately supported by staff in a process which the children found intimidating.

Hill and Tisdall (1997) have suggested a number of key elements concerning participation and decision-making that are essential for children and young people who are living away from their families: procedures for consultation with children; access to information and skills to enable children to express themselves well; decision-making which takes account of their views; assistance or representation by a trusted person of their choice; opportunities for complaint or appeal. Similarly Lansdown (1995) suggests that participation should underpin all adult–child relationships and that there should be procedures for implementation and a clear means of redress where children's participation rights are breached.

Hart (1992: 8–10) notes the difficulty of turning the rhetoric of participation rights into practice, and from his analysis has developed an eight-step ladder of participation which measures the extent and quality of children's participation. He describes the bottom three rungs as 'manipulation', 'decoration' and 'tokenism' that are non-participative and represent children's passive involvement rather than their active participation. If we consider these in the context of a children's home, an example of 'manipulation' might be when staff seek individual children's views in relation to a proposed project but the children are not given detailed information, involved in discussion or the decision-making process or given any feedback. The staff may seek to validate, that is engineer, the outcome on the basis that they have 'consulted' with the children. An example of 'decoration' may see children wearing T-shirts, with appropriate names or slogans but which they have not been involved in designing or choosing. 'Tokenism' might involve staff inviting one child to attend a meeting about a proposed project as a representative, without informing or preparing the child for the meeting or supporting the child to seek the views of other children. Tokenism can also be seen in case conferences and reviews where staff invite children to attend but do not provide them with the information or support they need to participate in the process.

There are only five steps that represent genuine and increasing levels of participation. The bottom of these, 'assigned but informed', is when a project is designed and planned by adults but participating children are well informed and included. The subsequent levels—'consulted and informed'; 'adult initiated, shared decisions with children'; 'child initiated and directed'; 'child initiated, shared decisions with adults'—reflect the increasing possibilities for children's participation (Hart, 1992: 9). These levels of participation can be extended to children in all decisions on matters of concern to them and most aspects of residential care, from purchasing policies to the recruitment of staff, if they are appropriately supported. Children's level of participation can increase as, through the process of participation, they gain experience and confidence that their views are valued. The challenge for residential homes is to work toward and achieve a situation where children's participation in all aspects of practice is regarded as normal, where their exclusion from participation is actively questioned by residential staff and social workers and the children themselves are sufficiently empowered to seek and receive explanations if their right to participation is denied.

CONCLUSION

This chapter set out to identify and discuss some of the common themes from previous inquires into the institutional abuse of children and to explore whether it is possible to reduce the risk of institutional abuse by operating a model that places children's rights, needs and participation more centrally. The authors argue that unless there is a commitment to children's rights that includes 'provision' and 'protection' rights and children's right to participation in matters of concern to them, their needs also will be neglected. Using the frameworks suggested, residential homes could start by developing practice that places rights, needs and participation more centrally and begin translating paper statements into concrete examples of practice.

Up to now the main response to concerns identified by inquiries has been to tighten and regulate the inspection process. Although this is important and has, as Utting (DOH, 1997) concludes, contributed to an improvement in the safety aspects of residential care, it has failed to address any of the issues with a child-centred response and will therefore not be fully effective in safeguarding children. The value of further inquiries into the institutional abuse of children has to be questioned: we already have a wealth of knowledge about the causes. We need to listen to children and take active steps to change practice in residential care by making children's rights central to the organisation of the service provided. A starting point is for all those concerned with the welfare of children in residential care to ask some pertinent questions concerning the degree of participation in the homes where they are working or intend to work, or where they have children already placed.

Although there is a greater understanding of children's rights, there is a deficit in the development of a children's rights perspective in practice. Having a commitment to the principles laid down in the Children Act 1989 and the United Nations Convention on the Rights of the Child is only a starting point. Most agencies can demonstrate this commitment to the principles on paper through procedures and mission statements, but research with children has not confirmed that it is evident in practice (Buchanan, 1995; NSPCC, 1995; Westcott, 1995).

Franklin suggests that to 'lean the ladder against the institution and see how few rungs children are able to climb' (Franklin, 1995: 14) will provide a graphic illustration of the very limited levels of children's participation in many institutions where children should be centrally involved, such as residential homes. The message for residential staff and social workers must be that if children are to be safe in residential care in the future, the levels and quality of their participation must improve. It is clear that a children's rights perspective that encourages and fully supports children's participation in decisions on matters of concern to them, both individually and relating to the residential units in which they live, is likely to be the most effective way of ensuring that they are protected, their needs are fully identified and policies which will meet those needs are implemented. The risk of institutional abuse can only be significantly reduced by a genuine commitment to children's participation that requires an exploration of power relationships between adults and children, and a shift in the existing imbalance of power in favour of children.

REFERENCES

Archard D (1993) *Children: Rights and Childhood*, Routledge, London.

Aymer C (1992) Women in residential work: Dilemmas and ambiguities, in Langan M and Day L (eds) *Women, Oppression and Social Work*, Routledge, London.

Barter C (1997) Who's to blame: Conceptualizing institutional abuse by children, *Early Child Development and Care*, **133**: 1–128.

Berridge D and Brodie I (1996) Residential child care in England and Wales, in Hill M and Aldgate J (eds) *Child Welfare Services*, Jessica Kingsley, London.

Berridge D and Brodie I (1998) *Children's Homes Revisited*, Longman, London.

Bloom R (1994) Institutional child sexual abuse: Prevention and risk management, *Residential Treatment for Children and Youth*, **12**, 2: 3–18.

Brannon C, Jones J and Murch J (1993) Castle Hill Report: Practice Guide: Shropshire County Council, Shrewsbury.

Buchanan A (1995) The Dolphin Project, in Cloke C and Davies M (eds) *Participation and Empowerment in Child Protection*, John Wiley, Chichester.

Cawson P (1997) Who will guard the guards? *Early Child Development and Care*, **133**: 57–71.

Cloke C and Davies M (eds) (1995) *Participation and Empowerment in Child Protection*, John Wiley, Chichester.

Department of Health (1991a) *Children In The Public Care*, A review of residential care carried out by Sir William Utting, HMSO, London.

Department of Health (1991b) *The Children Act 1989: Guidance and Regulations. Vol. 4: Residential Care*, HMSO, London.

Department of Health (1991c) *Inspecting for Quality: Guidance on Practice for Inspection Units in Social Services Departments and Other Agencies*, Department of Health, London.

Department of Health (1992a) *Inspection of Community Homes, Circular LAC(92) 14*, Department of Health, London.

Department of Health (1992b) *Choosing With Care: Report of the Committee of Enquiry into the Selection, Development and Management of Staff in Children's Homes*, chaired by Sir Norman Warner, HMSO, London.

Department of Health (1995) *Staff Supervision in Children's Homes*. Support Force for Children's Residential Care Publications.

Department of Health (1997) *'People Like Us' The report into safeguards for children living away from home*, chaired by Sir William Utting, The Stationery Office, London.

Department of Health and Social Services Inspectorate (1994) *Inspecting for Quality Standards for Residential Child Care*, HMSO, London.

Finkelhor D and Browne A (1986) Initial and long term effects: A conceptual framework, in Finkelhor D (ed.) *A Sourcebook on Child Sexual Abuse*, Sage, London.

Fox-Harding L (1991) *Perspectives in Child Care Policy*, Longman, London.

Franklin B (1995) The case for children's rights, in Franklin B (ed.) *The Handbook of Children's Rights: Comparative Policy and Practice*, Routledge, London.

Gooch D (1996) Home and away, *Child and Family Social Work*, **1**: 19–32.

Hart R A (1992) *Children's Participation. From Tokenism to Citizenship*, Innocenti Essays, 4 UNICEF Child Development Centre, Florence.

Hill M and Tisdall K (1997) *Children and Society*. Longman, London.

Jones J (1994) Towards an understanding of power relationships in institutional abuse, *Early Childhood Development and Care*, **100**: 69–76.

Jones J (1995) Institutional abuse: Understanding domination from the inside looking out, *Early Child Development and Care*, **113**: 85–92.

Jones J and Myers J (1997) The future detection and prevention of institutional abuse: Giving children a chance to participate in research, *Early Childhood Development and Care*, **133**: 115–125.

Joseph Y (1995) Child protection rights, in Cloke C and Davies M (eds) *Participation and Empowerment in Child Protection*, John Wiley, Chichester.

Kahan B (1994) *Growing Up in Groups*, NISW/HMSO, London.

Kellmer-Pringle M (1974) *The Needs of Children*, Hutchinson, London.

Kirkwood A (1993) *The Leicestershire Inquiry*, Leicestershire County Council, Leicester.

Lansdown G (1995) Children's rights to participation and protection, in Cloke C and Davies M (eds) *Participation and Empowerment in Child Protection*, John Wiley, Chichester.

Lansdown G (1998) Children's rights and the law, *Representing Children*, **10**, 4: 213–223.

Levy A and Kahan B (1991) *The Pindown Experience and the Protection of Children*, Staffordshire County Council, Stafford.

Madge N (1994) *Children in Residential Care in Europe*, National Children's Bureau, London.

Mitchell D (1997) in the News section of *Community Care*, 23 October: 3.

Morrison T (1996) *Staff Supervision In Social Care*, Pavilion Publishing, Brighton.

NCH: Action for Children (1994) *Messages From Children*, NCH: Action for Children, London.

NSPCC (1995) *Responding to Abuse in Care*, NSPCC, London.

Parkin W and Green L (1997) Cultures of abuse within residential child care, *Early Child Development and Care*, **133**: 73–86.

Pressley J and Holmes C (1996) Residential care for young people: Managerial or charismatic leadership? *Practice and Staff Development*, **5**, 1: 49–53.

Sinclair R (1996) Children and young people's participation in decision making, in Hill M and Aldgate J (eds) *Child Welfare Services*, Jessica Kingsley, London.

Smith C (1997) Children's rights: Have carers abandoned values? *Children and Society*, **11**: 3–15.

Stein M (1993) The abuses and uses of residential care, in Ferguson H, Gilligan R and Torode R (eds) *Surviving Childhood Adversity*, Social Studies Press, Dublin.

Summit R (1983) The child sexual abuse accommodation syndrome, *Child Abuse and Neglect*, **7**: 177–193.

United Nations (1989) *Convention on the Rights of the Child*, United Nations, Geneva.

Ward H (1995) *Looking After Children: Research into Practice*, HMSO, London.

Westcott H (1995) Perceptions of child protection casework, in Cloke C and Davies M (eds) *Participation and Empowerment in Child Protection*, John Wiley, Chichester.

Williams G and McCreadie J (1992) *Ty Mawr Community Home Inquiry*, Gwent County Council, Cwmbran.

INDEX

Index compiled by Mary Kirkness

Related titles of interest...

Out of Hearing
Representing Children in Care Proceedings
JUDITH MASSON and MAUREEN WINN OAKLEY
Wiley/NSPCC Series in Child Protection & Policy
0471 98642 9 186pp January 1999 Paperback

From Hearing to Healing
Working with the Aftermath of Child Sexual Abuse
Edited by ANNE BANNISTER
Wiley/NSPCC Series in Child Protection & Policy
0471 98298 9 212pp April 1998 Paperback

Child Sexual Abuse
Responding to the Experiences of Children
Edited by NIGEL PARTON and CORINNE WATTAM
Wiley/NSPCC Series in Child Protection & Policy
0471 98334 9 190pp August 1999 Paperback

Joining New Families
A Study of Adoption and Fostering in Middle Childhood
DAVID QUINTON, ALAN RUSHTON, CHERILYN DANCE and DEBORAH MAYES
Wiley Series in Childcare and Protection
0471 97837X 282pp November 1998 Paperback

Interviewing Children
A Guide for Child Care and Forensic Practitioners
MICHELLE ALDRIDGE and JOANNE WOOD
Wiley Series in Childcare and Protection
0471 970522 248pp October 1998 Hardback
0471 982075 248pp October 1998 Paperback

WILEY